Keep From All Thoughtful Men

Keep From All Thoughtful Men

How U.S. Economists Won World War II

Jim Lacey

NAVAL INSTITUTE PRESS
Annapolis, Maryland

Naval Institute Press
291 Wood Road
Annapolis, MD 21402

Library of Congress Cataloging-in-Publication Data
Lacey, Jim
Keep from all thoughtful men : how U.S. economists won World War II / Jim Lacey.
p. cm.
Includes bibliographical references and index.
ISBN 978-1-59114-491-5 (hardcover : alk. paper)
1. World War, 1939-1945—Economic aspects—United States. 2. United States. War Production Board. 3. United States—Economic policy–1933-1945. 4. Industrial mobilization—United States—History—20th century. I. Title.
HC106.4.L34 2011
940.53'1—dc22

2010049651

Printed in the United States of America

19 18 17 16 15 14 13 12 11 9 8 7 6 5 4 3 2 1
First printing

For Sharon, whose love, support, and encouragement made this and much else possible

Contents

Keep From All Thoughtful Men

CHAPTER 1

Economics and War

★ ★ ★

Approximately a generation ago, historians finally realized that much of what they had written about battle and war in the past had neglected the effects of logistics. While they may have been aware of the old adage "amateurs talk tactics, while experts talk logistics," they had largely ignored logistical concerns, except for a few feeble mentions of famine-induced disasters. The probable reason is that logistical studies are boring and recounting logistical matters invariably slows down the narrative pace of a campaign history. After all, who really wants to read about how many trains it took to move ammunition to the front in 1916 or about the hay consumption rate of one of Murat's cavalry divisions?[1]

Though historians begrudgingly allowed logistical concerns into the mainstream of military history, they have still largely barred the door to the study of economic matters. While no one has analyzed the divorce of economics from most histories of war, that failure probably has two causes: economics lacks drama, and it is often hard to understand. Among historians who research and write about armies sweeping across continents and who paint verbal pictures of brutal battlefield carnage, there is little desire to delve into the economics that drive the character and form of war. Furthermore, the "dismal science" of economics is not a subject military historians typically have invested much time in learning.[2] This neglect will likely widen as economics continues on its current path toward pure mathematics and model-based econometrics, and slips farther from its original moorings connected to political economy.

Over time, this historical oversight led to considerable misrepresentations of history. For example, the greatest historian of the ancient world, Thucydides, made only one mention of the Athenian silver mines in his history of the Peloponnesian War. In a speech, Alcibiades urged the Spartans to fortify Decclea: "Whatever property there is in the country will become yours, either by capture or surrender, and the Athenians will at once be deprived of the revenues of their silver mines at Laurium."[3]

Following Thucydides, two millennia of historians, for the most part, have identified Athens' failed Syracuse Expedition as the turning point in the Peloponnesian War. Actually, Athens made good most of the losses from that campaign in a remarkably short period and continued the war for another decade. What wrecked Athenian power were the successive economic hammer blows of losing the silver revenues from Laurium, isolation from the revenues of the Delium League, and, finally, the blockade that a Spartan fleet (financed by Persia) imposed between Athens and its Black Sea food sources.

Likewise, few historians focus on the discovery of two major silver mines in Macedonia as a major factor in Phillip's rise to dominance over Greece, or how that new wealth allowed Alexander to purchase the loyalty of his army by paying them twice the going wages of the most skilled masons.[4] In the Roman era, military historians marvel at the brilliant maneuvers and stratagems of Hannibal and his nemesis Scipio. Few ever mention, however, how the silver mines Hannibal controlled in Spain allowed him to keep his army in the field for almost two decades without financial support from Carthage. This factor also explains Scipio's strategy of cutting off Hannibal from this inexhaustible source of finance, while securing the mines for himself and Rome before launching his invasion of the African coast.[5] In fact, Caesar, in his war against Pompey a century and a half later, invaded Spain for the same reason: before the first winter of the war was over, he had exhausted the fifteen thousand gold bars and thirty thousand silver bars that he had seized from the Roman treasury.

Historians who focus on the military dynamics of the situation often wonder what was behind Caesar's propaganda statement, "I go to meet an army without a leader, and I shall return to meet a leader without an army."[6] The reality is that Caesar chose his main theater of operations not because Pompey had troops there, but because that was the location of the mines that would finance his war. Lost on most military historians is a fact Caesar knew well: the base of Pompey's power was Spain's wealth. Knowing it would take time to mobilize the wealth of the eastern portions of Rome's empire, Pompey had placed seven legions in Spain to protect that source of funds and recruits. Caesar knew that without access to Spain's mines Pompey would inevitably find it difficult to finance another army.[7] As it turned out, by Herculean efforts Pompey extorted sufficient money to raise an army, but it was a near-run thing and his raids on temples throughout Asia Minor and confiscation of their gold and silver did much to undermine his local support.[8]

In summary, for the 2,500 years that historians have studied war, they have largely neglected its economic sinews. As such, historians have mostly missed the way finance and economics have driven changes in operational and strategic methods, as much as if not more than technology, logistics, or even the operational brilliance of commanders. So, it is unremarkable that, while most military histories give at least passing reference to Britain's subsidies to its allies in the wars against France, there is precious little investigation into just how England revolutionized national finance so that a small, underpopulated nation could raise the funds required to fight wars on a global scale.[9]

So, it is also of little surprise that there are few military histories of World War II that focus on how economics drove Allied strategic decision making, an observation that until recently also has been true of the Axis.[10] There are, admittedly, passing references to Hitler's decision to send Kleist's panzers into the Caucasus for economic reasons, as well as his famous complaint, "My generals do not understand economics." There is also lip service paid to the fact that World War II was a war of production and materiel resources, won, in Churchill's words, "on a sea of oil."[11] Besides the work of a few economic historians who demonstrate little interest in the relationship between economics and military operations, however, serious military historians have largely failed to examine the economic decisions that drive war production or to relate them to the critical military choices of the war.

In considering World War II, this neglect has led historians to accept some startling fallacies and miss the true revolution that occurred in translating "economic potential" into the munitions of war. This book focuses on how a few almost-forgotten economists determined when the Normandy invasion would occur. In reinterpreting the strategic history of the war, it also challenges four main planks underpinning much of the extant literature. These planks have gained almost mythical status, each of which will be shown to be untrue:

1. The myth that Lieutenant General Albert Wedemeyer's prescient findings in his "Victory Program Report" became the foundation for strategic planning as well as the basic guidance for U.S. munitions production throughout the war is at odds with the demonstrable facts. The effects of Wedemeyer's Victory Plan were minimal, and what impact the report did have was almost uniformly negative.
2. The proposition that General George C. Marshall at the Casablanca Conference was a strong advocate for a second front in 1943 but British intransigence stymied his aims does not accord with the full historical record. General Marshall became aware immediately before the Casablanca Conference that the munitions production he expected the United States to produce in 1943—the basis of his strategy—would not be fully available until June 1944. Therefore, an invasion in 1943 was impossible.
3. To argue, as most historians have done, that President Roosevelt's insistence on setting what at the time appeared to be both astronomical and impossible production goals inspired and provided impetus to American industry to reach record levels of production, ultimately burying the Axis under a tsunami of U.S. munitions, is also incorrect. I will show that Roosevelt's ill-thought-out goals and his stubbornness about adjusting them came close to seizing up the entire production program and ending any practical chance of invading northern Europe in 1944. Furthermore, his insistence on producing what he called his "must items" threw U.S. production so out of balance that it endangered the conduct of military operations.
4. Finally, the myth that in the pursuit of total victory the American people sacrificed so that consumer production facilities could convert to war production is also demonstrably untrue. Consumer spending in America went up (as a percent of GDP) every year of the war, and virtually all wartime munitions production can be accounted for by GDP growth and not by limitations placed on consumer production.

There is also a factor more profound than these that economic and military historians have overlooked. World War II overturned the economic basis of major-state war, which had held true since the Battle of Marathon 2,500 years before. For more than two millennia, money had been the determining economic influence on war. As long as a ruler had the equivalent of cash on hand or access to a loan, he could continue to prosecute any war of his choosing. There were always sufficient armories to produce war materiel and enough people whose service was for sale.

Beginning in eighteenth-century Britain, this truism eroded as revolutions in the industrial and financial world began. Together, these fundamental changes eventually made possible a true nation-in-arms far beyond the dreams of the French Revolutionaries and their *levée en masse*. Industry could now produce armaments in quantities that were entire orders of magnitude beyond what the artisans of the past were capable of, while the Bank of England's *consols* could pay for them.[12] Britain had discovered that it was better for an economy to maintain a high level of liquidity by keeping as much specie in circulation as possible rather than hoarding cash and gold reserves for potential wars. By creating reliable programs for emergency debt finance, peacetime Britain could invest its income back into growing the economy while simultaneously ensuring a ready source of cash in the event of war.

Nevertheless, old habits die hard, and before the onset of World War I many looked with trepidation at the German war reserves stored inside the Spandau Fortress.[13] Rather than spend or invest a large segment of the reparations France paid after the Franco-Prussian War, Germany had stored away $70 million of gold to defray the costs of a future war. When, on the eve of war, someone reminded future British prime minister Lloyd George of this apparently massive gold reserve, he responded, "A mighty sum, but England will raise the last million."[14] It was a remarkable testament to his faith in Britain's capacity to finance a prolonged conflict, as well as proof that his government, if not historians, realized that the ability to raise massive sums of cash was still the determining economic factor in war.[15]

In any event, no one in 1914 could have envisioned the colossal sums of cash twentieth-century warfare would consume. The much-feared Spandau gold reserves proved insufficient to cover even two days of the war's expense during a major offensive. While methods of finance had improved considerably in the century and a half since Pitt the Elder, they still strained under the stress. Without the timely intervention of the United States and its untapped financial resources, the Allied financial system would have collapsed.[16] Accessing this American financial stream was by no means an easy task and the scope of the effort involved was daunting. By 1916 Britain was spending $5 million a day on the war, of which $2 million had to be raised in the United States. Still, it was not until the British credit crisis of 1917 that the United States began providing credits to the British government.[17]

While the Allied financial system adjusted to the demands of global war, industry also rapidly converted to meet new challenges. Though there were early shortages of materiel as the combatants either built or converted plants, once industry hit full stride it easily met war demands, particularly after the United States added its massive production potential to the Allied pool.[18] Reports of British Cabinet meetings of the period often reflect a concern about raising more millions, but have nary a word about running short of production capacity. While finance had closed the gap on production, it had not yet caught up. As long as the cash held out, there were always sufficient munitions available for purchase.

World War II reversed that situation. For the first time, the warring powers ran out of production capacity long before they ran out of money.[19] As U.S. Secretary of War Henry L. Stimson said after the war, "The one thing upon which the whole country was agreed was that the services must have enough money. At no time in the whole period of the emergency did I ever have to worry about funds; the appropriations from Congress were always prompt and generous. The pinch came in getting money turned into weapons."[20] As evidence that modern financial methods had closed the funding gap, the week after the United States entered the war, the head of the Federal Reserve, Marriner S. Eccles, announced he would throw the entire power of the Federal Reserve behind the war effort and that there were more than sufficient funds available to pay for the total mobilization of the country for war.[21]

Nevertheless, politicians and planners in the United States were slow to adjust to the new reality. Consequently, there were ferocious struggles between the military, civilian production experts, and the White House. From the beginning, each party knew it was in a war of production and that the Allied powers were counting on the United States to bury the Axis powers under an avalanche of war materiel. Roosevelt announced as much in his State of the Union speech one month after the attack on Pearl Harbor:

> It will not be sufficient for us and the other United Nations to produce a slightly superior supply of munitions to that of Germany, Japan, Italy, and the stolen industries in the countries which they have overrun.
>
> The superiority of the United Nations in munitions and ships must be overwhelming—so overwhelming that the Axis nations can never hope to catch up with it. In order to attain this overwhelming superiority the United States must build planes and tanks and guns and ships to the utmost limit of our national capacity. We have the ability and capacity to produce arms not only for our own forces, but also for the armies, navies, and air forces fighting on our side.[22]

It was also during this speech the Roosevelt laid out his "must items," which were to plague both the production experts and the military for the next few years. He announced that he had ordered government agencies to take all steps necessary to produce sixty thousand planes in 1942 and one hundred twenty-five thousand more in 1943. In this speech, Roosevelt also ordered that forty-five thousand tanks were to be built in 1942 and another seventy-five thousand the following year. Not quite finished, he also ordered fifty-five thousand antiaircraft guns and an additional 16 million deadweight tons of shipping to be built by the end of 1943.[23] When economists and industrialists questioned the feasibility of such plans, Roosevelt had a ready answer: "Let no man say it cannot be done. It must be done—and we have undertaken to do it."[24]

Unfortunately, Roosevelt's hopes were built on faulty assumptions. The reality was that even the United States could not achieve such monumental goals, and all of Roosevelt's cheerful optimism, cajoling, and demands for the impossible could not make it happen. In fact, his demanding the impossible actually meant that the United States would produce considerably less than if the government had told industrialists to produce an optimal amount. Unfortunately, few if any senior officers in military procurement ever grasped this point. But one can hardly blame them, since at this point in the war only a mere handful of people—unknown economists and statisticians—understood the concepts of industrial feasibility and optimal production goals.[25] These people and their contribution to victory in World War II remain mostly unknown, because military historians have greatly distorted the story of what has become known as the "Victory Program." The next two chapters will deconstruct the myth that a lone genius on the Army staff devised the strategic and industrial plan that would win the war, and will also correct the record so that those who did understand and undertake this endeavor get the credit they deserve.

CHAPTER 2

Unmaking the Victory Program

★ ★ ★

It has become an article of faith among historians that then–Major Albert Wedemeyer, a junior member of the Army's War Plans Division, foresaw and laid out America's mobilization and production effort during World War II. The basis of this claim lies in a nineteen-page document, "The Ultimate Requirements Study: Estimate of Ground Forces," that Wedemeyer completed in early September of 1941. The histories of World War II, which mention what became known as the "Victory Program," generally focus on this as a document of remarkable prescience and the basis of most of America's wartime strategic and mobilization planning. Ironically, such reviewers developed this opinion without ever reading the document. In fact, Wedemeyer's Victory Program was wrong in nearly every particular.[1] *Moreover, its effect on mobilization or future war plans appears to have been virtually nil. In fact, one searches in vain for documents, memos, or letters produced during the war that reference Wedemeyer's program.*[2] *In modern terms, Wedemeyer's version of the Victory Program is analogous to any one of hundreds of PowerPoint presentations given to Pentagon audiences every month—over in an hour and just as quickly forgotten.*

It was not until after the war that historians discovered Wedemeyer's Victory Program and created the myth of a lone genius who clearly saw the path the United States must follow. In *Chief of Staff: Prewar Plans and*

Preparations, a volume of the Army's official history of the war, Mark Watson devotes a whole chapter to Wedemeyer's work.[3] In only a single footnote does the reader learn that the chapter rests almost entirely on the author's conversations with by then–Lieutenant General Wedemeyer.[4] In fact, Wedemeyer's life-long marketing effort to secure his place in history appears behind virtually all of the uncritical acceptances of claims that he was the author of the Victory Program. In his own 1958 book, *Wedemeyer Reports!*, the general was not shy about claiming credit as the genius behind U.S. planning for the war. He went into great detail about how he formulated the Victory Program and how it influenced later deliberations.[5] Throughout his life, Wedemeyer's various efforts at self-promotion were unceasing. In an extensive oral history recorded by the Center for Military History in 1972, he again put the formulation of the Victory Program at the forefront of Joint Chiefs of Staff (JCS) planning for the war.[6] In the same interview, however, Wedemeyer lamented that he had never received credit for many of the other ideas, which he claimed originated with him, including the plan for Operation Overlord and the postwar Berlin Airlift.[7]

In 1990 the Center for Military History continued a long tradition of official scholarship crediting the Victory Program to Wedemeyer when it published Charles Kirkpatrick's *An Unknown Future and a Doubtful Present: Writing the Victory Plan of 1941*, which argued that Wedemeyer's Victory Program represented the most important strategic document of the war. Only in the preface does the author acknowledge that his entire work rests on extensive interviews with Wedemeyer, who oversaw every aspect of the writing and production of yet another official report glorifying his work.[8]

Wedemeyer's greatest postwar public relations coup, however, was to call his study the Victory Program, thereby confusing or conflating it with the actual "Victory Plan," which industrialists used to conduct their production planning. The actual title of General Wedemeyer's study was the more prosaic, "The Ultimate Requirements Study: Estimate of the Army Ground Forces," and the term Victory Plan occurs nowhere in the text.[9] The actual Victory Plan was a combination of a strategic policy document written by Chief of Naval Operations Admiral Harold R. Stark, and a production plan written by Stacy May, an economist in the Office of Production Management (OPM). The contributions of both will be examined in considerable detail later.

Churchill's comment that "history would be kind to him because he intended to write it" was not lost on Wedemeyer. To a large degree, Wedemeyer patiently wrote himself into the historical narrative step by step over the course of fifty years. As a result, historians have generally accepted the general's version that his Victory Program was central to America's planning in World War II. How did he get away with this historical scam? Mostly by focusing attention on the one thing his Victory Program got right. Wedemeyer had predicted that the United States could field a maximum military force of between 12 million and 14 million men, a figure remarkably close to the number finally mobilized—12 million at the peak.[10]

Late in life Wedemeyer provided an account of how he arrived at this number. He claimed to have inquired from a number of government agencies and Princeton University's Demographics Center as to the number of people it would take to maintain industry, agriculture, and government.[11] Once he had those figures in hand, he deducted the final total from the male population: what was left over was available for mobilization. Such a thoughtful approach would be more believable if any records of such inquiries could be found in the papers Wedemeyer later deposited at the Hoover Institution.[12] Moreover, Princeton's Demographics Center during the prewar period focused its research exclusively on fertility studies and third-world development, and would not have possessed the information Wedemeyer required.[13]

In most of his interviews, however, and in his own book, Wedemeyer claimed he reached this number by conducting a thorough study of military history to determine that a country could mobilize at most 10 percent of its total population before it would ruin its economic base and no longer be capable of supporting its war effort.[14] Given that the United States had a prewar population of approximately 140 million, it was a simple mathematical equation to arrive at the conclusion that it could mobilize only 14 million. Unfortunately, even the most elementary survey of military history fails to support Wedemeyer's assertions. Prior to the French Revolution and the advent of the *levée en masse,* it was unheard of for military forces to approach even 3 percent of a nation or region's population for any prolonged period. Even the highly organized Roman Empire found it impossible to sustain a mobilization level much greater than 2 percent.[15] Table 2.1 shows the military participation ratio that nations sustained prior to 1789.[16]

Even at the height of the Napoleonic Wars, the French had only 1.1 million of their population under arms, a bit less than 5 percent. By 1813, however, France could not even sustain that level of mobilization, though Prussia had managed by this time to mobilize 6 percent of its population. Of course, this Prussian achievement was possible only because Britain, through subsidies, was underwriting a substantial portion of Prussia's economic burden.[17] Russia,

Table 2.1 The Military Participation Ratio: The Principal European Powers, 1789

Country	Population	Army	Military Participation Ratio
Austria	20 million	300,000	1.5%
Britain	16 million	50,000	0.3%
France	24 million	255,000	1.6%
Prussia	9 million	200,000	2.2%
Russia	35 million	400,000	1.1%

Source: Strategy World n.d.

with a much larger population but an inferior economic base, was able to mobilize only 2 percent of its population for the great effort in 1813 to finish off Napoleon.[18]

By 1914 the spread of the Industrial Revolution had made it possible for Western nations to support far larger forces than ever before. One would expect that it was this conflict, which ended at the start of Wedemeyer's military career, that most influenced his conclusions. Once again, however, the actual mobilization numbers do not justify his maximum numbers of 10 percent.

As Table 2.2 indicates, France and Britain mobilized more than double the numbers of men that Wedemeyer argued was the maximum possible. In fact, France suffered casualties that exceeded Wedemeyer's maximum limit for total mobilization, while Germany and England were not far behind. If Wedemeyer had focused his studies on only American wars, he would have found some support for his 10 percent number during the Civil War, but in no other American conflict (see Table 2.3).[19]

So where did Wedemeyer's 10 percent figure come from? With no evidence of serious analysis on his part, one can only assume that he made up his estimates out of whole cloth.[20] Wherever it came from, Wedemeyer used that calculation as the basis of the rest of his strategic plan for the conduct of World War II. Rather than attempting to design military forces based on national objectives and what the military required to achieve them, Wedemeyer designed a force based entirely on what his fabrications suggested the country could support—in other words, the exact opposite of how one should make strategic plans.

Table 2.2 National Mobilization for World War I

Country	Population	Mobilized	Killed/ Wounded
Germany	67 million	16.5%	9%
Russia	90.5 million	13.5%	7%
France	41 million	21%	11%
United Kingdom	41 million	22%	8%

Source: Spencer C. Tucker, *The European Powers in the First World War: An Encyclopedia* (New York: Garland Publishing, 1996); Philip J. Haythornthwaite, *The World War One Source Book* (London: Diane Publishing, 1993); and Michael Clodfelter, *Warfare and Armed Conflicts: A Statistical Reference to Casualty and Other Figures* (Jefferson, NC: McFarland, 1992). A statistical round up can be found at http://www.spartacus.schoolnet.co.uk/FWWdeaths.htm (accessed 1 February 2008).

Table 2.3 American Mobilization Levels

Conflict	Population	Enrolled	Mobilized
Revolutionary War	3,500,000	200,000	5.7%
War of 1812	7,600,000	286,000	3.8%
Mexican War	21,100,000	78,700	0.4%
Civil War			
— Union	26,200,000	2,803,300	10.7%
— Confederate	8,100,000	1,064,200	13.1%
— Combined	34,300,000	3,867,500	11.1%
Spanish-American War	74,600,000	306,800	0.4%
World War I	102,800,000	4,743,800	4.6%

Wedemeyer's papers do contain detailed handwritten and printed copies of what he titled "The Army Troop Basis." None of these troop basis studies appear to have been completed prior to May 1942, however (and all were radically revised in December 1942). These "Troop Basis Estimates" appear to be just a detailed breakdown of the subunits of the divisions that the Wedemeyer study stated the Army should build, with a unit strength placed beside them. There are no tables of allowances included with the troop estimates, nor any details on production requirements or schedules of when the Army would require the materiel to equip these units.[21]

Is there a possible explanation for this? Yes. In a nutshell, determining a troop basis was Wedemeyer's assignment. Contrary to the picture the general painted for historians, he never had a role or responsibility in determining the materiel or production requirements for equipping such a force. It would have been strange if he had been given such an assignment, since the head of the War Plans Division, General Leonard T. Gerow, who assigned Wedemeyer his tasks, certainly knew he had no experience or expertise in the area. All of the consultations in the world would not have made Wedemeyer an expert logistician in just ninety days, and it would have been absurd for Gerow to assume he could undertake such a task.

Due to Wedemeyer's postwar influence and dedication to writing an oversized role for himself into the historical record, however, the Army's official history, which credits Wedemeyer's recollections as its source, recounts an untrue account.[22] According to Mark Watson, in May 1941 General Marshall asked then–Major Wedemeyer to undertake an assignment whose "immense reach, complexity, and importance were not surmised by the Staff itself until the ultimate product, 'the Victory Program' of 10 September 1941, was completed."[23]

In a recently discovered and never published history of the JCS, written immediately after the war by an officer who was serving on the JCS and whose account Wedemeyer did not influence, a very different picture emerges.[24] On 27 May 1941 General Marshall held a conference with his immediate assistants to consider the problems involved in the build-up of Army ground and air forces to the strengths required for the successful execution of the Army tasks under the new war plan—Rainbow 5. During the meeting Deputy Chief of Staff (Major) General R. C. Moore pointed out that the General Staff was "receiving pressure from newspapers and otherwise to go above the present supply objectives and to procure a war reserve. Moore then forcefully made the case that the only way to procure this reserve was by making a strategic estimate of the situation, based on the capabilities of Germany, Japan, Italy, and Great Britain. Marshall agreed, and ordered the General Staff and Air Corps to begin immediate preparation of estimates. In the War Plans Division, Major Wedemeyer was charged with preparation of estimates of the necessary ultimate strength of the Army, while Colonel Henry Aurand (acting, assistant chief of staff, G-4) began preparation of estimates on materiel requirements. In Guyer's version of events, on 31 May Colonel Aurand submitted a preliminary estimate of the time required for the build-up of Army ground and air forces. In a cover letter, Aurand explained: "From the information available to G-4, it will not be until after 1 July 1942 that the production of anti-aircraft and anti-tank equipment will be sufficient to supply all of the requirements so far set up. It will probably not be until 1 July 1943 that the ground Army, complete in all of its estimates, will be able to conduct extensive operations."[25]

After receiving this report, on 3 June the War Plans Division, with General Marshall's approval, informed the other General Staff Divisions and production agencies that the strategic estimate under preparation would assume 1 July 1943 to be "the earliest date when the United States armed forces can be mobilized, trained, and equipped for offensive operations."[26] This estimate became the basis for the Army proposals then incorporated into the "Victory Requirements Program."

The War Plans Division's proclamation makes several key points that are important to this study. First, it clearly establishes that Wedemeyer was not the only officer tasked with producing an estimate for what victory required. Colonel Aurand, who as a professional logistician would have possessed the expertise to determine munitions requirements, was assigned a large portion of the task.[27] Moreover, contrary to Watson's account, he was not tasked just to provide information to Major Wedemeyer. In fact, Aurand completed his materiel estimates a full three months before Wedemeyer submitted his study.[28] It is also clear that Aurand's submission became the basis of Army estimates presented to the civilian production authorities.[29] A footnote in Guyer's history states that General Marshall forwarded a memorandum, titled "Ultimate Munitions Production Essential to the Safety of America," to the chief of naval operations (Admiral Stark) on 7 June 1941 for inclusion in the combined requirements study to be sent to the White House, three months before Wedemeyer submitted his final work.[30]

More crucially, this production requirement estimate had a major effect on future strategic planning because it placed the idea firmly in Marshall's and the joint planners' minds that the Army would have all it required for extensive offensive operations (northern Europe) by 1943. Once this date was implanted as a possibility, it proved difficult to get Marshall to move away from it as the point when the United States could begin decisive operations in Europe.[31]

Since Wedemeyer's force design had no relation to what the American military would have to accomplish to win the war, it is no wonder his so-called Victory Plan was also wrong in many other respects. Wedemeyer's Victory Plan called for the creation of 215 combat divisions (actual number built: ninety). Sixty-one of those divisions would be armored (actual number built: sixteen), sixty-one would be motorized (none of these was built), and twenty would be airborne or mountain divisions (six were eventually built).[32]

His strategic assumptions proved even wider off the mark. Wedemeyer's study stated that the Germans would quickly defeat Russia and would be able to focus their entire military force in the West; that a 1943 Allied assault on Europe would face four hundred full-strength German divisions; and that Japan was unlikely to enter into a war with the United States because it would be fully occupied with China. This final point was a remarkable statement to make in a report finalized only two months before the attack on Pearl Harbor.

Astonishingly, as late as 2005 the Army Center for Military History published a history of the American Army that claims Wedemeyer foresaw a two-front war with Germany and Japan—a claim that is directly contradicted by his actual so-called Victory Plan.[33] Because he did manage to "guess" the approximate number of men mobilized for the conflict, however, many historians have supported claims that Wedemeyer's program provided the basis for industrial mobilization. With his plan in hand, industrialists for the first time supposedly possessed a document that would guide them in the rearmament of the United States.

Even that claim is false. There is no indication that any of the key individuals involved with industrial planning and rearmament gave Wedemeyer's plan any consideration at all.[34] In fact, except for the military histories of the conflict that were directly influenced by Wedemeyer's decades-long campaign to enhance his own reputation, there is no evidence that anyone involved in industrial production ever heard of the plan's existence.[35] Furthermore, if the experts who managed the rearmament program had seen Wedemeyer's plan, they would have found it of little value.[36]

Although the nineteen-page Wedemeyer study did not include a listing of munitions or materiel required to equip and maintain this force, Wedemeyer in his autobiography claimed that he consulted at great length with the logistics experts in G-4 and the Army's Quartermaster and Ordnance branches to get just such estimates.[37] Although the Wedemeyer Papers stored at Stanford's Hoover Institution include numerous munitions spreadsheets, he incorporated none of this information in his study. In fact, almost all the spreadsheets within Wedemeyer's collected papers are Air Force and British studies of their respective requirements. What spreadsheets do exist detailing Army munitions requirements are dated after Wedemeyer had finished his study and appear to be copies of the refined product of Colonel Aurand and his G-4 staff.

In fact, long before Wedemeyer ever began working on his plan, a few farsighted economists and production experts had begun clamoring for information on military-munitions requirements. For months the production organizations had banged their heads against the military bureaucracy without result. It was not until after the war that General Marshall and other senior officers admitted why the services had remained silent: the Allies did not have an agreed-upon global strategy for the war until after the Trident Conference in May 1943.[38] Without answers to key questions such as when or even if America would invade northern Europe or whether there would be a single thrust in the Pacific or two mostly autonomous thrusts, there was no way for JCS planners to provide production experts with reliable estimates of their requirements.

In a 1948 speech General Brehon Somervell, who commanded Army Services Forces and was responsible for coordinating production with strategy, seconded the production experts' frustrations. Somervell acknowledged it was impossible to build a realistic production plan without knowing "the size of the forces required, the kind of war you are going to fight, and the possible theaters of operation." He went on to admit this was impossible because "it was not until after we were well into the war that the size of the forces we expected to employ was determined." He then admitted that if the United States had possessed a strategy for the war early on "it would have been of immeasurable help in building production plans.[39] This not only explains why the military could not answer the production experts' questions, but also underlines that not even the military paid much attention to Wedemeyer's strategic formulations. If they had, they could have easily created basic "tables of allowances" from his required ground force estimates and told the production agencies to build from those tables.[40]

One other major problem the production experts encountered early in the mobilization deserves mention now. There was great reluctance on the part of those in the military, particularly procurement officers, to ask for much. In the first place, their estimates of requirements to fight a global war were woefully low, but the refusal of most procurement officers to ask for even this bare minimum compounded this difficulty.[41] It was neither in their nature nor within America's military culture to ask Congress for large appropriations. As one historian has noted, "The War Department was to a lamentable extent, cowed by the force of isolationist sentiment on Capitol Hill and was trained to be timid in requests for appropriations."[42] The officers who were the most successful in peacetime were those who Congress identified as economy-minded. Unfortunately, sailors or soldiers who are economy-minded rarely win wars.

In one 1940 example, production czar Donald M. Nelson asked textile manufacturer Robert Stevens to probe around and find out what the Army needed in textiles. Stevens then asked a military procurement officer for an estimate of how many parachutes the Army would require during the war. In due time, he received the answer that nine thousand would suffice, to which Stevens replied he would ask for two hundred thousand. When a procurement officer berated him for his wildly high estimate, Stevens defended his number by saying, "The President wants to build 50,000 planes and they will have an average crew size of four. I simply multiplied."[43] In the event, the United States produced and used almost 10 million parachutes during the war.

According to Robert Sherwood, "Although Secretary of War Stimson and General Marshall were well aware of the urgency; the generals and colonels charged with the implementation of policy were trained to rigidly adhere to established tables of organization." It was their job to take the number of American soldiers currently authorized by Congress and multiply that by the various items of equipment required. "They had been trained to believe that if they asked for more than the irreducible minimum they would find themselves detailed to instruction in some boy's military academy in South Dakota . . . where promotion was apt to be slow."[44]

The simple fact was that the military, despite years of planning and having sent hundreds of senior officers to the Industrial Staff College, had absolutely no idea on the eve of war of what the services would need to fight.[45] Founded in 1924 "to train Army officers in the useful knowledge pertaining to the supervision of procurement of all military supplies in time of war and to the assurance of adequate provision for the mobilization of materiel and industrial organizations essential to war-time needs," the Army Industrial College had graduated more than one thousand officers by 1941, few of whom were actually prepared to assist in mobilizing industry for total war. For almost the entire period from 1924 to 1941 the school had focused its students on learning and refining the Industrial Mobilization Plan (IMP), which would have placed the military in charge of all production (including civilian production). When Roosevelt scrapped the IMP and placed the military in a secondary role behind the civilian production agencies, the Industrial College cadres became bewildered and ineffective. Worse still, anyone who might have had any inclination of what was required was too afraid to ask for it. In the event, Wedemeyer's work did nothing to enlighten them. That guidance had to come from other sources.

CHAPTER 3

The Real Victory Program

★ ★ ★

If the Wedemeyer Plan did not determine or predict the future strategic direction or production priorities of the United States, what did? The answer lies in two parts. The first is the military dimension that rested almost entirely on a memorandum written by Chief of Naval Operations Admiral Harold R. Stark. This memorandum later became the basis of a joint memorandum (signed by Admiral Stark and General Marshall) to the president. From a historical point of view, this study is noteworthy in two respects: it was the only strategic guidance the president kept in his office, and it is rarely mentioned in the U.S. Army's official histories of the war.[1] *However, there was one exception: someone commented, "Admiral Stark's document constitutes perhaps the most important single document in the development of World War II strategy."*[2]

The second key portion of the actual Victory Plan was an economic spreadsheet prepared by Stacy May, a statistician on the War Production Board (WPB). Though a number of other people played a role in May's formulations, he was the driving force behind the creation of a combined "balance sheet," which then became the basis of all early production planning for the war. In fact, two British economic historians have gone so far as to argue that May's work was the cardinal concept of the real Victory Program.[3]

Plan Dog

Prior to the outbreak of World War II, the code name for America's strategy for a future war was "Plan Orange."[4] This plan, worked out over decades, basically identified Japan as America's primary future enemy and called for the United States to send its fleet across the Pacific to seek a decisive naval engagement with the Imperial Japanese Navy at the earliest possible date. In 1940, Admiral Stark became convinced that both assumptions were wrong: Japan was not America's most dangerous enemy, and America's entire concept of how to fight a future war was off the mark.

In a single day, working alone in his study, Stark created the outline for a new strategic plan. Afterwards, during the last week in October, he met with key naval staff members for several hours a day to discuss his concepts.[5] By 2 November 1940 he had sufficiently satisfied himself with the concept to produce a draft memorandum, which he forwarded to Marshall for the Army chief of staff's review and concurrence before presenting it to the secretary of the Navy.[6]

It is easy to see why Marshall immediately concurred with Stark: the central point of Admiral Stark's analysis was the recognition that American security depended to a large extent on the fate of Great Britain. Stark's opening assertion, "if Britain wins decisively against Germany we could win everywhere; but that if she loses the problems confronting us would be very great; and while we might not *lose everywhere*, we might, possibly, not *win* anywhere" (emphasis in original), directly coincided with Marshall's strategic formulations.[7] Should the British Empire collapse, it seemed probable to Stark that the victorious Axis powers would seek to expand their control— economically at first and then politically and militarily—into the Western Hemisphere. For Stark, the consequences of a British defeat were so serious for the United States that he declared Britain ought to be assisted in every way possible. Stark also made it clear that he did not believe Britain had the manpower or materiel to conquer Germany, and that U.S. assistance would be required for ultimate victory.[8]

In a passage certain to endear his analysis to Marshall, Stark declared, "The only certain way of defeating Germany is by military success on shore; for that, bases close to the European continent would be required.[9] Although most mentions of Plan Dog in the historical record claim that plan was formulated by Stark in relative isolation, Guyer claims that Admiral Stark and General Marshall had "long and continuous consultations concerning national defense policy plans and preparations."[10] Guyer goes on to say that Marshall agreed with the conclusions of the Stark memorandum, and had emphatically expressed these same concepts in a June 1940 meeting, concerning the dangers that would result for the United States from a German-Italian victory in the invasion of France. During this meeting, Marshall also posed a question of the grand strategy: How would the United States meet simultaneous threats in both the Atlantic and the Pacific? He then answered his own question: "Are we not forced into reframing our naval policy, into one that is purely defensive in the Pacific, with the main effort in the Atlantic?"[11]

As for Japan, Stark also placed it on the second tier of enemies and thereby reversed decades of Navy assumptions and planning.[12] The Navy's Orange Plan had contemplated the eventual economic starvation of Japan, followed by the complete destruction of that country's military power. The Navy assumed that Plan Orange would require several years, and would absorb the full military, naval, and economic energy of the American people. In his Plan Dog memorandum, Stark claimed that this focus was no longer feasible. As Stark saw it, because the need to send large forces to Britain required major naval efforts in the Atlantic, few resources remained for employment in the Pacific, where the United States would remain on a strict defensive.[13]

As Stark saw it, America had to choose between four major strategic options, which he stated as questions:

(A) Shall our principal military effort be directed toward hemisphere defense, and include chiefly those activities within the Western Hemisphere which contribute directly to security against attack in either or both oceans?
(B) Shall we prepare for a full offensive against Japan, premised on assistance from the British and Dutch forces in the Far East, and remain on the strict defensive in the Atlantic?
(C) Shall we plan for sending the strongest possible military assistance both to the British in Europe, and to the British, Dutch and Chinese in the Far East?
(D) Shall we direct our efforts toward an eventual strong offensive in the Atlantic as an ally of the British, and a defensive in the Pacific?[14]

As far as Admiral Stark was concerned, there was no doubt that "Option D" was superior to the others ("Option D" is what gave the plan its name—"Dog" being the letter D in American military parlance).[15] As he further argued, "I believe that the continued existence of the British Empire, combined with building up a strong protection in our home areas, will do most to ensure the status quo in the Western Hemisphere, and to promote our principal national interests."[16]

On 12 November 1940 Admiral Stark forwarded the plan, with Marshall's concurrence, to Frank Knox, secretary of the Navy, who immediately forwarded it to the White House. There is no record that Roosevelt ever approved the plan, but from Marshall's and Stark's perspectives it was just as important that the president did not disapprove it. Although Roosevelt, Stimson, Knox, and Secretary of State Cordell Hull were never called on formally to approve Stark's and Marshall's proposals, which were adopted by the joint board as a basis for redefining national defense policy and strategy, "the Secretaries of War and the Navy were in full agreement with the proposals, while tacit approval was given by the President."[17] Knowing that Roosevelt had just won an election by promising to stay out of the war, both officers realized he could not officially comment on the memorandum. However, knowing that the president was never slow to demolish an idea he did not favor, the two took his silence as tacit approval.[18]

When the first plenary session of American-British-Canadian (ABC) staff talks got under way on 29 January 1941, Plan Dog became the basis of agreement, essentially restated as ABC-1.[19] This agreement, later integrated into the Navy and Joint Rainbow 5 Plan, placed Germany at the center of Allied efforts and became the foundation stone for subsequent discussions about strategy during the war.[20]

The Production Victory Program

Although by early 1941 the United States had cast a new strategic conception of how it would fight a future global war, the planners had yet to match that strategy against national resources and capabilities. In reaction to the production chiefs' continuous requests for guidance from the military planners, on 9 July 1941 the president wrote letters to Secretary of War Stimson and Secretary of the Navy Knox ordering them to, "Explore the munitions and mechanical equipment of all types which in your opinion would be required to exceed by an appropriate amount that available to our potential enemies." Roosevelt further directed that both departments establish munitions objectives that could be used to determine "the industrial capacity which this nation will require."[21]

In no uncertain terms, Roosevelt had just asked the war secretaries for a munitions Victory Program. For the first time he had gone beyond asking what it would take to defend the United States, but now asked for assumptions based on an all-out effort in a global war.[22] The president's letter was referred to the Joint Board, and that Board sent a response to the president on 11 September. The response, signed by both Marshall and Stark, was essentially a restatement of Plan Dog: "The Joint Board is convinced that the first major objective of the United States and its Associates ought to be the complete military defeat of Germany. If Germany were defeated, her entire European system would collapse, and it is probable that Japan could be forced to give up much of her territorial gains, unless she had already firmly established herself in such strength that the United States and its Associates could not afford the energy to continue the war against her."[23]

This report was supposed to include two annexes laying out the production estimates of the Navy and the Army. Unfortunately, the one complete copy of the report available has only the Navy estimate included.[24] This estimate is actually close to what the United States produced in terms of combat ships, though it misses the mark considerably in terms of the requirements for the merchant marine and landing craft. The accuracy of the combat ship estimates reflected the fact that the Navy was working with a friendly Congress and a president who had formerly been an assistant secretary of the Navy. Unlike the Army, Congress approved the Navy's shipbuilding program, which included appropriations, on a multiyear basis. This removed the guesswork from the Navy estimates because its shipbuilding program had the effect of law. This was to have serious ramifications later when the entire production program was found to be unfeasible. The Navy never had to take its fair share of the cuts because Congress had approved its programs.

The Army's production and manpower requirements were not included, but according to one source they mainly consisted of estimates of what the Army required to reinforce the Philippines and what the Army required for immediate hemispheric defense.[25] Apparently, the Army staff was unwilling at this point to defend its previously delivered estimates assembled by Colonel Burns and Colonel Aurand.[26] As we have seen, Wedemeyer's force predictions were impractical, and their impracticability was compounded by the fact that G-4 personnel were unable to convert their tables of allowances" into production requirements.[27] In reality though, the White House, and particularly presidential adviser Harry Hopkins, refused to pay much attention to production estimates coming from the military, with one exception: those of Colonel James Burns.

Time magazine described Burns as Harry Hopkins' munitions workhorse—a man who knew more about the materiel and munitions needs of the Allied powers than did anyone in Washington.[28] In 1941 he was a fifty-five-year-old congenial Irishman who seemed to know and get along with everyone. Later promoted to general, he would direct all Army munitions production and distribution throughout the war. In 1941 he was Hopkins' de facto executive officer as well as the soldier to whom Hopkins would most likely turn for advice on production recommendations and capabilities.

Long before Wedemeyer supposedly began toiling on his estimates, Burns was making his own tabulations. As early as 1938 Burns had been working on estimates of what the time lag would be from the moment a decision was made to build a 1 million- or 2 million–person Army until industry could reasonably equip such a force.[29] This work, plus his selection to represent the Army on the Office of Production Management's (OPM's) Planning Committee (which also included close presidential adviser and friend Harry Hopkins), provided Burns with a greater familiarity with the capabilities of American industry than did any other officer in the War Department.[30] Thus, in response to a plea from William S. Knudsen—Donald Nelson's predecessor as the chief coordinator of U.S. production—for more detailed knowledge of the Army's requirements, Burns went to work in the spring and summer of 1941 to provide a rough outline of requirements. Burns also prompted G-4 to begin its own work in this area, which accounts for Colonel Aurand's remarkably quick turnaround on his portion of the Victory Program. Knudsen had earlier told the secretary of war he had two critical questions that required immediate answers: "How much munitions productive capacity does the country need and how rapidly must it become available?"[31]

Drawing on his two years of familiarity with the question, Burns took little time in producing his estimates. Though rough in outline, the secretary of war signed off on Burns' program and had it delivered to Knudsen.[32] Through Hopkins, it soon made its way to the president and became the first firm statement of long-range Army objectives. It also became the basis for planning by the OPM and industrialists and was the underlying basis of the numbers presented by Colonel Aurand in his portion of the Victory Program, "Ultimate Munitions Production Essential to the Safety of America." Its key points are outlined in the following chart.[33]

Working in a rush, Colonel Burns sent a copy to the Army for approval, with the blunt demand for a reply within thirty minutes of receipt. Marshall replied personally, "I concur in the above quantity objectives, but I consider

Ground Army		
Production for a combat Army of	1 million men	1 October 1941
	2 million men	1 January 1942
	4 million men	1 April 1942
Air Army Production sufficient to meet air needs comparable to those of a ground Army of each stated size at each date; i.e.,		
Annual production capacity of	9,000 planes	by 1 October 1941
	18,000 planes	by 1 January 1942
	36,000 planes	by 1 April 1942

it of imperative importance that means be found to advance the date for the needs of the first million herein scheduled for October 1, 1941."[34]

From later discussions held at the White House and from the recorded planning activities of the OPM, it is clear that Burns' numbers became the basis for determining military production requirements to support a growing Army. Possibly because Burns' numbers arrived so closely to when Wedemeyer was completing his work, later historians confused the two. Every official history states that Wedemeyer delivered his Victory Program (*Ultimate Requirements Study Estimate of Army Ground Forces*) to the president on 11 September 1941. However, that claim is incorrect. It was a restatement of Stark's Plan Dog that was delivered on this date. Moreover, a side-by-side comparison of Wedemeyer's plans and assumptions with what the president actually received on 11 September shows that it incorporated none of Wedemeyer's conceptions in the final product.[35] Since the Army munitions requirements are not with the copy in the president's safe, it is a reasonable assumption that they were not delivered at this time—at least not in usable form—making Burns' and Aurand's estimates the War Department's default position.[36]

The production people, now led by Donald Nelson, still found the new 11 September document and the included production estimates nearly worthless for planning purposes because it consisted mainly of a troops estimate. While the Army might have a good idea of what it took to equip a million-person

Army, the production experts had no clue: how many tanks, artillery pieces, blankets, and so on, in the end would that Army need? On 17 September Nelson had to request a new estimate of requirements. The War Department complied with a document that stated this was a "tentative" list of requirements for a "hypothetical" question about the needs for defeating "potential" enemies.[37]

Economist Robert Nathan later outlined some of the frustrations the production people confronted:

> We were trying to find out what the military requirements would be under varying assumptions and circumstances so we could have a basis for planning what raw materials, what factories, what machinery, what tools and what components we would need for the production of armaments. First I went to the Army and the Navy. When I asked them about military requirements, they asked "are we preparing for a land war, a sea war, or an air war, a defensive war on the U.S. continent?" I was not in any more of a position to tell them what kind of war to prepare for than I was to tell them how to build a bomber or a tank. There seemed to be no way to get those requirements because they indicated that such numbers did not exist.
>
> I remember asking them: "What are your varying assumptions about defense? You must have some assumptions and some lists of quantities of weapons and planes and ships needed under varied assumptions." They said, "We have no estimates of requirements under varying assumptions. If you tell us how many tanks you want, we have tables of allowances and can tell you how many tons of steel or how many pounds of this or that go into a tank, but we do not know whether this is to be a one-million-man Army or a ten-million-man Army." I then said, "Give us the requirements for a one-million-man, and a five-million-man, and a ten-million-man Army." Their reply was: "We are not going to do all of that work unless we have some indication of what kind of prospective hostilities we will face."[38]

In late 1941, after much prodding from civilian production agencies, the Army and Navy Munitions Board (ANMB) finally delivered a list of raw material requirements required to support a 4 million–person military establishment. Apparently, the ANMB assembled this report without referencing the work done by the Army's G-4 or its operations planning section, and there is no indication that the ANMB even knew of Wedemeyer's work. In any event, the civilian production experts at the OPM found themselves less than impressed with the new ANMB estimates and forwarded a blistering note to Nelson, pointing out just how awful the military estimates were. For instance, over the next two years the Army claimed it needed 500 million pounds of aluminum, twenty-five thousand tons of copper, and 13 million pounds of silk. The civilians, however, placed these estimates at 1 billion pounds of aluminum, 1 million tons of copper, and 3 million pounds of silk. According to the letter's author, Robert Nathan, the Army's IMP bore no relationship to realistic demands. As for the Navy, Nathan considered their estimates as nothing more than wild guesses and stated the Navy did not possess the experts on its staff to undertake any meaningful estimates.[39] It is impossible to determine the source of the ANMB's raw materials estimates, but given that they were off the mark by orders of magnitude, it is not unreasonable to assume ANMB might also have fabricated estimates out of thin air.

The Consolidated Balance Sheet

Despairing of receiving a requirements list from either the War or Navy department, the production organizations took matters into their own hands. Stacy May, an economist/statistician working with the Supply Priorities and Allocations Board (SPAB), became so incensed with the poor quality of the military estimates that he created his own.[40] From Colonel Burns' memorandum, the production experts knew they would need to construct a 2 million–person Army by early 1942. By using that as a base, they could double the requirements on a prearranged schedule, as the Army size multiplied. What May needed was to create a template for a functioning Army around those numbers and then determine if there were sufficient raw materials and industrial capacity to build such a force.

May had come to Washington from the Rockefeller Foundation where, according to his boss, Donald Nelson, he had led a rather sheltered life among his graphs, research, and papers on social and economic trends.[41] He was the first head of the Bureau of Research and Statistics at the National Defense Advisory Commission (NDAC) and continued in that position through succeeding production bureaus.[42]

Upon arriving in Washington, May met with Jean Monnet, who Robert Nathan and Robert Sherwood, in separate histories, both refer to as "the unsung hero of World War II."[43] Monnet had first involved himself with war production when he had headed the French delegation to Britain to coordinate inter-Allied activities on the outbreak of the war. When France surrendered, Monnet immediately did two things: he cabled the American government to ship all war materiel ordered by France to the United Kingdom, and then he closed the Anglo-French Coordinating Committee on his way to asking Churchill for a job.

Churchill immediately took him on as an adviser, whereupon Monnet began an unceasing quest to convince anyone who would listen that, if the British wished to survive, they must depend on America for the bulk of their industrial production. At a meeting of the War Cabinet, Monnet once placed a scaled map of England, Scotland, and Wales over the Northeast United States and told them that the map underneath held double the industrial production of the United Kingdom, and that it in turn represented only a tenth of U.S. industrial capacity. He was fond of telling people that the whole industrial strength of the United States, should it be directed toward war making, would construe "power never dreamed of before in the history of Armageddon."[44] Because of his obsession with enlisting U.S. production into Britain's service, Churchill eventually sent him to the United States as part of the British supply and munitions board, directed by Arthur Purvis.

When he arrived in the United States, Monnet announced he had but one goal: to convince America to put its industrial capacity behind winning the war against Hitler.[45] He has been described as a man of calm, cool reason, but one completely focused on his objective from which he never deviated.[46] Nathan later described him in the following terms:

> He was a master operator at a critical time, when his rare talents were desperately needed. Monnet formulated issues and solutions in ways that evoked constructive and positive responses. His statements about American production being needed to win the war attracted much support, since no one had stated the problem in those terms before. Monnet's operating and maneuvering were unbelievably creative, persistent, and ultimately effective. He would send cables to Roosevelt from Churchill or vice versa, and then he would prepare the reply for the other to send. He worked very closely with Robert Patterson and Jack McCloy, then Deputy and Assistant Secretaries of War. He knew Supreme Court Justice Felix Frankfurter, who was very close to the President and himself not an amateur manipulator. Monnet once said in a meeting with Frankfurter the words "arsenal for democracy." Frankfurter immediately asked him to "never use that phrase again." Monnet asked, "Why?" Frankfurter said, "I want that phrase for

> President Roosevelt."[47] And sure enough, Roosevelt later said, "The United States would be the arsenal for democracy."[48]

One of the issues on which Monnet constantly harped was his conviction that all would be lost unless Britain and America established franker military ties and closer industrial collaboration. This was an idea that May had developed independently, and the two became natural allies.[49] Monnet and May together became the disciples of close production collaboration and relentlessly pushed the idea on those who would listen. But this collaboration required the mutual exchange of detailed information, which both sides considered military secrets and were reluctant to share. Undeterred, throughout the winter of 1940–41 May kept pushing the argument that if the United States were really interested in helping Britain, both countries needed to produce a coordinated list of what they wanted—not as of that moment, but for a year or more in the future. May also argued that the United States had to know what Britain could produce, what its materiel potential was, and what its stockpiles were. However, such information was considered by both the British and the Americans as a deep military secret. There was no precedent for this level of intimate sharing of knowledge, and neither side knew how to do it, or even if it was possible. Even during World War I, neither Britain nor the United States had ever told the other what it was producing. While there had been some military integration, there was no industrial integration during the Great War.[50]

The best the British were able to say in 1940 and 1941 was, "We want as much as we can get of everything."[51] Of course, May would answer, "We knew that the British wanted all they could get of everything, but we had no way of knowing what came first, what they could do for themselves, and what their long-range planning was like."[52]

A luncheon held in late March 1941 had an interesting follow-up. Attending it were Monnet, May, Purvis (chair of the British Supply Commission), and John McCloy (assistant secretary of war). From this meeting came unanimous agreement that there had to be a complete exchange of information between the United States and the United Kingdom, and that the British likely would confront defeat unless they learned how to get the most from the United States in the way of munitions and supplies.[53] After some argument, the participants agreed that the figures for the British and American resources needed to be combined in one report. May's staff then built a huge book with comprehensive categories and tabs, but with its columns blank. Then they filled the American columns with figures: total industrial and raw materials capacities, total industrial and raw materials potentials, as best they could figure those numbers out at the moment.[54]

Once the American half of the document was completed, Secretary of War Stimson sent May to Britain to fill in all of the blank columns with British information. For two months in late summer and early fall 1941, May conferred with the War Cabinet, the British chiefs of staff, and British production experts. Together they compiled a composite set of accounts that recorded all American and British war production potential.

One of the first problems May encountered was that Churchill had been right when he observed that the British and Americans were "two people divided by a common language."[55] British and American experts spent countless hours laying out a glossary of common terms to ensure that each term meant the same to both parties. Without this common lexicon, the joint requirements ledger May was building would have conveyed more misinformation than information. For instance, when the Americans said "car" they were referring to an automobile, while the British were more often than not referring to an armored vehicle. In terms of production values, each misunderstanding of that term alone equated to more than three tons of steel.

The completed document went by various names: sometimes the Stacy May Document, sometimes the Stimson Balance Sheet. The name that stuck was what the British called it—"The Anglo-American Consolidated Statement."[56] The report itself was a statement of statistical fact. It made no attempt to set targets for production, but restricted itself to realistic forecasts of output under existing programs and of stocks up to the end of 1942.[57] Whatever its designation, it was a comprehensive listing of the British, Canadian, and American military requirements, current and potential production, and potential material stocks.[58]

The cold rows of figures were not flattering to the United States. With 2.5 times the combined population of Britain and Canada, America's installed munitions production capacity was lagging far behind its ultimate potential and what the other two nations were producing. The stark numbers clearly demonstrated that the United States was a long way from being the "arsenal of democracy."[59]

When it was completed, May took the massive thirty-five pound document and returned to the United States. He made his way through Dublin, Baltimore, and then by taxi to Washington, all without escort. As Nelson later said, it was a German spy's ultimate fantasy: a plump, fortyish, dignified, preoccupied, American statistician, all alone and carrying what everyone who knew of its existence considered the most important document in the world.[60] For the production experts, May's report provided a sure measuring stick for use against Army and Navy orders. As the Army "expanded (which it did, from 2,000,000 in 1940 to 4,000,000, then 6,000,000 then 8,000,000 and beyond) our production requirements would necessarily expand in systematic ratio."[61]

Despite its defects, the requirements under this real Victory Program represented a far more realistic statement than any previous study. They were also, when judged against any previous standard, enormous. So enormous, in fact, that the feasibility of the program was immediately called into question.[62] In fact, because of an initial feasibility analysis conducted after May's return, the program underwent significant modifications. Nelson, however, did not receive a final report on the feasibility of the Victory Program in terms of national industrial potential from Stacy May until 4 December 1941, three days before Pearl Harbor.[63]

So, in the final analysis, what was the actual Victory Program? It certainly did not have anything to do with the study Wedemeyer produced. Rather, it was a combination of two documents. The first, Plan Dog, written by Stark, became the basis of Anglo-American military strategy codified as ABC-1. It later provided the backbone for America's basic strategic plan—Rainbow-5. Although Plan Dog outlined how America was going to fight the war, it was the Anglo-American Consolidated Statement, formulated by the now almost forgotten Stacy May, that determined what materials were available for the build-up of Anglo-American military forces.

There is, however, one further matter for those interested in how the Allies formulated requirements after May created the Anglo-American Consolidated Statement. While May's work indicated what the requirements were for an 8 million–person Army, it did not say how long it would take the American economy to shift production and grow sufficiently to supply those requirements. In effect, May's work told the military what it could have to win the war, while Stark's plans told how the materiel could be put to good use. What still remained unanswered was the very serious question of when it could be made available.

Two economists were already working on the answer to that question. What they came up with was far from pleasing, and led to some of the fiercest and nastiest military-civilian debates of the war. In the end, their pronouncements did more to determine military strategy and the timing of the great Allied offensives than all of the Allied national leaders and military commanders combined. Today, though, history has largely forgotten Robert Nathan and Simon Kuznets.

CHAPTER 4

The Economist's War

★ ★ ★

Nobel Laureate Paul Samuelson commented in 1945, "the last war [World War I] was the chemist's war, and this one has been called the physicist's war. It might equally be said that this has been the economist's war."[1] Even so, for the most part the contribution of economists to victory in World War II has disappeared from histories that are more interested in the actions of the great generals and the swirling tides of military operations.[2] Without the calculations of economists, however, World War II would likely have lasted much longer and cost the Allies hundreds of thousands if not millions more casualties.

How economists infiltrated into almost every area of the federal government is a story in itself. For our purposes, it is sufficient to state that it was rapid and pervasive. Just fifty years before World War II there had been only one individual in the government with the title of economist, and that person was listed as an "economic ornithologist." World War I saw a few trained economists brought to Washington in policy positions, but their influence remained constrained to providing advice on price administration and shipping. They had little impact on mobilization planning. It was the Great Depression that brought economists into Washington policy circles, first by the hundreds and then by the thousands. By the time World War II began, the federal government employed an estimated five thousand economists.[3]

These economists made two major contributions that had a significant impact on World War II. First, they completed the financial revolution begun by the British in their wars with France, a revolution that made it possible to fund a war waged on an unprecedented scale. Second, they created the concepts of national income accounts, GNP, and GDP, which together provided the statistical basis for determining the growth and production potential of the American economy.[4] Admittedly, their figures and calculations remained inexact, but, when put in the context of the scale of what the government would demand for mobilization in a global war, they sufficed.

Moreover, World War II was the first war where money was truly no object. While there were a number of practical concerns about the best method of financing the conflict and the inflationary impact of massive spending policies, there was never any concern in the United States about the nation's ability to finance the war. Everything American industry could turn out the government could afford to buy. This was also true of Britain, which instituted similar policies in purchasing all the munitions produced by its industry. The financial crisis in Britain came in 1940, when its industry could no longer meet wartime production requirements and the need arose to tap American industrial potential.[5] Within months, Britain had shipped its entire gold reserve to New York and exhausted its credit. To alleviate this payments crisis, Roosevelt pushed Lend-Lease through Congress just in time to avert a financial disaster that could possibly have forced Britain's withdrawal from the war.[6]

The Financial Revolution

The Roman statesman Cicero once noted, "Endless money forms the sinews of war."[7] It was not until the twentieth century, however, that governments discovered how to tap their economic systems to provide "endless" streams of money. Although the three historical methods of financing government spending (raising taxes, borrowing, and printing money) remained, governments had become more sophisticated in the employment of these tools. Focusing on these three methods, of course, generally ignores other possible funding sources in war, such as commandeering assets, both at home and in conquered areas; liquidating existing assets (as Britain did to purchase American industrial output); or asking for voluntary contributions. For the most part, however, such additional methods played a minuscule role in the financing of the Allied war effort, particularly in the United States.[8]

Orthodox economic thinking at the beginning of World War II held that taxes should finance wars on a pay-as-you-go basis.[9] This viewpoint had wide support across the political spectrum since most politicians considered the printing of money as inflationary and debt financing as a burden on future generations. Moreover, most believed that adding additional debt to the national balance sheet was particularly reprehensible because the initial burden of paying it off would fall on the same young men who had fought the war.[10] Economists also believed that turning on the printing presses would at best represent an emergency stopgap measure that would rapidly lose its effectiveness as hyperinflation outpaced the presses.[11]

An examination of World War II's financing, however, indicates that the printing press played a much greater role than commonly assumed, particularly in the early war years.[12] Although this rapid expansion of the monetary base would have crippled the economy if it had continued for too long, it was at the time critical to jump-starting rapid increases in production.[13] In the first place, the government-instigated monetary contraction, which had extended the length and depth of the Depression more than any other single factor, had not been rectified by the time the United States entered the war. Thus, there was room to expand the stock of money without sparking inflation, particularly because the government had halted the production of high-ticket durable consumer items and because Leon Henderson, head of the Office of Price Administration (OPA), had begun instituting relatively effective price controls. For business to expand would require immediate working capital, and there was plainly not enough of it available in the economic system in 1941.[14] In short, the in-circulation monetary base in 1941 was too small to support the daily activities of the massive American economy as it mobilized for war.[15] Unless the government added cash to the system quickly, there was a real possibility the entire mechanism would seize up.[16]

The *Federal Reserve Bulletin* for December 1942 noted that the government had financed 75 percent of its expenditures in the first year of the war through borrowing, with the remaining 25 percent financed through taxation.[17] This is somewhat disingenuous because it fails to reflect on how the Federal Reserve System creates money. Since the start of the Federal Reserve System, the primary method of adding liquidity to the monetary system was by altering the reserve requirement that members of the system had to keep on deposit with the Federal Reserve. In peacetime this is a highly effective method, but in a crisis several overlapping factors often led to lag times between reserve rate changes and expansion of the monetary base. In the emergency of global war, when the funds necessary to finance rapid expansion are needed immediately, the government could not tolerate this lag.[18]

In spring 1942 the Federal Reserve's principal method of adjusting the monetary base became a fixed buying rate on Treasury Bills. Under this policy, as the *Federal Reserve Bulletin* stated, "Member bank reserves are almost automatically supplied, with the initiative being taken by the member banks rather than by the Federal Reserve System."[19] The importance of this policy lay in the fact that, in effect, it authorized the member banks to purchase any volume of U.S. government securities, purchase other securities, or make loans as they desired, provided that among these securities they acquired sufficient Treasury Bills to exchange at Federal Reserve banks for whatever additional reserves may be needed because of the accompanying expansion in reserves.[20] That is, the government had turned the formulation and execution of monetary policy over to the commercial banks with a blanket authorization to produce as much wartime monetary expansion as they found profitable.[21]

How did this work in practice? As the public purchased government securities, the payments were credited to U.S. government accounts in various commercial banks. This process automatically reduced the amount of reserves that banks were required to hold on hand. Eventually Treasury transferred these excess reserves to the various regional Federal Reserve banks, which used them in payment for the purchase of war supplies and other government expenditures. The government's admonition to keep these reserves fully invested at all times, coupled with the natural desire of profit-making institutions to increase their holdings of interest-bearing investments, encouraged banks to use their reserves to purchase large amounts of government bonds, both during bond drives and on the secondary market. The banks made most of such purchases directly from the Treasury, when possible; otherwise, they bought them from private investors. The need to keep reserves employed until they were called for by the central bank caused banks to make sizable loans to customers for the purchase of government securities, most of which these customers later sold to banks. Both the direct purchase of government debt and the funding of customers to do so tended to increase a bank's future reserve requirement. This increase showed up several months later, when the Treasury spent its new deposits and the funds reappeared in the accounts of banking customers. The announced policy of the Federal Reserve System to purchase Treasury Bills at a fixed rate, however, eliminated any fear that the bank might have trouble meeting future reserve requirements. As long as this policy continued any bank could purchase any volume of U.S. government securities for its own account, or could loan any volume of money to its customers for any purpose without fear of being embarrassed by its inability to meet future reserve requirements.

In short, the Federal Reserve gave the banks a license to print money. Two things, however, stopped the banks from undertaking an unbridled monetary expansion that could have led to hyperinflation and financial ruin. First, the U.S. banking system remained largely fragmented, with more than sixteen thousand national and state-chartered banks across the country.[22] The many thousands of bankers across the country simply lacked the economic sophistication to spot the opportunity presented to them. More important, though, were memories of the Great Depression and the numerous banking panics of previous decades. Though on a practical basis the new Federal Reserve wartime policies had eliminated the need for reserves, most of the Depression-scarred banking community still thought it prudent to hold sufficient reserves on hand for emergencies.[23]

What the government was doing was issuing debt in quantities so huge that it would be impossible for the economy to digest those sums without massive interest rate increases to make bond purchases attractive. To clear the debt, the Federal Reserve became the buyer of last resort and purchased as much of the debt as necessary to keep the price and interest rate at a previously agreed pegged rate: this is called monetizing the debt.[24] These purchases created government-owned deposits on the books of the central bank, which equated to the banking system receiving additional reserves; banks then used those reserves to expand their asset holdings while creating additional deposit money.[25] Thus, one must consider the portion of the debt issued by the government that banks or private investors, using bank financing, bought back as printed money, although the Federal Reserve resisted such thinking at the time.

This means that 75 percent of the government's expenditures in 1942 were not, in reality, financed through debt securities. Instead, the government funded a substantial portion of its purchases through money creation.[26] Estimates are that as much as 42 percent of 1942's wartime spending was the result of turning on the printing presses, while actual non-government-financed bond sales paid for approximately 34 percent, with taxes paying the remaining 24 percent. This situation had reversed by 1944, when taxes and a much-reduced amount of debt sales sufficed to cover expenses.[27]

If politicians and economists agreed that money creation was the worst possible measure to finance the war and taxes were the best, how did the reverse become policy, at least in the United States during the early war years?

The overriding problem facing the U.S. government during World War II was how to raise the staggering amounts of money required by war.[28] If it performed the job well, the government could stabilize the economy, which would make preserving the soundness of the currency immeasurably easier. If it performed the job poorly, the entire economy could be destroyed.

For example, most historians agree that Germany's failure to adequately address its war financing needs was a contributing factor to the general disruption of its economy in the aftermath of World War I. By failing to adequately tax its economy to meet wartime expenditures, the Germans left it up to their central bank to raise the necessary funds on a credit basis. This negligence, plus military defeat, contributed to the ruinous inflation that wiped out the value of most of German society's economic assets in the early postwar period.[29]

During World War II, the Treasury Department had the responsibility of raising sufficient funds to wage the war. In this regard it focused on keeping interest rates low, thereby minimizing the cost of servicing debt.[30] The Federal Reserve's principal concern was to ensure that the means used to raise funds were as noninflationary as possible. To the extent that these funds did not come from taxation or borrowed savings, the United States had to raise its financial wherewithal through the banking system. In other words, the federal government used the banks to create sufficient credit.[31]

In the process, the Federal Reserve confronted a dilemma. On the one hand, the system had to supply the banks with the reserves required to support credit expansion. On the other hand, it was the system's responsibility to neutralize the inflationary potential of newly created money. There was no satisfactory way to neutralize the money that would not raise the cost of debt substantially or contract available credit. The most the Federal Reserve could do was go about its business with sufficient care to slow the impact.[32]

That inflation remained low, or at least within reasonable limits, was the result of three realities. The first was creation of the OPA in 1942. That organization possessed sweeping powers to control prices and establish rationing programs on products in short supply. The second was that conversion to wartime production brought a halt to the manufacture of almost all big-ticket consumer durables, such as automobiles and refrigerators.[33] The wartime boom may have given consumers more cash than they had previously, but it did not give them much to buy with that cash. The third, and in many ways most important reality, was the self-restraint exhibited due to consumers' postwar expectations. Virtually all Americans had vivid memories of the Great Depression and believed that the current prosperity was a wartime boom.

There was widespread expectation and trepidation that the Depression would return as soon as the war ended. Many, therefore, took the sensible precaution of saving rather than spending their windfall.

Was it necessary to go this route? During the six fiscal years from 1 July 1940 to 30 June 1946, the federal government spent $387 billion, of which $330 billion was for national defense. The Treasury raised $397 billion, of which taxation garnered $176 billion, or 44 percent.[34] Moreover, politicians were aware that taxation provided many benefits over the other two methods of finance. First, taxation distributed the cost of the war while it was being fought rather than imposing the costs on future generations and was therefore considered more ethical and fair. Taxation also fought inflation: it had an almost dollar-for-dollar impact on inflation because consumers cannot spend a dollar on goods that has been taken away by the government. Finally, taxation alleviated many negative postwar economic effects: greater amounts of wartime borrowing meant greater postwar taxation in order to service the resulting debt. Furthermore, large amounts of government securities in private hands at the end of a war could easily provide sufficient liquid assets to stoke serious inflation, as was to happen in 1947–49.[35]

So why did the government not raise tax levels to cover the expense of war? First was the need to provide incentives to workers. During the war the government wanted every worker to make a maximum effort to increase production levels. Taxes not only discourage workers by making them feel poorer, but also have a negative impact on the human desire to earn extra dollars if they believe those dollars will only end up in the hands of government. Moreover, politicians are reluctant to place tax burdens on constituents to whom they eventually will find themselves accountable. When faced with a vote on a tax increase, politicians can easily forget about the burden to future generations in favor of keeping today's voters happy.[36]

By far the major determining factor in financial decisions was the one that received little coverage from the economic historians of the period—namely, time. The emergency was now, and the need to pay for the war was immediate. This need was particularly pressing in the first year of major rearmament, when the American economy had to provide resources to build or expand factories and emplace the infrastructure on which the expansion of the military establishment depended. Passing new tax laws through Congress and then establishing the apparatus on which to assess and collect those taxes would have represented a time-consuming affair. Though Congress authorized a new tax structure in April 1942, it was almost a year before substantial new revenues began to find their way into the treasury.[37] Bond drives that focused on sales to private individuals had the same problem, as it took months for the government to organize and publicize them.

The maturity of the Federal Reserve System, born in the early days of World War I, provided an efficient system, already in place, to raise vast amounts of cash in a remarkably short time. It was not without risks but, properly managed, the system provided a stopgap until taxation and bond drives could begin to assume the bulk of governmental funding requirements. Even after taxation had reached its maximum wartime limit, the Federal Reserve continued to guarantee sufficient bank liquidity to ensure that bond drives always met their goals without ever going over the 3 percent interest cost on offered bonds. By any measure, the American banking system, which was controlled by the Federal Reserve System, provided the Allies with a financial engine that relatively easily assumed the burdens of war finance. Although the strains on it were enormous, every indication is that the Federal Reserve could have created substantially greater funding without collapsing the system, if the war had continued.[38]

The Federal Reserve banks themselves absorbed approximately $22 billion of the public debt, while also creating a favorable environment for absorption of roughly $95 billion more by commercial banks. Moreover, from June 1941 through December 1945 investors other than Federal Reserve commercial banks absorbed approximately $129 billion of government securities.[39] In total, this was close to all of the government's spending on the war, and even in 1945 these sources were far from tapped out. In fact, the continuing high levels of savings that propelled the postwar boom could easily have provided additional war funds, if required. For the first time in history, a government had exhausted production capabilities long before it had exhausted the funding sources required to pay for new munitions. Such a state of affairs could not have continued forever, but it lasted long enough to win the war.

The Federal Reserve held true to the promise it had made almost immediately after Pearl Harbor, when it issued the statements that the "system's powers would be thrown completely behind the war effort" and that there were "sufficient funds available to prosecute the war on a massive scale until victory." At the time, many politicians doubted this was possible.[40] There is no record, however, that any economist during the period doubted the system could fulfill the Federal Reserve's boast.[41] Governments, through their economists, for the first time in three thousand years had devised methods to pay for total war, over an indefinite period. When the test came, these methods proved effective at managing the fiscal machine. It remains to be seen how economists were able to determine how much the country could produce over a fixed amount of time.[42]

The Statistical Revolution

The statistical revolution is the story of two men, Nobel laureate Simon Kuznets and economist Robert Nathan. Although these men and their activities remained closely connected, in order to delineate the narrative their story must be told in two parts. The first outlines Kuznets' pioneering work in the field of national income accounting. The second examines how Nathan applied Kuznets' work to determine the feasibility of the Victory Program. Interestingly, Nathan was a former student of Kuznets and later was employed by the latter to help work on national accounts for the Commerce Department in the 1930s.[43] Still later, on the eve of war, Nathan moved to the Office of Production Management (OPM) to build a statistical abstract of the country's ability to support an expanded war effort.[44] When Nathan later took over the Bureau of Planning and Statistics, a division of OPM, he immediately rehired his former boss and teacher, Kuznets, as his deputy, to help make sense of the masses of economic data assembled to manage war production activities.[45]

Simon Kuznets was the recipient of the third Nobel Prize in economics and was a pivotal figure in the transformation of economics from a speculative and ideologically driven discipline into an empirically based science.[46] Born in Pinsk, Russia, in 1901, he and his family emigrated to the United States in 1922. He entered Columbia University and earned his B.A. in 1923, his M.A. in 1924, and his Ph.D. in 1926. In 1927 he went to work for the private National Bureau of Economic Research (NBER) where he remained, with brief interruptions for government service, until 1961.[47]

From 1932 to 1934 he served in the Department of Commerce, where he constructed the first official estimates of U.S. national income and laid the basis for the department's national income section. His work during this period established the statistical base that later allowed Nathan to engage in a major battle with the Joint Chiefs of Staff (JCS) and bring about a dramatic change in U.S. strategy for fighting the war, particularly the war in Europe. It is almost impossible to overestimate the effect of Kuznets' work on the planning and conduct of America's wartime mobilization. While the United States would still have undertaken the production miracle that swamped the Axis, it would likely have taken years longer and been accomplished only after a great waste of resources.

To see why and how this was so one must understand what national accounts are, how they came into being, and what they were designed to accomplish. National income and product accounts are the comprehensive set of accounts measuring the total value of final goods and services (often called GDP) produced by the U.S. economy and the total incomes earned in producing that output. This integrated set of accounts and similar detailed sets of regional and industrial accounts allow for the comprehensive analysis of the impact of alternative policy actions, or external events, on the economy, as well as on detailed components of final demand, income, and regions of the country.[48] Though the work behind these national accounts often appears arcane and filled with drudgery, the final products have become instrumental in setting policies that keep a modern society functioning.

The concept of national income goes back to Sir William Petty and Gregory King, who developed estimates of English national income during the seventeenth century. Later economists, including Adam Smith, debated the concept of national accounts and how economists could measure them. Economists were not, however, able to create practical methods to determine or influence government policy until the early twentieth century. For centuries, measurement and application had lagged behind economic theory due to the absence of detailed accurate data on which to build estimates.[49]

Prior to World War I, published national income estimates were the work of individuals.[50] Most of these attempts were not rigorous and primarily concerned the collection of data on the burden of the public debt or on various taxation schemes. It took the exigencies of a world war to prompt the first American attempts at national product estimates for senior government officials to analyze and use. Adolph C. Miller, an economist with the Federal Reserve Bank of New York, prepared estimates to evaluate the "surplus over necessary consumption and maintenance of capital that could be devoted to the war effort."[51] Moreover, during the war the NBER undertook its first project to study national income—its size, year-to-year variation, and distribution. The purpose of these estimates was to provide an impartial and trustworthy source for use as a basis for correcting social and political problems.[52]

It was not until 1926, however, that the first official government estimates, from the Federal Trade Commission, were presented. These estimates, prepared by Francis Walker, showed the value of national product produced by U.S. industry for the years 1918–23. Unfortunately, after completion of this first report the government halted all follow-up work due to a lack of funding. Washington bureaucrats realized the need for such reports only several years later as the economy sank into the Great Depression and the government began to feel the keen lack of a suitable statement on national accounts that politicians could use to guide their efforts to rehabilitate the sinking economy. The NBER (a private organization) tried to provide the required data for policy makers, but it failed to update its earlier estimates and it took many months to calculate new ones. Congress became fully aware of the extent of the problem when in 1931 it called government and private experts to testify on the current economic crisis. Congress was astounded to discover that no expert could provide any national account figures more recent than 1929.[53]

At the time, the Depression had been worsening for two years. Nearly a quarter of U.S. workers were in the lines of the unemployed, while many of those who still had jobs were working on a part-time basis. Asset values had plummeted, the banking system was collapsing, deflation was reversing the gears of the economy, and sales were insufficient to maintain businesses. Farm income, on which one-fourth of the population depended, had fallen by half. Neither the public nor elected officials understood the workings of an economy that appeared to be perpetuating the crisis, nor did they know quantitatively its scale and scope. The most up-to-date estimates of national income—that is, economy-wide income—were for 1929, a boom year, that had been marred only by the October stock market "crash," after which the economic slide began.

Realizing that it was trying to direct economic policy without the necessary tools, in June 1932 Congress passed a law ordering "That the Secretary of Commerce report estimates of the total national income of the United States for each of the calendar years 1929, 1930, 1931, including estimates of the portions of the national income originating from agriculture, manufacturing, mining, transportation, and other gainful industries."[54]

The person originally placed in charge of this project, Frederick Dewhurst, soon quit, and the Commerce Department borrowed Simon Kuznets from the NBER to take over. Kuznets had already been working on a new set of estimates for the bureau, where he had been busily remaking the nation's basic economic models.[55] To help him, the Department of Commerce provided Kuznets with a small staff of assistants, among whom his former student, Robert Nathan, was the leading light.

Almost a year to the day after assuming control over the project, Kuznets provided Congress with the Commerce Department's first complete set of estimates. These estimates indicated that between 1929 and 1932 national income had dropped by more than 50 percent. Incomes in manufacturing had dropped by 70 percent, while incomes in construction had dropped by more than 80 percent. Government was the only industry that had grown over the period, although the federal government remained relatively small—federal tax receipts claimed only 3 percent of GDP in 1932.[56] The finished product, *National Income, 1929–32*, was printed as a Senate document in 1933.[57] The report—261 pages of tables and explanation—was the Senate's first bestseller, and the initial run of 4,500 copies immediately sold out at twenty cents a copy.

The report also found that between 1929 and 1932 national income had fallen by more than 50 percent and national income paid out had fallen by 40 percent, while business savings had become negative in 1930 and remained negative through 1935 as businesses drew down their financial reserves or borrowed to remain in operation, when fixed costs and wages exceeded revenues. In terms of the new statistics, this meant that national income paid out exceeded national income produced.[58] The United States was, in economic terms, a losing proposition.

Soon after completion of the estimates, Kuznets returned to the NBER and Nathan took over the ongoing work on future economic estimates. By May 1938 Nathan was presenting estimates not only of total income, but also of income per capita broken down by types of payment and individual states. In addition to business taking an interest for the first time (to help in marketing efforts), these new, more-discrete estimates became the basis for targeted federal relief efforts in each of the states. From this point, the government published these estimates annually, and these statistical methods remained basically unchanged until the mid-1950s.[59]

Economic historians credit Kuznets with transforming the field of national income accounting by bringing a far greater precision to the task than economists had ever achieved before. He accomplished this by rooting his estimates firmly in classical economic theory and by solving numerous problems related to using imperfect raw data to create the theoretical conception of "national income."[60] In later publications, the Department of Commerce heralded the creation of Kuznets' national income estimates as one of the great inventions of the twentieth century.[61] Nobel laureate Paul Samuelson said of them, "That for the first time the President, Congress, and the Federal Reserve had a methodology to judge whether the economy was contracting or expanding, and whether it needed a boost or should be reined in a bit." Without measures of economic aggregates like GDP, Samuelson believed policy makers were adrift in a sea of unorganized data. The GDP and related data acted like beacons that helped policy makers steer the economy toward key economic objectives.[62]

During the 1930s, national income statements became regularly issued products of the Department of Commerce and were generally accepted as the broadest readings on U.S. economic conditions.[63] The public followed them closely, while the Roosevelt administration and Congress used them to plan and evaluate fiscal policy. By the time Commerce first provided GNP figures in 1942, national income statements had already become the most cited U.S. macroeconomic statistics. The Roosevelt administration realized that these new measures provided an authoritative means of describing the dire economic conditions that its proposed New Deal programs would address, thus it included them in the marketing of these programs to the public.

For example, within two weeks of the release of the first national income report, Secretary of Commerce Daniel C. Roper was already citing the more than 50 percent drop in national income between 1929 and 1932 in speeches around the country explaining New Deal programs.[64] Although few if any policy makers thought about it at the time, it did not take a great logical leap to see that, if the government could use these statistics to drive policies for the Depression-era economy, then they would prove an equally valuable tool in managing the economy and military production during a major conflict.

To see just how valuable a policy instrument they proved, one can note the long-term effects engendered by these estimates. According to the U.S. Bureau of Economic Analysis, the national accounts contributed to a reduction in the severity of business cycles and a post–World War II era of strong economic growth. Prior to World War II the lows of the business cycle were much more severe and more frequent. There were six severe depressions between 1854 and 1945, each with an average duration of nearly three years. Including recessions as well as depressions, the average downturn between 1854 and 1945 was twenty-one months, with a contraction occurring on average once every four years. During the postwar era the length of the average contraction has been halved to eleven months, with a contraction occurring once every five years.[65] The postwar era also stands out as a period of unprecedented growth for the United States. Real GDP per capita and real wealth have almost tripled since 1948. This period of economic prosperity has not only dramatically improved standards of living but also has contributed to large improvements in social conditions, cutting poverty in half, raising living standards, and adding to leisure time. Bank runs, financial panics, and depressions that were recurring problems before World War II became a thing of the past. This success was due in significant part to the timely, comprehensive, and accurate data on the economy provided by the national accounts.[66]

In 1935 Nathan began writing a series of annual survey articles presenting the national income statistics for the preceding year, analyzing them in detail. The next year, the Department of Commerce published a statistical compendium, *National Income in the United States, 1929–35*, which presented revised and extended statistics and explained the concepts behind the report.[67] Roosevelt began citing national income statistics in speeches as early as 1935, for example, in his statement of September 1935 on the state of the economy and the federal budget. In April 1938, in his message to the Congress requesting additional spending for the new recovery program to address problems caused by the 1937 recession, the president described economic developments over the period 1929–37 in national income terms.[68] And he described the goal for the program in national income terms as well: "We must start again on a long, steady, upward incline in national income." Starting with the annual budget message to the Congress in January 1939, which presented his fiscal year 1940 budget, the president cited national income statistics as the primary measures of the state of the economy.[69] In his 1939 message, he also highlighted the importance of these measures to economic policy by suggesting how different levels of national income would generate different levels of federal tax receipts.[70]

The critical element to grasp from the president's use of national income statistics to support his policies is that he trusted their accuracy and apparently believed that he could use them to plan national economic strategy. This trust and belief was not limited to the president. His advisers, government economists, and any politician who thought of himself as a "New Dealer" shared the president's faith. This common shared faith in the efficacy of national income statistics would be of critical importance in the final showdown between the economic planners and the military over the feasibility of the Victory Program.

Gross National Product and World War II

The Department of Commerce launched GNP statistics to answer a policy question for which the national income accounts undertaken by Kuznets and Nathan were proving inadequate. Could the nation meet the Victory Program requirements? If so, at what costs would it be to the civilian standard of living and price stability? As was the case for national income accounts in 1932, the GNP concept elucidated in 1942 was not new, having been discussed and partially formulated during the 1930s. While economists made progress in developing theoretical and statistical standards for GNP, it took a policy requirement (the requirement for economic information during world war) to push the U.S. government to develop an authoritative, consensus-based statistical measurement. When finished, GNP made up the other side of the national income equation—the production side, to match the income-earned side (approximated by national income). It thus helped provide a more complete picture of the economy.

In his budget message to Congress in January 1940, four months after Germany had invaded Poland, Roosevelt asked for a modest defense supplemental appropriation for fiscal year 1940 and a likely increase in defense spending for fiscal year 1941. In 1940 defense expenditures had reached more than $1 billion, approximately 14 percent of the budget. In his January 1941 budget message, Roosevelt asked for $25 billion in defense expenditures, 62 percent of the budget, reflecting a "world at war." In his January 1942 budget message, President Roosevelt asked for $53 billion for defense, 90 percent of the budget, reflecting "a nation at war in a world at war." It was the computations of the economists creating national income and GNP accounts that provided the president and his advisers with the basis for estimating what the United States was capable of supporting in terms of a rapid and massive growth in military spending.

During the week before the January 1942 budget message and shortly after the attack on Pearl Harbor, the president announced the goal of increasing the share of national income spent on war production from the current 17 percent to 50 percent by 1943. Such an increase in the speed and scale of the mobilization program was beyond experience, and was "A national effort of gigantic magnitude," according to the president. To accomplish this task, the United States would have to sustain major economic dislocations as it readjusted to a wartime economy.

The U.S. rearmament program, begun in 1940, had already boosted national income above the 1929 level for the first time, to achieve an almost 25 percent increase before Pearl Harbor. The rise was steep, and by December 1941 national income was almost 40 percent above its level of less than two years earlier. Putting the country on full war footing would boost income even more, but purchases of consumer goods and services, which had boomed in 1941, would find themselves stymied because the country would need to cut back production for civilian purposes to make way for the war's programs.

Rationing, wage and price controls, and other consumption-damping regulations were on the table. Statistics measuring the total amount as well as the composition of goods and services being produced were a base requirement for evaluating the risks of shortages of civilian goods and services and the bidding up of prices, but those statistics were not available in the United States at the beginning of 1942. National income sufficed at that time as an informed measure of the economy's size, but it was not up to the task of evaluating production constraints and trade-offs because it measured only the income earned in production and not the greater market value of the goods and services produced. In these early days, using current economic statistics for mobilization planning was akin to a corporation bidding on contracts without knowing the capacity of its factories or the financial facilities at its disposal.

Within two months of the January 1942 budget message, the Department of Commerce produced the first GNP statistics. These figures distinguished only among major categories of expenditures, but they succeeded in bringing the war-production trade-offs into the picture. Earlier statistical analyses tended to provide overly grim assessments of the risks of shortages of civilian goods and inflation because, among other errors, they underestimated the productive capacity of the United States. When first published in March 1942, GNP offered a new framework for assessing the feasibility of the 1943 war program by comparing it with 1941 national output. Two months later, the Commerce Department provided historical GNP statistics for 1929–41.[71] The January 1942 budget message had foreshadowed the new statistical terms presented in the GNP, mentioning for the first time in a fiscal policy context "consumer durable goods" and "industrial plant and equipment."

Understanding the pressures of the proposed huge war expenditure program required consideration of competing expenditures in the economy—most simply, expenditures for the war versus expenditures for everything else. The expenditure components of GNP provided the material for that comparison. Because economists measure GNP in market prices and therefore include taxes and depreciation allowances, not included in national income, this estimate exceeded national income in 1941 by 25 percent ($23 billion) and provided a better approximation of aggregate U.S. productive resources. The inclusion of business taxes and depreciation resulted in a production measure that was more appropriate for analysis of the war program's burden on the economy, in part because those flows were potential sources of program funding. For example, during wartime, business might delay spending for the replacement of capital goods (i.e., old factories, machine tools) to free up resources for the production of more war materiel.

Economists define GNP as a comprehensive measure of the production of goods and services in the economy valued at market prices. In addition to being measured as the sum of production components, one can measure GNP as the sum of expenditures on goods and services for final uses, plus the change in business inventories. Put in other terms, GNP represents the sum of value added by all industries in the economy.

Because data on expenditures were not fully available in early 1942, Nathan and Kuznets had to use other estimates to approximate GNP figures in their early feasibility estimates. They accomplished this by adding business taxes and depreciation to the existing national income statistics, using the budget and other government sources to obtain approximations of government spending. They estimated investment ("gross private capital formation") from business records, including tax returns, and estimated durable goods sold to consumers from census bureau and other government data.

Before GNP became available, analysts sometimes erroneously subtracted projected defense expenditures from projected national income, producing a residual that was interpreted as the amount of production left for nonwar goods and services. For example, in early 1942 analysts subtracted the president's proposed 1943 defense expenditures of $56 billion from projected 1943 national income of $110 billion, leaving a residual of $54 billion. Comparison of the 1943 residual with the same residual for 1941, $81 billion, indicated that the government would have to find a way to cut income by a third if the resources required for the war program were to be available. The assessment was overly grim: national income fell short of the total market value of goods and services produced, of which defense spending was a component.

Substitution of GNP for national income in such an analysis revealed that the effect of war mobilization on living standards would be less dire than predicted and that an even larger war program might be attainable. This was true not only because GNP was larger in value than national income (because analysts measured it at market prices, not factor costs), but also because the expenditure composition of national product showed how the income generated from national production was being spent. The expenditure composition of GNP suggested that, despite a potentially large forced reduction in nonwar spending, the nation could absorb much of the decrease by reductions in private investment and consumer purchases of durable goods rather than in consumer purchases of nondurable goods and services—purchases of food, clothing, and shelter—in other words, basic needs. The analysis suggested that only a 4 percent, price-adjusted reduction in the consumption of nondurables and services below the 1941 level would be required to meet the president's war program goals for 1943, while private investment would have to decline by 80 percent and the consumption of durables by 70 percent. Put another way, the GNP analysis showed that economic growth brought about by increases in employment and productivity spurred by the war program and the diversion of heavy industry from civilian to war production could provide more than 90 percent of the additional resources needed for the 1943 program.[72]

This puts the final nail in the coffin for the idea that the United States paid for the Victory Program by reducing the amount of resources available for consumer purchases. As the consumption of nondurable would only be reduced by 4 percent, the president and his economic team knew early in the war that mobilization would require little consumer sacrifice and that they could achieve virtually all required production by economic expansion. Almost all that was asked of consumers was that they postpone purchases of large durable items such as cars and washing machines.[73] Furthermore, economic statistics for the war indicate that consumer spending in the United States actually increased throughout the war.[74]

In summary, the revolution in economic statistics reached a point in 1940 where those few economists intimately familiar with their intricacies could use them to determine, with a considerable degree of accuracy, how much and how fast U.S. industry could expand to meet wartime demands. It was a truly remarkable coincidence that such a valuable statistical tool was created and perfected in the decade just before it was needed to help win humanity's greatest struggle. Moreover, Kuznets, May, and Nathan, the three men in America with the firmest grasp of what the statistics said about the production potential of the United States, by the time the war started, were all firmly ensconced within the Planning Division of the OPM. Here they were able to lay the groundwork for America's great wartime economic expansion. There was one big change in their relationship, however. Kuznets' former student and employee, Robert Nathan, was now the boss, while the other two men worked for him.[75]

CHAPTER 5

The Production Organizations

★ ★ ★

To comprehend the debates over feasibility, the historian requires some knowledge of the various organizations responsible for military procurement, along with some understanding of their relations with each other and the personalities involved. Clarity will not be attained by exhaustively detailing every organization that the president authorized from 1939 until the end of the war. This section, therefore, will highlight the main developments and then focus on the final organization this book concerns itself with, the War Production Board (WPB). It should be noted that the WPB was not the final or most powerful of the war production agencies. This distinction belongs to the Office of War Mobilization and Reconversion (OWMR), which was created after the events discussed in this work took place, and which therefore is not covered in any detail here.[1]

In response to the attack on the Low Countries and France in May 1940, Roosevelt had established the Office of Emergency Management inside the Executive Office of the President. This new organization helped coordinate and direct emergency agencies, which were beginning to proliferate. Three days later he created, by executive order, the National Defense Advisory Commission (NDAC), with the Office of Emergency Management serving as a secretariat for this new advisory commission. Congress had passed legislation sanctioning these bodies in 1916 and had never repealed its authorization. The Commission was made up of key cabinet officials— the secretaries of war, the Navy, commerce, the interior, agriculture, and labor—whose departments were essential to mobilizing for war. Its seven civilian leaders (chosen with typical political astuteness by Roosevelt) were Edward R. Stettinius Jr. (adviser for industrial materials matters), William S. Knudsen (adviser for industrial production), Sidney Hillman (labor), Leon Henderson (price stabilization), Chester C. Davis (agriculture), Ralph Budd (transportation), and Harriet Elliot (consumer protection). They reported individually and directly to Roosevelt. The NDAC (the emphasis lay on the third word in the title—"advisory") met often, but it had neither a chair nor decision-making authority.[2]

However it was divided and subdivided, and no matter the caliber of the people in it, the NDAC was not the agency to supervise industrial mobilization: it had no formal leader (critical in an organization with powerful men who saw themselves as equals), and, more importantly, it possessed no authority. According to Robert Nathan, the NDAC's two cochairs, Knudsen and Hillman, got along very well, but did not accomplish a great deal. Nathan further related that Knudsen, although he was a very dedicated, loyal, and patriotic man, was neither politically nor broad policy oriented. As for Hillman, Nathan claims he did not know much about either defense mobilization or the problems involved in the conversion of the peacetime economy to war production.[3]

The NDAC, however, did bring Nathan into the military planning arena for the first time as associate director of Research and Statistics. In this position he worked directly for a man he had never met before, Stacy May. Nathan later related that May was a good operator and was deeply committed, and that he developed a great respect and affection for him. Nathan was put in charge of studying military requirements and soon found that assignment to be nearly hopeless.[4]

According to Nathan, the military would not hazard a guess as to what any future conflict would look like. Many years later he still believed that establishing the requirements for alternative scenarios could have been accomplished easily and that useful rough approximations could have been provided. At the time, however, Nathan did not possess enough clout to break that bottleneck; he was frustrated that other higher-level officials also seemed to lack the authority to force the military to provide the required data. Much later, he wrote in disgust, "It was very frustrating, and we got nowhere."[5]

NDAC was not totally ineffective, however. William Knudsen proved particularly successful in generating the facilities that would eventually lead to construction of the greatest air armada in history. British and French purchases in early 1940 (and only the British thereafter) helped lay the foundation for unprecedented growth in the aviation industry, but Knudsen's work on the conversion of the automobile industry for aircraft production was certainly essential. Creative funding to build the necessary aircraft manufacturing plants was also an initiative of the NDAC. Leon Henderson, a commission member, and Donald M. Nelson, an adviser to the commission, came up with a five-year amortization scheme to permit industrialists to write off plant construction costs more rapidly than the tax code allowed, if these were expended for building munitions factories. Knudsen carried the ball for this proposal in testimony before the Senate Finance Committee, where it passed eleven to ten in July 1940, spurring new construction at a critical time. After Pearl Harbor the government generated the funds for most factory construction, but Roosevelt would have found it impossible to get this kind of direct funding in the political climate of 1940.[6]

Although by general agreement Knudsen was not the right person for the job at NDAC, because he was not capable of dealing with the political currents or forcing his will on a diverse group of political appointees, one cannot overstate the importance of his contribution in moving the aircraft industry toward mass production. In 1946, in a talk at the Industrial War College, Knudsen outlined the problem:

> The first thing that confronted us was President Roosevelt's appeal for fifty thousand airplanes a year. We had been making about fifteen thousand in ten years at that time.
>
> We got all the airplane manufacturers together and talked with them. They were leery because there was a lot of money per unit in airplanes. They cost all kinds of money, around ten dollars a pound. I knew that, of course, but I didn't take much stock in it, because I knew if they ever got the quantity, the cost would come down. It so happened that we started with ten dollars a pound and ran it down to 3.6 dollars per pound simply by getting quantity manufacturing.
>
> I had the dickens of a time getting them to understand that you could have certain units of the airplane made by other kinds of manufacturers. The first fellow who had a wing contract in Detroit lost seven hundred thousand dollars on the wings. He didn't know what he was about. I had to hold his hand for about twenty-four hours, down here in Washington. As a matter of fact, he became an outstanding airplane manufacturer of parts, and not only got his seven hundred thousand back, but quite a considerable amount more.

> There were either no drawings or the drawings were very crude and rough. I am not giving away any secret when I tell you that the airplane manufacturers spent a lot of time telling me that nobody else could do what they did.[7]

Up to the eve of World War II, the production of airplanes and aircraft had been a job for specialists and craftsmen. What drawings existed were basically guidelines to be used by experts, who cut out the pieces and fitted them together by hand, milling here and there until they had constructed a superb piece of equipment. This was a nightmarish situation for industrialists, who thought in terms of mass production. The blueprint was an indication of what had to be done, but it was not an exact mathematical guide. Detroit engineers had to disassemble several aircraft and their engines into their component parts, weigh and measure each piece, and then create an entirely new set of blueprints for each aircraft with mass production in mind. When Packard undertook this job with the Rolls-Royce engine, it took a regiment of engineers and an investment of more than $6 million—but after that they were producing engines as easily as roller skates.[8]

Without Knudsen's early pushing, with the full weight of the NDAC behind him, the aircraft industry would have accomplished none of this preliminary work in time for the mass conversion of Detroit's auto industry in 1942. As a result, by 1944 the United States was producing twice as many aircraft in a month as it had produced in all of 1939. Where Roosevelt's call for an air force of fifty thousand aircraft had once seemed impossible, America produced more than three hundred thousand planes in less than half a decade. Much of this success resulted from the mass-production techniques brought to bear on the problem by the auto industry, but the aircraft industry did more than its share. With NDAC's encouragement, its leaders formed several councils to coordinate the sharing of technology, research, specialists, and excess material. The industry president at North American Company went so far as to call in department heads, engineers, and designers and told them, "From now on, we are giving our competitors anything we have—processes, methods, even tools and materials—that we are not planning to use immediately. Anyone failing to do so would have his name handed to the draft board."[9]

One practical result was that when a Douglas plant building dive-bombers found itself short of two thousand feet of binding braid, critical for the aircraft's final assembly, it was able to find excess in a North American Company plant nearby. Following the North American president's directions, the firm rushed the excess over to the Douglas plant, which finished the bombers. These same dive-bombers were then rushed to the Pacific where they arrived just in time to join the carrier group heading for Midway, where they launched the decisive strike that turned the tide of the war in the Pacific.[10] If NDAC had brought about only that one achievement in the year it existed, it was enough.

Another NDAC commissioner, Leon Henderson, who was responsible for price stabilization and who later became the director of the Office of Price Administration (OPA), came to the fore at this time as a power with whom leaders of industry had to reckon. Henderson was an early New Dealer, but more importantly he was an outspoken "all-outer."[11] All-outers were civilians who fervently believed that the United States would soon confront war with Japan, Germany, or both, and who wanted an all-out effort begun immediately to prepare for such a contingency. All-outers were still rare enough in Washington's 1940 power circles that everyone knew who they all were. Because he was an early New Dealer, Henderson enjoyed unparalleled access to the White House and was not shy in assuming the political power of the president onto himself. Although he had no legal power to establish price limits while part of NDAC, that fact did not stop him from employing political power to keep prices in check whenever possible. Throughout 1940 and 1941 many executives got calls from Henderson saying, "I hear you are going to raise prices. I trust you won't. It will go bad for you if you do."[12]

Henderson was a driven man who had only one goal—beating the Axis powers. When the president offered him the role of U.S. price administrator, Bernard Baruch told him that if he took it he would be the most hated man in the country.[13] Undeterred, Henderson plunged into the job. He did become, arguably, the most hated man in the country, at least among the segment of the business population that wanted to raise prices, but he did the job and held inflation substantially in check throughout his tenure. In 1940, however, his powers remained circumscribed and there were limits to how hard and how far he could push, leaving the always active Henderson time to delve into other matters.

Understanding that the scrap metal shipments to Japan were a major contributor to its rearmament, Henderson was determined to cut them off. He approached the State Department and attempted to persuade Secretary Hull to use his executive powers to halt such shipments. On the advice of the department's bureaucrats who were loath to upset the volatile diplomatic balance with Japan, however, Hull refused to act. Taking matters into his own hands, Henderson contacted British purchasing agents and helped them (using his price administrator powers) to cut deals to buy up the entire U.S. supply of scrap metal. The State Department howled in protest, but Henderson blithely ignored the shouts.[14]

On another occasion, Henderson heard the president comment that the United States would find itself short on copper once it began a total mobilization for war. Henderson looked into the matter and, along with Edward Stettinius, went to meet with the man then in charge of the purchase and stockpiling of strategic raw materials, Jesse Jones.[15] According to Henderson, "Jesse had his own ideas on what he was going to do and he left Stettinius a bit dejected about how little he seemed prepared to do." As the meeting ended, Henderson thanked Jones for his time and informed him, "I will go ahead on other fronts to see what I can do."[16]

Jones, alerted now to a serious threat to his position, asked, "Young man, what do you have in mind?" Henderson replied, "I am going to ask Congress to amend the law establishing a price administrator to allow me to buy copper." With that, Henderson departed and went first to visit Will Clayton, who was then setting up a commodities trading organization to purchase strategic materials on a worldwide basis. Henderson outlined the problem to Clayton, who assured him he had come to the right person and that he would take care of it. Henderson asked, "How much do you think you can buy?" To which Clayton replied, "I will start with the entire global supply and go from there."[17]

This diversion into Henderson's activities is necessary because he will later figure prominently at the critical moment in the feasibility dispute to be addressed shortly. When Henderson voiced his opinion, it was impossible for the military to ignore him. He had direct access to the White House, was thoroughly familiar with the intricacies of war production, and was famous for doing whatever was necessary to make sure the services received everything they needed to win. It was widely acknowledged that if Henderson said something was impossible, then there was no use arguing over the matter: if there was anything that would help the war and was even remotely possible, Henderson would roll over any and all opposition to get it done.

Despite the unceasing efforts of men like Henderson, most still deemed NDAC a failed institution. This was mainly Roosevelt's fault. Although NDAC could advise the president and cajole industry, Roosevelt would not provide it with the authority to force industry to obey its orders nor, in many cases, would he even assist in ensuring that NDAC had the information necessary to be effective. For example, in 1940 when the president called for industry to tool up to build fifty thousand airplanes per year, Roosevelt did not direct the military to tell NDAC what kinds of aircraft to produce or the numbers of each model, so the military did not bother telling industry what it aimed to build. Everybody knew that the Army needed tanks in great numbers after Germany's lightning war against Poland and France, but nobody told the NDAC what kind of tanks to build, when to build them, or where to deliver them.[18]

Few were satisfied with NDAC—not its members, nor the president, nor mobilization gurus like Bernard Baruch, who had been the U.S. production czar in World War I. Acknowledging that his own organization was failing, Knudsen proposed to the president in November 1940 that a director of industrial mobilization be placed in charge of all administrative organizations dealing with planning, procurement, export and import control, raw materials, production, transportation, labor, price control, domestic requirements, and statistics. Knudsen's proposal would have vested the director of industrial mobilization with the power to supervise and direct almost the entire home-front effort. In its essentials, it restated the Army–Navy Industrial Mobilization Plan (IMP), a scheme already rejected by the president.[19] It would have placed in the hands of the proposed director of industrial mobilization the functions that eventually came to be performed by the WPB, the OPA, the War Manpower Commission, the Foreign Economic Administration, as well as other agencies. In effect, the position would have created a copresident, and consequently something that Roosevelt was not ready to consider.[20]

By this time Congress was voicing its concerns and dissatisfaction with NDAC. On 21 November 1940 Senator Robert Taft announced that he would introduce a bill to create a War Resources Board under a single administrator.[21] Unwilling to let Congress dictate how or who should run U.S. war production, Roosevelt preempted Taft and, again by executive order, created the Office of Production Management (OPM). He appointed Knudsen as director general, and, because he considered labor support essential to winning the battle of production, he appointed Sidney Hillman as associate director general. The secretaries of war and the Navy were members of the OPM policy council, but Knudsen and Hillman were to run the office, rationalize war production, and coordinate the many other government agencies involved in producing for rearmament.[22]

At a press conference on 20 December 1940, the president outlined the structure of the new OPM and ridiculed the idea of an economic "Czar, Poobah, or Akhoond of Swat" who would embody all the characteristics necessary for handling defense mobilization.[23] In the president's analysis the problem had three elements: the element of the buyer and user combined, and the elements of management and labor. Apparently, the OPM was to consist of these "three elements," divided among four people—the director, Mr. Knudsen; the associate director, Mr. Hillman; and the secretaries of the Department of War and of the Navy. Production, purchasing, and priorities were to be under the policy supervision of these four individuals.[24]

Economic agencies proliferated like weeds in the first months of 1941, which saw the birth not only of OPM, but also of the OPA, Civilian Supply, the Coordinator of Information, the National Defense Mediation Board, the Petroleum Coordinator, the Office of Scientific Research and Development, the Office of Civilian Defense, and the Economic Defense Board. Most of these agencies came into existence as units of the Office for Emergency Management, and were quartered in the White House. Roosevelt considered that rapidly changing conditions required administrative arrangements that he could make and unmake on the fly, and this in turn called for maintaining presidential initiative in matters of emergency governmental organization. The legal basis for this initiative had been provided in 1939 with the creation of the Office for Emergency Management under presidential auspices. Thus, in addition to serving as a means for assisting the president in general management, the Office for Emergency Management became something of a holding company for emergency agencies and a legal device permitting flexibility in emergency organization.[25]

For the moment, however, OPM was the center of everyone's attention. The president chartered the office to increase and regulate the production and supply of defense materials, equipment, and factories. OPM was also tasked to analyze and summarize the requirements of the two services, as well as of foreign governments. Moreover, OPM was charged with ensuring supplies of raw materials, formulating plans to further mobilize defense facilities, and planning for the future creation of new industrial plants.

OPM's charter made it appear as if the president had centralized his vast powers in a single organization, but once again Roosevelt was playing a smoke and mirrors game. Despite its impressive list of responsibilities, OPM could only "advise"; usually that advice could go only to the president and not to those intimately involved in production matters. As just one more presidential advisory body with no statutory enforcement powers, Roosevelt had doomed it from the start.[26] Moreover, the organizational structure of OPM appeared to be designed to run as inefficiently as possible. Instead of one leader, it had two, who were supposed to coordinate their activities and decisions. Because the two men in charge, Knudsen (with a business background) and Sidney Hillman (a labor official), were not forceful leaders and the secretaries of the Department of War and of the Navy remained substantially uninvolved (preferring to work production matters through their own Army and Navy Munitions Board [ANMB]), OPM was ineffective even in areas where it clearly could have contributed.[27]

A poor organizational structure compounded the leadership failures. Its three divisions—production, purchases, and priorities—each functioned more or less independently, with little interaction.[28] In fact, their primary method of contact with each other was Knudsen's staff conferences, which inevitably focused on the detailed minutiae of production—Knudsen's strength—and not the establishment of a grand national program.[29] The fact that each division was allowed to maintain its own contacts with the armed services, other agencies, and Congress exacerbated the negative effects of this decentralization. With no firm hand on the rudder and with each division possessing its own contacts and base of political support, the inevitable bureaucratic disputes were more drawn out and bitter than they needed to be. Industrialists often had to visit with and gain the cooperation of each division separately in order to ensure that projects would not be held up by OPM's internecine warfare. Moreover, each of these divisions replicated within itself all of the administrative areas and functions required to make any bureaucratic structure work, with one important exception. There was only one central statistical division to collect and prepare data for all three divisions. To accomplish this, Knudsen formed the Bureau of Research and Statistics, which he tasked to act as a clearinghouse for all statistical and economic information for the entire OPM. It was here that Stacy May ensconced himself.

A snippet of how bad the overall problem was can be seen in the role the executive secretary, Henry Emmerich, a lifetime civil service employee, undertook for himself. With no leadership from the top, Emmerich attempted to fill the void. Since Knudsen had begun keeping his codirector, Hillman, in the dark about production, Hillman stopped informing Knudsen about labor problems. Emmerich began keeping abreast of what was taking place in both areas and then briefing his two bosses about what the other was doing. Emmerich also began acting on his own initiative to try to coordinate the activities of the three main divisions. Without Emmerich's seizure of the initiative, there is little doubt that the entire OPM apparatus would have collapsed.[30] In the end, Knudsen's leadership style and the competition between the separate divisions crippled OPM.

Although OPM made some progress in coordinating the construction of new munitions facilities, it failed to do much of anything to convert consumer production facilities to munitions production. At its root, this failure reflected the outlook of OPM's leaders. Although both Knudsen and Hillman agreed that military production was a national priority, they were both reluctant to force consumers to pay for the transition from civilian to military production. Knudsen, with his General Motors background, proved reluctant to force the hand of industry before it was necessary, while Hillman did not want to do anything that might deprive his labor constituency of items they were beginning to demand in quantity as the economy rapidly improved.

By April 1941 "guns and butter" was no longer an option. Critical shortages were developing in basic materials and equipment. Constructing new production facilities was going to take too long, and, by absorbing more resources during construction, would exacerbate both consumer and military production problems. Reducing the production of consumer durables, however, would immediately increase the supply of materials for military production, and would place America's most modern plants at the disposal of the munitions production authorities. The automobile industry, for instance, was absorbing 18 percent of total steel production, and 80 percent of rubber production. Moreover, it controlled the nation's largest collection of engineering talent.[31]

That April, Stacy May concluded that the combined demands of the Army, the Navy, the Maritime Commission, and the British would total $49 billion. This represented almost two-thirds of the country's GDP and was unachievable without a rapid reduction in consumer production. When these arguments finally worked their way up to the president's attention in early May, Roosevelt became increasingly insistent that OPM start ordering the curtailment and conversion of civilian industries.[32] Roosevelt was brought over to this point of view by his close adviser, Harry Hopkins, who in turn had become convinced of its necessity when he was presented with an early feasibility analysis completed by Stacy May. Because of its importance to future arguments, it should be noted that this was the first time a presidential decision concerning military production was made almost solely on the basis of "national income" statistics; this demonstrates that Roosevelt and Hopkins were convinced of their merit.

The numbers, however, had not convinced Knudsen and he continued to lead the cause for gradual curtailment of the civilian sector. He maintained that the nation should and could meet its defense needs with the least possible disruption of the civilian economy.[33] This battle of the bureaucrats lasted through May, but along the way Knudsen made a major error (from the perspective of his own cause) by agreeing to the creation of a separate agency to control civilian prices. The Office of Price Administration and Civilian Supply (OPACS) with Leon Henderson at its head reported directly to the president. The executive order that created OPACS was meant to limit its functions to the civilian area.[34] Henderson was not the kind of man, however, to limit himself to the letter of his instructions and soon found an opportunity to expand his authority. When on 31 May 1941 Congress gave the president power to determine priority allocations for the civilian as well as the military sectors, both Knudsen and Henderson immediately claimed this new power for their own organizations. While Knudsen consulted with his confidantes, Henderson acted. In a particularly clever maneuver, Henderson issued orders that protected every consumer sector that his office considered essential to the efficient operation of the economy. By staking out portions of the economy where he was all-powerful and would tolerate no intrusions, Henderson basically had informed OPM that everything he had not fenced off was available for immediate conversion to munitions production. In fact, he was offering a large portion of civilian production for rapid conversion to munitions production.

Still, Knudsen moved slowly. In July he announced that OPM had cut a deal with the automobile industry to gradually reduce production by 20 percent over the course of the coming year. Unimpressed, Henderson ordered Detroit's announced price increases rolled back and then sent his deputy to Detroit to tell automobile industry executives that OPACS was not happy with the pace of curtailment and that Henderson was not overly solicitous of the industry's goodwill.[35] When industry executives resisted Henderson's entreaties, on 20 July 1941 he unilaterally ordered a 50 percent cut in scarce materials (e.g., steel) going to the automobile industry. Knudsen objected, but knew he was losing the battle. By August OPM had received industry agreement to begin cutting back production immediately and to make overall cuts of well over 40 percent.[36]

Soon after this, the president removed Henderson's power to restrict raw materials from industry. Apparently, the president did not feel himself politically powerful enough to defeat business interests in the Congress over the issue. In order to strengthen his hand for future arguments on this point, on 9 July Roosevelt ordered the Army and Navy to lay out their requirements for a major war—the Victory Program. But the immediate effect of Roosevelt's temporary limitation of Henderson's power was to ignite a new round of bureaucratic warfare. As the infighting continued, Roosevelt asked one of his personal advisers, Judge Samuel I. Rosenman, to look into the matter and recommend organizational changes. To Rosenman the answer was obvious: the president needed to combine OPM and OPACS into a single agency with one forceful leader.[37] In typically Roosevelt fashion, the president used the parts of the recommendation he liked and discarded the rest. On 28 August 1941 he created the Supply Priorities and Allocations Board (SPAB). Although World War I industrial czar Bernard Baruch and his own presidential advisers strongly advocated placing this new economic administration under one person, Roosevelt still was not ready to appoint what would in effect be a copresident—at least not until he had been thoroughly tested and proven to not represent a political danger, if not always pliant to Roosevelt's whims. Instead of doing away with failing organizations, Roosevelt placed SPAB on top of them. The OPM was still supposedly in charge of setting priorities, while the president transformed Henderson's price control office into the independent OPA.

What really doomed this set-up was the convoluted leadership arrangements, which Roosevelt either created or allowed to stand. Because of his reputation as America's number one buyer, Donald Nelson became the head of SPAB.[38] Within that organization, Nelson was Knudsen's boss, but Nelson still held his position as the head of purchasing for OPM, where he worked for Knudsen. Within the OPA Henderson was now his own boss, but he also still held his old job at OPM. Nelson then confounded matters further by ordering that SPAB should do most of its work through and in coordination with OPM, although SPAB remained superior to OPM in the power hierarchy. This led to some interesting procedural arrangements. For instance, Nelson as head of SPAB could transmit directives to OPM. Once these directives arrived at OPM, Nelson could then interpret or reinterpret them as he saw fit before transmitting any orders to industry, therefore ignoring, if he wished, the desires of the SPAB board.[39] Furthermore, although Nelson was in charge of the board, Roosevelt placed other powerful persons on the board, including Vice President Henry Wallace and Harry Hopkins.[40] These arrangments had two major effects: first, Nelson could never be sure of his own power on the board when several of its members had daily exchanges with Roosevelt, and second, they created numerous "unofficial" power centers within a single organization. Any business or military claimant who was unhappy with a decision made by a member of the SPAB had numerous avenues in which to get the decision modified or overturned.

Although the leadership arrangements within SPAB were awkward, they reflected the political realities of the moment. Actually, though, SPAB was a step forward from what had come before. By this time, American rearmament had reached a point where it was essential to create an organization whose decisions could not be ignored and that had a powerful bite. Since Roosevelt was still not ready to concentrate economic decision making in one person, however, SPAB was the best possible compromise.[41] The infighting within and among powerful groups ensured that SPAB's decision processes would often be bloody and result in compromises. On the other hand, once decisions did emerge, SPAB had the power to enforce them. As one example, SPAB determined that it could not justify the resources required to complete the St. Lawrence Waterway Power Project in light of the current mobilization emergency. It fell to Donald Nelson to tell Roosevelt that SPAB wanted to kill off a project everyone knew was the "apple of the President's eye." On hearing the news, Roosevelt commented, "Don, you're killing one of my children." Nelson replied, "I know Mr. President, but it has to be done." The project was closed the following week and nothing was heard about the matter again.[42]

The SPAB leadership also revealed one important, but mostly overlooked, fact about Roosevelt's thoughts. By this time, the president had gone far beyond his original conception of mobilizing enough of American industry to provide the Allied powers, short of war. It is now clear that he considered the entry of the United States into the war almost inevitable and the SPAB membership reflects his thinking. Wallace, Hopkins, Henderson, Hillman, and Nelson were all-outers. The president could count on them to counter the more conservative impulses of Knudsen, Secretary of War Stimson, and Secretary of the Navy Knox. This latter group had worked together to stymie the efforts of the all-outers within OPM, but they were now being pushed aside by the SPAB members. When Knudsen was the head of OPM, he used his influence to check the all-outers in favor of business interests that wanted a slower and more measured conversion to war production. The secretaries of War and of the Navy supported Knudsen so as not to antagonize firms they viewed as critical to their current production efforts.[43] The removal from OPM, at presidential direction, of many of Knudsen's business supporters—such as John Biggers and Edward Stettinius, who were viewed as drags on mobilization—further undermined Knudsen's continuing efforts to bridle the likes of Leon Henderson and the other all-outers.

Given its organizational weakness, SPAB's accomplishments were rather remarkable. For instance, the SPAB board was the first to realize that the priorities system established for the use of key industrial materials was breaking down, due to a predictable inflation in the number of production contracts requiring a top priority. Because everybody wanted everything now and certainly ahead of everyone else, too many systems received A-1 ratings, forcing OPM to create new higher ratings. When too many projects claimed the new higher ratings, a new priority rating system was established that rated material from A-1-A through A-1-J. And after that system also seized up, OPM imposed an AA band on claimants as a type of super-priority. It was a vicious cycle and a crash was inevitable.[44] As one of its first undertakings, SPAB launched a frontal assault on the priorities system.[45] With no reliable requirements estimates available from the military and no hope of the situation improving any time soon, however, the civilians used their own best judgment as to military needs. For example, at the end of September 1941 a SPAB staff report to Nelson stated that the Army estimates the military provided were based on imaginary and arbitrary assumptions. As for the Navy, the report found that when the number of ships was increased, ammunition requirements only went up enough to account for target practice. There were no estimates about what might be required to fight a war, despite the Navy already being committed to combat operations in the North Atlantic. To make up for these estimation shortfalls, civilian production experts began doubling and in some cases tripling what the military was asking for without ever going back and reconciling the new numbers with the War or Navy departments.[46]

It was rapidly becoming obvious not only that the civilians did not trust the military to come up with reliable requirements estimates, but also that they were becoming confident they could substitute their own judgment on many matters previously reserved to those with military expertise. Nowhere was this clearer than in the battles over increasing steel production, when the all-outers on SPAB went toe-to-toe against business, their supporters at OPM, and the military services. As Robert Nathan recalled decades later,

> In the fall of 1940, the Division of Research and Statistics sent to the National Advisory Commission a report stating that for an all-out defense effort the United States would need at least a 10-million-ton steel expansion. The steel industry's response was, in essence, "This is absurd, only 6 years or 7 years ago we were functioning at only 15 to 20 percent of capacity." That was true. Even in 1940, the American steel industry was producing at about 60 to 65 percent of capacity. The steel industry's view was that we should not build new capacity because at the war's end there

> would be another depression or recession and the industry would be left with even more idle capacity than in the Great Depression. They favored deep cuts in steel supplies for the civilian sector rather than adding new capacity. We pointed out that steel capacity had to be enlarged even if consumer uses were drastically reduced.
>
> Fortunately, this became a high-level issue. The government decided to offer attractive incentives, and we did get a 10-million-ton steel expansion. By the time Pearl Harbor was attacked, United States steel capacity was approaching 80 million tons rather than the 70 million tons of capacity that existed in mid-1940.[47]

In a speech given after the war, though, Nathan remembered the steel debate as a "long bitter fight" that finally had been decided by a directive from President Roosevelt ordering a 10 million–ton increase in steel production.[48] In addition to steel, SPAB pushed hard for production expansion of other key war commodities in the face of constant resistance from business and the military. In the case of aluminum, for instance, Nathan related,

> We pushed hard for much more aluminum capacity expansion than was under way. At that time the only aluminum producer in the United States was Aluminum Corporation of America (Alcoa). Henry Kaiser and the Reynolds Company were given incentives and support for building new plants to produce aluminum. Also, Alcoa greatly expanded its capacity. Later another company entered the field. The United States had four aluminum producers instead of one. This was of great importance because the United States had been producing airplanes for military use only at the rate of a few hundred a year. Within one year after Pearl Harbor we were producing over 1,000 [tons of aluminum] a week and by the end of 1943 the production reached about 2,000 [tons] a week.[49]

At this point, it is important to understand why business was so resistant to major increases in production. In most situations, a business expansion based on guaranteed government contracts would appear to be almost a license to print money and that businesses would be expected to jump at the opportunity. There were three main reasons that this was not the case. First was the political atmosphere. In 1940 and even late 1941, most Americans remained adamant that the United States should remain out of the war. In the years after World War I, many Americans became convinced that crafty British propaganda had drawn them into that war. This time they were determined to resist such pressure. With national heroes such as Charles Lindbergh touring America to spread the gospel of noninvolvement and no rearmament and others leading massive rallies advocating a policy of "America first," it was by no means clear that America would enter the war in the immediate future. Business interests feared the government would force them to expand in order to support a military that America would never build, and leave them with a huge load of expensive, possibly even ruinous, excess capacity.

Moreover, most business executives found their regular current business environment unpredictable. Even though the economy was expanding at a rapid clip in 1940 and 1941, no one was sure the expansion would last. The Depression had been a grueling time for American business. Those firms that survived the lean decade of the 1930s had learned caution and conservatism. During the 1930s there had been several moments when it appeared the worst had passed and a growth trajectory had returned. Each of those instances proved to be a false dawn, however, with the economy quickly reversing itself, usually within a single quarter. Each of these experiences left business and industry wary; by 1941, although this time the growth trend appeared sustainable, no one was ready to move too quickly toward an optimistic vision.

Hard-headed business interests were not the primary reason why American business failed to answer the clarion call to action until after the attack on Pearl Harbor, however. Before World War I, according to Donald Nelson, the United States had no munitions industry such as that found throughout Europe, which had existed for hundreds of years. There was, in fact, a strong feeling in the United States against the "merchants of death," of whom von Hindenburg had said, "They understood war and were both brilliant and pitiless." After World War I, politicians, reacting to their constituents' sentiments, cracked down on the so-called munitions barons.

Bethlehem Steel Corporation provides a sterling example of this process. Before the end of World War I, Bethlehem Steel was making almost all the munitions necessary to wage modern war. Postwar tax laws were such that Bethlehem had no other recourse than to destroy its whole munitions empire—literally to wreck it physically. The new facilities were too expensive to maintain and pay taxes on, so Bethlehem demolished them. One month there was a munitions production behemoth that might have dwarfed Krupp or Vickers, and the next month there was no trace of it left. This fate befell scores of other firms, too. The largest rifle-manufacturing firm in the world, the Eddystone plant of Remington, was swept away. Half-finished ships rusted and rotted because shipyards had gone out of business. The world's biggest merchant marine faded to a shadow of its former self. Machine-gun plants and the beginnings of a promising military plane industry disappeared. All that was left of the engine of war production that made von Hindenburg shudder was reduced to the plans in the files of the War Industrial College.[50]

In short, ramping up production to ensure Allied victory in World War I not only had forced American businesses to absorb crippling financial and economic losses, but also had seen the top executives of the firms demonized as "merchants of death." Chief executive officers were now understandably reluctant to undertake actions that would lead to the pillorying of their own reputations.

SPAB had a considerable impact in the allocation of scarce materials between the American military and those of America's future allies.[51] The services had already come to terms with Lend-Lease for the British, but when Roosevelt announced his intention to supply military aid to the Soviet Union, the military chiefs rushed to the barricades, claiming they needed every bit of production to equip American forces. Roosevelt ignored his military advisers, however, and in early October approved the Moscow Protocol with Britain, which agreed to the sending of large shipments of military materiel to the beleaguered Soviet Union.[52] On 23 October SPAB issued orders for allocating materials and equipment to meet the protocol's undertakings.[53] Since German armored columns were already deep inside European Russia and pushing toward Moscow, these orders met bitter resistance from the military. Most military experts agreed that the USSR's life expectancy could now be measured in weeks, so the military could not see any justification for shipping precious munitions and raw materials in a futile attempt to prop up a losing cause. According to Army analysts, the best one could hope for was that the Soviets might be able to hold at the Urals and become a nuisance for the Germans in the future. Accomplishing this feeble outcome, at the cost of America's own military capabilities, remained a hard sell for many months. So, although SPAB's material allocation decisions were in accordance with the president's direct orders, they had to be fought over in every board meeting. On a weekly basis, the military, and particularly the Navy, citing expert opinion that the USSR was about to collapse, strenuously objected to the shipment of raw aluminum and machine tools to the Soviets.[54]

After losing a series of battles within SPAB, the Army and Navy teamed up in an attempt to create a super-priorities committee on which the military would have the dominant role and that would not contain the SPAB members who supported the president's Soviet policy.[55] In this new conception, Hopkins, Nelson, and Henderson were to be removed and Stettinius returned.[56] With a SPAB super-board consisting of Stimson, Knox, Knudsen, Stettinius, and Wallace, the War and Navy departments were sure they could dictate mobilization policy, or, at the least, determine the level of assistance that would be made available to the Soviet Union. Roosevelt in no uncertain terms quashed the Knox–Stimson proposal for a super-board, but the attempt had firmly drawn the battle lines for the future.

How the military thought it was going pull off this coup is still hard to understand. Advocating the removal of Harry Hopkins, who by this time maintained his residence in the White House, demonstrates a remarkable political naiveté on the part of senior military officers. In the end, the military had to execute an ignominious retreat, but bad blood remained. Fortunately, Hopkins, with his close relationship with the president, could shrug off any military hostility. In fact, Marshall and the other JCS soon found him to be a great asset in their dealings with the president, so any residual hostility from the ANMB and other military staffs remained muted. As for Henderson, he always gave the impression of a man who lived for conflict. He noted his enemies, marked his time, and focused his energies on winning the war of production.[57] Nelson was most affected by this early squabble. He was the man those leading the military side of the production and mobilization apparatus identified as the primary obstacle to achieving their desires. Unfortunately, Nelson's personality and desire to manage by consensus made him an easy target in the upcoming internecine warfare. He represented the kind of target who was unaware of how to defend himself and was unlikely to do so even if he knew how. The consequences of his inability to get into the mud and fight were almost ruinous, and disaster was averted only because Henderson and Nathan were bureaucratic in-fighters of the first order.

While these debates continued, SPAB was conducting a rapid but comprehensive analysis of the American economy. In its first meeting, on 9 September 1941, Leon Henderson convinced Nelson to produce a study that would compile scheduled, overall military, civilian, and foreign requirements through mid-1943.[58] Stacy May, who recently had returned from the United Kingdom with the completed Anglo-American Consolidated Statement, undertook this new assignment. On 10 September SPAB began a systematic review of all the requirements necessary to defeat the Axis and stabilize the home front. The accuracy of these estimates rested on fundamental assumptions about the size of the defense effort required and on the barest essentials needed to keep the civilian economy functioning at peak efficiency. Once completed, there still remained an enormous statistical problem of translating these numbers into quantities of raw materials and required production capacity.[59]

In an attempt to help May and his research staff undertake this task, in mid-September Nelson again asked the Army, Navy, Maritime Commission, and Lend-Lease administration for clear statements of their estimated requirements, based on military objectives over the next two years.[60] In response, the War Department submitted what staff officers termed a comprehensive set of estimates covering domestic and foreign needs for Army-type equipment.[61] As for the Lend-Lease administrator, his staff sent only partial requirements because staff was still in the process of compiling data. Astonishingly, the Navy Department and the Maritime Commission both refused to forward any estimate and claimed that the country would actually have to be at war before they could determine what was required for victory.[62] Undeterred by the quality or scarcity of the data, Stacy May and his team substituted their own best judgment based on previous military estimates and an incomplete Joint Board plan.[63]

In early November May turned his attention to creating requirements estimates for all production programs, industry by industry. He worked out estimates for what raw materials would be required on a monthly basis—not just for war production, but also for industry, civilian use, and essential public services.[64] This was the first instance where someone bothered to integrate the needs of the civilian economy and the rest of government into the economic planning for war. The developing Victory Program was no longer just a statement of military requirements, but also was a realistic appraisal of what the United States would require to win the war and keep the country functioning at peak capacity.[65]

Despite some defects, the requirements May outlined in his study were superior to any previous standard. Because of its immense size, however, a number of individuals immediately called its feasibility into question. A feasibility study was required and its conduct fell to Robert Nathan, who at this time was working for Stacy May. His analysis went on through most of November and forced major alterations in the program.

What Nathan found was astounding. As of November 1941 the total defense effort in the United States, including Lend-Lease, added up to $60 billion. According to Victory Program estimates, however, the United States would have to spend at least $165 billion by October 1943 if it were to have the materiel necessary for an all-out offensive against the Axis powers.[66] Thus

Nathan concluded that the entire defense program would have to be doubled if there were to be any hope of attaining the objectives of the Victory Program. This meant that the United States economy would have to reach a GDP level of $150 billion by 1943, and at least half of this total would have to be dedicated to war production. Once he completed his analysis, Nathan announced that the program was feasible, but only in terms of a wartime economy with a high degree of central control. The problem was that on 4 December 1941, when Stacy May delivered Nathan's final report to Donald Nelson, the country was not at war.

Three days later Stacy May was looking out the window of his apartment, which overlooked the Japanese embassy, listening to the first reports of the attack on Pearl Harbor and watching embassy officials burn papers on their lawn.[67] The United States was now at war and May was one of the few who understood what was going to take place in America. Starting the next day the country began turning what von Hindenburg called its "pitiless" industrial might toward war. If America's World War I production had shocked von Hindenburg, he would have found himself dumbstruck at the avalanche of munitions that soon began flowing out of America's "pitiless" factories. On some level this bothered Stacy May. A one-time pacifist who had volunteered to be an ambulance driver in the First World War so as not to be thought of as shirking his responsibilities, he knew that his work made much of what would become known as the production miracle of World War II possible. May also understood that there was evil in the world, however, and that the United States had to confront it. Long after the war, when he was asked about his previous pacifism, he simply replied, "I was wrong."[68]

CHAPTER 6

The War Production Board and Two Wars

★ ★ ★

In the immediate aftermath of the attack on Pearl Harbor, Roosevelt accepted that both Office of Production Management (OPM) and Supply Priorities and Allocations Board (SPAB) were failing in their primary responsibility to increase munitions production efficiently. To ensure that new astronomical production goals were met, he created a new organization to replace both SPAB and OPM: the War Production Board (WPB). To head the WPB, Roosevelt first selected Supreme Court Justice William O. Douglas. After what some thought was rather unseemly political maneuvring by Harry Hopkins, however, Roosevelt dropped Douglas in favor of Donald Nelson, a man Hopkins thought would be easier to manage and control.[1] *In selecting Nelson for the head job, Roosevelt purposely pushed Knudsen out of the leadership role. In doing so, he did not show him the courtesy of personally informing Knudsen that he was being cast into the wilderness.*

To soften the blow, Roosevelt, at Nelson's urging, made Knudsen a lieutenant general in the Army and sent him on a roving mission to increase production in factories across the country.[2] Though Knudsen had his detractors as head of OPM, in this new role he received nothing but well-earned praise: if there was one thing Knudsen knew, it was how to build things. In fact, understanding how to build things was so important to him that when his teenage son asked for a car, Knudsen delivered it to him in pieces and told him to assemble it himself.[3] Over the course of the war, Knudsen visited thousands of plants. It was later estimated that on average these visits increased the productivity of each plant by between 10 and 20 percent.[4] In other words, he single-handedly increased war production by billions of dollars.

Nelson's predecessors and their organizations were doomed to failure because Roosevelt was never ready to confer on them the power necessary to achieve required or expected results. By comparison, some have termed the executive order creating the WPB as an almost perfect instrument.[5] In Executive Order 9024 (16 January) Roosevelt placed almost total power and authority to direct the country's mobilization in the hands of Donald Nelson. The chair of the WPB was given full powers to direct all federal departments and agencies in all matters dealing with war procurement and production. The key words, however, did not come until the end of the order when Roosevelt did what he was never prepared to do before—turn over ultimate power: "The Chairman may exercise the powers, authority, and discretion conferred upon him through such officials or agencies and in such a manner as he may determine; and *his decisions shall be final*" (emphasis added).[6]

This was the ultimate power to control every facet of the economy and the mobilization of the country for war. Unfortunately, Nelson was not the man for the job.[7] Given more power than any of his predecessors—or, for that matter, more than anyone thought Roosevelt would ever allot to another individual—he seemed to be in mortal fear of ever using it.[8] As part of this executive order, Nelson received the power to control all Army and Navy procurement and contracting functions. Inexplicably, though, and with almost disastrous results, one of his first acts as chair was to abrogate this responsibility and hand it back to the military.[9]

On 12 March 1942 Nelson made an agreement with Under Secretary of War Robert P. Patterson to "perfect the governing relationships between the Army and the War Department" (he made a similar agreement with the Navy on 12 April).[10] In the agreement, Nelson laid out the overall responsibilities of his organization as giving general direction and supervision to the war supply system in accordance with strategic directives and plans. The agreement also allowed the War Department to retain its role in procurement, however, although the military was supposed to use WPB directives to guide its purchasing programs.[11]

Nelson had high hopes that this and his similar agreement with the Navy would lead to a harmonious partnership between the WPB and the military contracting authorities and that it would provide a jump-start for increased production. As he explained to the Truman Committee on 21 April 1942,[12]

> I have gone even to the point of being overzealous in seeing that the contracting power is kept within the Army and Navy.
>
> We had one of two courses to take when we took this job. Many urged that we set up a buying organization independent of the Army and Navy. I knew, sir, that that would be just dead wrong and didn't even consider it for five minutes, because it would have been impossible to have gotten the kind of men that we wanted to come here and do that job with the contracting power without having subjected themselves to great criticism. So, in setting it up, we were very careful not to take a bit of authority away from the Army or Navy. As a matter of fact, we enhanced that authority.[13]

After the war, Nelson presented other reasons for his transfer of procurement and contracting authority back to the Army and Navy. According to him, the shifting of the massive procurement machinery would have led to unconscionable delays in war production during the critical early months of 1942. He further maintained that it would have been difficult to separate contracting from inspection of the finished products for conformity with military designs geared to strategic and tactical needs.[14] Finally, Nelson claimed the complicated and time-consuming process of getting the mass of laws altered to accommodate the shift of procurement responsibilities to a civilian agency.[15]

These reasons now appear as hindsight justifications for what many, even at the time, regarded as a disastrous decision. It is unlikely that there would have been any delay in war production because the assumption of contracting power by WPB did not require the elimination of one organization and the creation of another. Nelson could have accomplished this transition slowly and smoothly by starting with a small oversight group to manage the overall contracting system in order to ensure that orders remained within the economy's ability to meet them. Furthermore, the problem of separating inspections from contracting appears to have been a fabrication. When civilians finally did seize total control over production with the advent of WPB's successor agency, the Office of War Mobilization and Reconversion (OWMR), allowing the inspection function to remain with the military did not prove to be a problem.[16] Finally, virtually all the legislation required to shift procurement authority to the WPB was already prepared and there was a compliant Congress waiting to approve it. In fact, when these laws eventually were submitted for a vote, they were debated and cleared Congress in a single day.[17]

Despite Nelson's high hopes for harmony between the military and WPB, his decisions to allow the Army and Navy to control contracting almost crippled war production. The services saw an opportunity to reinstitute the defunct Industrial Mobilization Plan (IMP), which would have placed them in charge of all production, including that part of total production required to keep the civilian sector functioning, and they were quick to act.[18] Their job was made easier when Nelson compounded his mistake of allowing the military to let contracts without supervision with two other mistakes that were just as serious. First, he decided to maintain the priorities system that had been in place under OPM; second, he allowed the Army and the Navy to establish their own priorities for contracts they let.[19]

A case can be made that Nelson had to allow the services to maintain contracting responsibility because they already had the organization and staffing to accomplish this task, while the WPB was still in its infancy and not prepared to assume that responsibility.[20] Even if one accepts such a proposition, however, the WPB was sufficiently staffed to provide oversight of both the size of the military's overall contracting activities and of the priorities system. The result of Nelson's failure to assert control of military procurement was growing chaos throughout the entire production system since military orders far outstripped industry's capabilities.

Reorganizations within WPB and the Army

As Nelson was completing his negotiations with the under secretaries of the Army and Navy, both the War Department and the WPB itself were reorganizing to meet the circumstances of global war.[21] For the most part, the WPB did not change its previous OPM structure very much. The biggest change was in the overall leadership (Knudsen out, Nelson in) and the increased power conferred on WPB that had been denied to its predecessors.[22] Virtually all the bureaucratic organization that made up SPAB and OPM survived to be incorporated into the WPB.

Organizational units dedicated to production, purchases, civilian supply, and materials went on much as they had for the past year. The groups responsible for planning and requirements received increased power, and were made into separate committees reporting directly to Nelson: the Requirements Committee and the Planning Committee. The Requirements Committee took over the supervision of most of the allotments of raw materials from the materials branch. Hence, it was responsible for organizing the priorities system. This committee eventually came under the control of Ferdinand Eberstadt, who managed to simplify the priorities system through the institution of the Controlled Materials Plan (CMP); the CMP, in a single stroke, restored some semblance of order to the production scheduling chaos.[23]

To run the Planning Committee, Nelson selected Robert Nathan, who promptly hired Simon Kuznets as the committee's chief statistician and economist.[24] The other members of the group were a study in contrasts. Thomas Blaisdell, earlier a teacher of economics and later a staff member of the National Resources Planning Board, was quiet, even-tempered, well-informed, and scholarly. After coming to Washington in 1933, he had acquired broad experience in a half-dozen different jobs, including the directorship of the Temporary National Economic Committee monopoly studies of 1938–39. The final member of the committee, Fred Searls, was tough-minded and conservative, a highly successful mining engineer. Formerly vice president of the Newmont Mining Company, in 1941 he became a consultant with the ordnance branch of the War Department and held that position during the entire period of his service on the Planning Committee. Serving without administrative responsibilities, this committee dedicated itself from the beginning to the job of evaluating planning for the optimum utilization of America's economic resources for the war effort. Stacy May was allied to this group, but in a distinctly separate office, as director of the WPB's office of progress reports.[25]

The Planning Committee was freed from all administrative duties and was specifically designed to analyze what was happening in production and to study the impact of the Victory Program on the American economy. According to Nelson, who formed the committee at the end of February, this committee was to, "Assist him in developing plans and policies for maintaining the proper balance and relationships of the war production program and in determining the fullest use of the materials, facilities, and services needed for the realization of the program."[26] The formal order establishing the committee added the task of "anticipating future trends of war production and recommending to the WPB Chairman policies for overcoming obstacles to the full realization of the war production program."[27] In a memo to Nelson in early April, Nathan laid out what he viewed as the Planning Committee's central task: "To evaluate and plan for the most effective utilization of our economic resources and the largest effective dedication of those resources to the war effort. This means that it must plan for maximizing total production, and for applying the largest feasible proportion of that total output to the war effort. This objective entails both the establishment of over-all programs and the creation of mechanisms to implement these programs."[28]

Nathan did not hesitate to use his broad mandate: within weeks of the Planning Committee's creation, it was conducting a wide variety of production -related studies. In addition to completing Nelson's first demand—to look at the feasibility of the entire munitions program in relation to shipping capacity—Nathan also had teams looking into a number of other areas, including military construction, the construction of new industrial facilities, rerating of military and civilian programs, manpower issues, raw materials flow, and a host of others. To convey some idea of the scope of the Planning Committee's activities, a nugget from *Time* magazine's comment at the time is priceless: "Most important, in WPB's second week, was a step which went almost unnoticed outside its own offices. On Nelson's desk each morning bald statistician Stacy May began to place a fat progress report: day-by-day, company-by-company of deliveries of armaments and armament parts stacked against the quotas. Before this, a lazy or corrupt producer could sit motionless for months without having anyone the wiser. Under Nelson's WPB, any failures show up at once in the morning report on his desk."[29] Despite this wide range of interests, the Planning Committee made its most important contribution in the sphere of long-term production planning: analyzing trends in civilian production in relation to national income, studies of national income and GNP, the examination of industrial capacity, and all other resource factors that operated as limiting elements of production. These studies, largely the work of Simon Kuznets and Stacy May, aimed to bring production objectives into line with overall capacity, and led to specific recommendations that had far-reaching effects on the magnitude and composition of the nation's production program.[30]

Unlike what one might expect from a policy group made up of statisticians and economists, Nathan's natural forcefulness ensured that the Planning Committee would aggressively push to have its recommendations followed. In an almost perfect example of understatement, the official history of the WPB states, "As many of the recommendations touched on important organizational and personal interests, this prodding for action resulted in opposition to the Committee by a few affected individuals in the services."[31] If one replaces the word "opposition" with "all-out bloody bureaucratic warfare" one gets much closer to the true picture. Even as the WPB and its subordinate Planning Committee mobilized the nation to wage a global war, WPB was waging its own internal war, mostly against the Army's Army Service Forces

(ASF) and its leader, General Brehon Somervell. Eventually WPB would win the battle over feasibility, but only at considerable cost. When the dust settled, the Army, and to a lesser extent the Navy, accepted reduced production goals, but Nelson and the WPB were crippled and the Planning Committee was completely dissolved.

Army Reorganization: Creation of Army Service Forces

In mid-February 1942 General Marshall called his staff together, briefed them on his plan to reorganize the entire Army, and gave them two days to comment on his plan.[32] The reorganization had been long in coming, but the catalyst appears to have been a 25 July 1941 memorandum from General Leslie McNair to Marshall, in which the former outlined the situation of a number of newly established bases, and discussed the broad questions of their command, operation, and administration. McNair concluded that several agencies and departments oversaw these bases and therefore no one controlled or coordinated them.[33] McNair's memorandum, although confined to the organizational problems of the country's new bases, came on top of a push by the Air Force for greater autonomy, broader command problems being experienced by the newly established Army General Headquarters, and the expanded burdens being imposed on the Army by an increasingly complex global situation. In this unsettled command and organizational environment, McNair's memorandum became the spark that lit the slow fuse toward reorganization.[34] Throughout the summer, the Army staff debated various reorganization proposals, all foundering either on the problem of Air Force autonomy or the command relationships between Washington and the possible theaters of war. In late July Colonel William K. Harrison Jr., the War Plans Division's representative on one of the reorganization committees, put forward his own idea for reorganization, on which he apparently had been working privately since late 1940.[35] Eventually, Harrison's memorandum became the basis of the Army's 1942 reorganization, but at the time it was killed by the chief of the War Plans Division, General Gerow, who later stated that he did not believe that Marshall was ready for the huge upheaval the plan's adoption would cause.[36]

On 30 August, in place of the Harrison memorandum the War Plans Division offered a revised version of the structure the Army was currently working under. Although McNair concurred with this approach, he did so with serious reservations.[37] By mid-September, however, McNair had reversed himself and come out against the War Plans Division's recommendation. It was left to the Air Staff, however, to finally kill off the plan. In late October, General Spaatz, chief of the Air Staff, writing for Army Air Force Chief General "Hap" Arnold, prepared a detailed memorandum pointing out that, while the proposed organization might work in peacetime, it would fail utterly in the event of the United States being drawn into the current global conflict.[38] The report concluded "that the functioning of GHQ [general headquarters] as now contemplated is not in consonance with the proper operation and control of theaters of operation, and is restrictive of the responsibilities charged to the Army Air Force."[39]

After several weeks of discussion, Spaatz concluded and informed Gerow that if the War Department's reorganization was going to be able to meet anticipated needs and control all theaters of operations it would have to remain under one head: General Marshall. Marshall could not possibly handle the burden of all that detail, however. Therefore, Spaatz concluded, the department should be reorganized so that it could delegate detailed responsibilities to subordinate commanders. Asked for a model, Spaatz resurrected the Harrison memorandum as an example of what he envisioned.[40]

Although Spaatz gave the Harrison proposal his full support, others convinced Marshall to allow the current system to persist a bit longer in the hope that it would settle comfortably into its expanding responsibilities. By the first week in November, however, Marshall had become convinced the current system was breaking down and, noting "command failures," he called a meeting for 4 November 1941. As the meeting began, Marshall became incensed when he discovered that the bombs he had ordered sent to Singapore in September had not yet arrived. This turned out to be one of a number of management failures that the meeting discussed. Marshall finally exclaimed, "We can have no more of this! This is the poorest command post in the Army and something must be done about it, though I do not yet know what we will do."[41] Taking his boss' uncertainty as further proof that he still was not prepared for a radical reorganization, Gerow floated various proposals to the other staffs, which basically amounted to maintaining the current organization, but making a number of small refinements around the edges. As most of November went by, Gerow was unable to get other staff sections to concur with his plans. Moreover, as the pace of activities increased, he also became convinced that the current system was unworkable.[42] By this time, Marshall and his immediate staff were dealing with forty different major commands and 350 smaller commands.[43]

In the meantime, Army Air Force Chief Arnold weighed into the argument in a long memorandum to Marshall that detailed the problems with the current system and advocated the adoption of a structure close to that set forth in the Harrison memorandum.[44] Marshall, in turn, sent Arnold's memo to General Stanley Embick, who, although close to retirement, was often used by Marshall as a sounding board for new ideas and concepts.[45] Embick concurred with Arnold, and Marshall ordered a thorough study on the matter in early December. This time, however, Marshall did not ask for a study of how to refine the current organization. He wanted to know how best to implement the proposals sent by Arnold, which in turn were a restatement of the basic Harrison memo. To undertake this task, Marshall selected General Joseph McNarney, who was then serving as his representative in London. On 7 December 1941, McNarney received orders to report immediately to Washington. Before he could assume his new duties on the Army Reorganization Committee, however, McNarney was selected to participate on the Roberts Commission, which was sent to Hawaii to determine what part of the actions of Army and Navy officers had contributed to the disaster at Pearl Harbor.[46] McNarney did not report back to Marshall until late January, whereupon Marshall informed him of his new duties on the Reorganization Committee. McNarney later related that Marshall showed him all of the minutiae that had arrived on his desk for a decision since Pearl Harbor and told him that he had been trying to make the current system work for six months, but that now he wanted to implement a new system that worked.[47] As was typical of Marshall, he had arrived at a decision as to what had to be done and given it to a competent officer to accomplish. Marshall then got out of McNarney's way and awaited the results.[48]

McNarney was briefed by General Marshall on 25 January 1942. By that afternoon he had selected a small team to assist him, including Harrison. The next morning the team began its work. On 31 January McNarney finished and went to brief Marshall with his final product. McNarney claimed that his new organization was designed for the current war, but he also informed Marshall that if his plan was submitted to staff divisions and other interested parties the result would be numerous nonconcurrences and interminable delay.

The following week, Marshall called a meeting of his senior staff and received their concurrences to the plan. With that, Marshall ordered McNarney to create a team to develop the implementing instructions for the organization. Keeping in mind McNarney's recommendation not to submit the reorganization plan to the branch chiefs (chiefs of infantry, artillery, etc.),

Marshall asked that those working on the project keep their activities a secret from everyone who did not have a need to know.

McNarney knew he had to work fast. The longer he took to prepare the reorganization's implementing instructions, the more time the forces opposed to change would have to organize and prepare their defense of the status quo. So, at the first meeting of the implementation committee he announced, "This is not a voting committee . . . not a debating society . . . but a committee to draft the necessary directives to put a new organization into effect."[49] Taking Marshall's request for secrecy to heart, McNarney also warned the implementation committee, "I'd like to impress upon you that this is confidential and this is not to be discussed except with the people with whom it is actually necessary to get work done. This reorganization at the moment is confidential and is not the subject for open discussion."[50]

Despite this admonition, the branch chiefs got word of what was in the air and fought a desperate rearguard action to protect their positions. Led by Chief of Artillery Major General Robert M. Danford, they used whatever influence they had to maintain the status quo and convince Marshall that the reorganization was a foolish idea. In one memorandum to Marshall, Danford stated, "I profoundly fear, and predict a creeping paralysis in efficiency when the dead hand of divided responsibility settles again upon the Infantry and Field Artillery. From the depths of my own experience and convictions I can but earnestly beg that we not sacrifice the gains that have been made in what is the very bone and sinew of the team that must win our battles—the Infantry and Field Artillery."[51]

When this failed to convince Marshall, Danford followed up several days later with another missive: "We are at war—the most desperate in our history. Experimentation is not in order. The chiefs of arms . . . are about to be eliminated by a stroke of the pen. So far as field Artillery is concerned, that elimination is contrary to war experience."[52]

Marshall took this second message from such a distinguished officer seriously and sent a copy of the memorandum to McNair for comment. McNair, also an artilleryman with a long and distinguished career, considered Danford's memo a perfect example of advocating "branch consciousness," as opposed to the integration of all arms into a unified and balanced fighting team. In a memo back to Marshall, McNair stated that this "galaxy of bureaus" would have no place in the kind of organization required to fight the war.

Armed with McNair's support, Marshall forwarded all of the documents from the debate to Secretary of War Stimson and asked the secretary to approve the reorganization as outlined by McNarney.[53] Stimson considered the reorganization a good thing and sent a draft over to the White House for Roosevelt's review. On 26 February Roosevelt informed Secretary Stimson that he was "sure" the reorganization was a "good thing to do." Two days later Executive Order 9082 appeared, directing that the reorganization be put into effect 9 March 1942.[54] *Time* magazine editorialized on the reorganization the following week:

> The Army took a big piece of brass out of its hat last week. President Roosevelt ordered the most sweeping reorganization in the War Department's history. An organization hitherto as strangely assembled as Topsy's hair was streamlined to bullet-shape. Out the window went bottlenecks, bureaus and bric-a-brac—and the fusty old general staff setup. *All old sections were packed into three new ones: Air Force, Ground Force and Supply. On top remains Chief of Staff George C. Marshall* (emphasis added).
>
> Under him three men will steer the Army of the future: Air Force—Lieut. General Henry H. ("Hap," for happy) Arnold, white-thatched, genial, 55, veteran flyer, ex-juvenile fiction writer; Ground Force—slender, studious Lieut. General Lesley J. McNair, 58; Supply—soft-spoken, hard-driving Major General (likely soon to be Lieutenant General) Brehon Somervell, 49.[55]
>
> Most dramatic, most drastic change was the centralization, under one head, of the old, hydra-headed bureaus of Army supply. General Somervell will see that the Army has what it needs when and where needed. Onetime New York City WPA administrator, where he was a whopping success, Somervell is quietly hot-tempered, moves in on what he wants with a sophistication belying his contention that he is "just a country boy from Arkansas trying to get along in the big city."[56]

At a stroke, the Army had created a massive Service of Supply (later renamed the Army Service Forces, or ASF) and placed one man at its head—General Brehon Somervell.[57] On Somervell's shoulders fell the entire responsibility for the procurement of all supplies and their disbursement throughout the United States and to every combat theater.[58] Somervell, according to one biographer, was an instrument, not a maker of high policy, and not a deep thinker. But he had ideas on logistics, and he fought for those ideas with vigor and conviction. Distinguished by ambition, energy, and managerial brilliance, Somervell was a formidable figure who reveled in big tasks and was enough of an SOB to get them done. Through force of personality, shrewd accumulation of power, and sheer ability, he carved out a dominating role for himself in procurement, supply, and movement of materiel forces. Thus he became a powerful influence in America's conduct of the war.[59]

Moreover, it is important to note that during the Depression Somervell, while still a military officer, had been in charge of the Work Progress Administration (WPA; renamed Work Projects Administration in 1939) in New York City. In that position he had been in almost constant contact with presidential adviser Harry Hopkins, who was then the director of the WPA, arguably the most important of the New Deal organizations established by the Roosevelt administration. As a result, Somervell and Hopkins had become friends and had developed a deep respect for each other's professional abilities.

Somervell would use this direct contact with the White House many times during his battles with the civilian production experts, particularly in his dealings with Donald Nelson. Finally, it should be noted that Somervell, like almost every other general in World War II, was always solicitous to Marshall's needs and desires and worked hard never to disappoint him. This desire to always give Marshall what he demanded was to have serious ramifications in the disconnect between the resources Marshall thought he would have in 1943 and what would actually be available.

The 9 March reorganization played havoc with the Army procurement and production apparatus, which just weeks before had been completely reorganized and placed under the authority of Under Secretary of War Robert B. Patterson.[60] In the new organization, Somervell's ASF took over those parts of the Office of the Under Secretary of War that were engaged in procurement functions and related matters.

The secretary's procurement branch thus came under the ASF's director of procurement and distribution, who also was made responsible for "the direction/supervision and coordination of the procurement and distribution of supplies and equipment, in accordance with approved programs and directives." Embraced within this broad delegation of authority was the responsibility for planning, scheduling, and accelerating production. All this work was lodged in a procurement and distribution division, which in the initial directive for the organization of the ASF was designated as one of its "operating" components.[61] This usurpation of authority was presented to Under Secretary Patterson as a fait accompli: he had no knowledge of the reorganization plans before Stimson actually forwarded them to the White House.[62]

After some hesitation and some fence-mending by Stimson and Marshall, Patterson signed on to the transfer of power from his office to the ASF, and even found the grace to forward a memo to his staff stating, "This unification of command under the vigorous leadership of General Somervell will enable us to perform our huge task with greater dispatch and better coordination."[63] As part of this fence mending, Marshall agreed that Somervell would have dual reporting channels. On military matters, Somervell reported to Marshall, but on business matters he reported to Patterson.[64] While this may have been the only practical solution to the tangle of bureaucratic politics, it unfortunately made it a simple matter for Somervell to "neglect" to brief Marshall about negative developments in the production process throughout most of 1942.

The creation of the ASF created a procurement organization that, rather than work cooperatively with civilian agencies, was to pit itself in competition with the WPB. Although there were to be many players in this drama, the coming contest of wills was to be fought primarily between Nelson, ably assisted by Nathan, and General Somervell.

The Personalities

Under any circumstances friction between the civilian production agencies and military procurement officials could hardly be avoided. The scale of the enterprise and the myriad overlapping jurisdictions guaranteed a considerable amount of bureaucratic battling. The fact that these fights became bloody, prolonged battles of wills, however, resulted from the interactions of the key personalities involved.

As suggested earlier, Nelson was probably a weak choice to head WPB from the start. Hopkins had maneuvered the president into selecting Nelson because Hopkins considered him controllable. Hopkins had not foreseen that the qualities that made Nelson controllable also made it impossible for him to take a firm stand on any matter, or to make decisive decisions in a timely manner, however. Personally he was warm, friendly, and likeable.[65] According to one person who worked closely with him, Nelson was by nature neither a meditative nor a reflective person but had more or less unconsciously developed a philosophy. Instinctively he had a distrust of coercive laws and coercive regulations and he believed in persuasion over coercion. For Nelson what was necessary was to persuade people, to keep them advised of what you were trying to do, and to ask for their cooperation. Nelson had another trait: he thought that differences could be resolved if you allowed time to elapse—that a great many issues that seemed acute would lose their acute character and be more readily capable of solution. Those two qualities as the war progressed became more and more pronounced.[66]

Leon Henderson's deputy and intimate, David Ginsberg, said of Nelson, "He and Leon were good friends. They met often and he liked him. While we both thought Nelson was friendly and nice we did not regard him as much of a manager. He was weak and was always fearful of a contest. He was a good policy man without the ability to execute. Leon and I used to speak about Nelson often. Usually we talked about how friendly and cooperative he was, but that he did nothing to help us get the job done."[67]

That Henderson would like Nelson is a bit of a surprise, since, as Ginsberg related, "Henderson spoke abruptly, was always direct and never polite."[68] Ginsberg also states that Nathan liked Nelson a great deal. While Nathan continued to like Nelson personally, however, his professional respect waned over time.[69] Initially, however, all of the economists around Nathan supported Nelson's elevation to the top job. This was mainly because his predecessor, William Knudsen, never believed their claims that the American economy was capable of significantly greater war production without affecting the civilian economy. Nelson did believe them, or at least claimed to, but as they later discovered he was reluctant to fight for their cause.[70]

Nathan came to understand that his boss was not much of a match in a toe-to-toe fight with Somervell, who in temperament was Nelson's polar opposite, but he blamed much of the problem on Somervell, who, according to historian John Millett,

> drove himself as hard as he drove his subordinates, perhaps even harder. He was not afraid of responsibility, he was not loath to cut red tape, and he rode roughshod over opposition. Somervell's energy and determination to overcome obstacles regardless of cost alienated some and occasionally disturbed others, but he did get things done. Senator Harry S. Truman once commented to his colleagues on the Senate Committee on Military Affairs: "I will say this for General Somervell, he will get the stuff, but it is going to be hell on the taxpayer. He has a WPA attitude on the expenditure of money."
>
> With Somervell's sense of urgency and drive went also a quick temper. No one knew this limitation better than did Somervell himself. Because

> of it there were some misgivings at the time he was being considered to head the ASF. Intellectually alert, he was inclined to be impatient with persons who were slower than himself in reaching a decision and in taking action. Continued indecisiveness aroused his anger, as did a failure to carry out instructions or a surrender to what seemed to him to be surmountable difficulties.[71]

Early in the war a journalist described Somervell in these words:

> He is out of the tradition of the Elizabethan Englishman, all lace and velvet and courtliness outside, fury and purposefulness within. While the bureaucrats in mufti are conscientiously trying to transform themselves into fire-eaters and nail-chewers, "Bill" Somervell is working just as conscientiously to water down his own triple-distilled potion of the grapes of wrath. His problem is not to work up a temper but to control one. . . . When goaded beyond endurance, rather than trust himself to act, he will shut himself up in the office until a judicial calm descends.[72]

Between these two men stood Robert Nathan. Nathan was described as

> a huge hulk of a man with a kettledrum voice. He is no dreamy brain-truster. Rather, he is more like a wrestler than a thinker and talks more like a barker than a savant. Yet when faced with a thorny problem, his mind can slip to the solution with the ease of a rabbit slipping through briar. He dictates letters on heavy subjects with the mechanical evenness of a victrola recording. He seldom corrects a letter, seldom rewrites any part of a ten-page memorandum. Details do not sidetrack him. He uses them instead, to fill the main structure of his thinking, and the end product is to the point and frequently blunt: "The only trouble with that plant is the guy running it. Fire him."[73]

In short, Nathan was no shrinking violet and in situations where Nelson was reluctant to enter into the political fray, Nathan either took on the job himself or propped up Nelson with enough backbone at least to continue inching forward. His writings and comments after the war left no doubt that Nathan understood that Nelson was not up to facing the Somervell challenge. But he also saw Somervell as the source of most of their problems:

General Somervell never ceased to attack the War Production Board and undermine the authority of Donald Nelson. He truly was a constant thorn in Nelson's activities. Nelson was intelligent, dedicated and a committed leader. But he was not tough enough to cope with Somervell's maneuvers and manipulations and dubious scruples. Nelson was not the only target damaged by Somervell. The highly competent General Aurand was another victim whose level of contributions to the war effort were diminished by Somervell's dominating demeanour.[74]

Nelson was commonly referred to in the press as the Economic Czar because of the authority delegated to him by the President. But Nelson never had the slightest intention to take over and operate the procurement function of the Services. He was a practical man with a lot of business experience and was sensitive and sensible about the essential role of government in the mobilization challenge. He was fully aware of the adverse consequences of divided and uncoordinated functions and responsibilities.

The same cannot be said of General Somervell. He seemed to believe there were two enemies. One included Germany, Italy, and Japan on the military front and the other included civilians on the home front. He felt that the civilian population was being coddled. But his principal enemy was the War Production Board and the other non-military government agencies. Nelson agreed that procurement for military purposes should be in the hands of the military. But Somervell never ceased to demand expansion of that function to embrace practically every aspect of war production. He never acknowledged or accepted any responsibility for delays, or failures, or problems attributable to his endless manipulations. I used to say that Somervell would come into a meeting with a knife in his hand, which he would stick into Donald Nelson's back; Nelson would pull it out and say, "pardon me General; isn't this yours?" and Somervell would reply, "Yes, Don, thank you." Immediately Somervell would place it in his other hand and stick it into the other side of Nelson's back. And Nelson would repeat the same response.[75]

According to Ginsberg, Nathan and Henderson both loathed Somervell. Along with Somervell's detestation of Nelson as a weak and ineffective administrator, this mutual hatred was to prove a volatile brew in the feasibility dispute, which came to a head in October 1942 after simmering for most of the year.[76]

CHAPTER 7

War and Feasibility

★ ★ ★

Upon his return from London with the Anglo-American Consolidated Statement, Stacy May combined that document with projected Lend-Lease orders and initial procurement figures resulting from the recently passed Defense Aid Supplemental Appropriations Act to begin building the outline of the actual Victory Program. Before this, both military and production experts had been working with estimates based on planning assumptions with little reference to actual orders. The start of mobilization brought real orders and a more practical, experience-based understanding of what building a military force capable of fighting on a global scale required from the economy.

As discussed earlier, throughout most of 1941 the military still maintained a culturally based aversion to ordering anything near what the Victory Program would require. It was only after Stacy May completed his first feasibility study in early December 1941, however, that anyone knew just how far the procurement process had fallen behind requirements. May forwarded his findings to the head of the War Production Board (WPB), Donald Nelson, on 4 December 1941.[1] Because this study became the baseline document for most of the debates between the civilian production experts and the military it deserves a careful analysis. In its opening paragraph, May admitted that it would have been desirable to have more and better data.

He also maintained, however, that time was of the essence and that it was doubtful if more intensive analysis would yield additional results that would be commensurate with the time involved with a new analysis.

It was the second paragraph of the report's conclusion that should have captured the immediate attention of military planners, however, but it failed to do so: "As you will observe, it is our conclusion, after carefully reviewing all of the important limiting elements, that *three-fourths of the Victory program can be achieved by September 1943. We believe the entire program can be accomplished by the spring of 1944*" (emphasis added).[2] Note that this document demonstrates that as early as December 1941 the economists in WPB already knew that sufficient munitions to conduct operations in northern Europe would not be available until approximately May 1944!

By assuming that the military would be in an all-out offensive against the Axis by spring 1943, May made some rough estimates of materiel the military would require, based on military estimates matched against his Anglo-American Consolidated Statement. After tabulating what was already on order by both the U.S. military and foreign powers, May matched the plan to what the government could reasonably expect the American economy to produce.

What he found was extraordinary. The entire military program as then outlined by military sources could be completed by the spring of 1944, and three-quarters of it could be completed in the summer of 1943, without any all-out push to increase U.S. economic output. Furthermore, such an effort would grow the U.S. economy by about $10 billion annually through 1943 without any extraordinary effort. If the United States was to undertake a mobilization effort equal to what it achieved upon entering World War I, however, it could grow the economy to $140 billion by the end of 1943—a 60 percent increase over 1941. Such a massive effort to maximize national income would mean the United States could spend $45 billion on defense in 1942 and $65 billion in 1943 out of a total national income of $130 billion. May believed that this defense spending level was achievable since both Britain and Germany were currently devoting similar percentages of their national income to war production. Moreover, May contended that this level of spending would not cause undo suffering among the general population. Even under the maximum war production effort scenario, he advocated that there would still be $60 billion available for civilian consumption. This was more civilian consumption than was achieved in the first years of the Depression and was about the average of 1935–39 consumption.[3]

In short, three days before the United States entered the war, a small number of key economists and statisticians within the war planning boards already knew exactly how much of the materiel called for by the current Victory Plan estimates could be produced and when it would be available. They also knew that the United States was capable of a far greater effort than was currently being called for and that this could be accomplished without severely curtailing consumer consumption. Moreover, if anything, the civilians were grossly underestimating the materiel and munitions the nations would require in order to win the war. In reality, the completion of the original Victory Program would be just sufficient to start waging major offensive operations in 1943. It would take much more to actually win the conflict. Therefore, May's 4 December 1941 report informed Nelson that the United States would not have all that it required to reenter the continent of Europe until 1944. All the planning by the Joint Chiefs of Staff (JCS) and their respective staffs to launch Allied forces onto the European continent in 1942 or 1943 represented nothing more than a pipe dream to the economic experts. They could concoct all the plans they liked for a 1943 invasion, but the economists could have told them in 1941 that the forces they planned for would not be there.

May's Victory Program, which rested on the data Nathan and Kuznets had collected on national income and on May's own Anglo-American Consolidated Statement, also included all Lend-Lease appropriations and his best estimate (as a civilian with no military training or education) of requirements for an all-out offensive. In order to achieve a common reference point and to make the study align with the way national income accounts were tabulated, May translated the estimates into a financial basis, as seen in Table 7.1.[4]

To make his estimates work, May made three important assumptions. First, that the munitions required in the future but not yet contracted would be similar to the items already contracted for. Second, that there would be no new large merchant shipping program and that ship production would remain stable through September 1943. Finally, that all production and disbursement would continue at the rates already scheduled or contemplated. In the event, none of these assumptions was to be realized, but for the time being America had the embryo of a war production plan.[5]

It is important to remember that May finished this report before the outbreak of war and that there was no way for May or Nathan to foresee how America's entry into the war would confound each of these assumptions. As he stated in the report, however, "To the extent that there may be substantial increases in requirements for new merchant ships beyond present contempla-

Table 7.1 Financial Analysis of the Victory Program

	Financed Program (billions)	Added Need by September 1943 (billions)	Minimum Foreseeable Additional Requirements (billions)	Estimate Total Requirements by September 1943 (billions)
Army-type equipment	$23	$55	$15–$16	$93–$94
Navy-type equipment	$14	$4	$0–$1	$18–$19
Industrial facilities	$7	–	$1–$3	$8–$10
Required housing construction	$5	–	$1–$2	$6–$7
Merchant ships	$3	–	$0–$1	$3–$4
Other	$9	–	$5–$7	$14–$16
TOTAL	$61	$59	$22–$30	**$142–$150**

Source: Memorandum from Stacy May to Donald Nelson, 4 December 1941, Planning Committee Document, National Archives, Record Group 179, Box 1.

tions or in the disbursements for other purposes, the Victory Program will call for larger outlays."[6] In the event, America's entry into the conflict also saw an almost immediate doubling in requirements for merchant ship production and a marked ramp-up in the speed of production capabilities and financial disbursements.[7]

Another key conclusion of the report did capture the military's attention and later became the basis of the Army's resistance to cutting back on its production requirements for the war. May found that the military had programmed less than $75 billion in spending through September 1943. Achieving the goals of the Victory Plan, however, required at least $150 billion. "Thus," May announced, "The entire program to date must be doubled and achieved by September 30, 1943, if the Victory objectives are to be attained." This was not the end of it. Although May had called for a doubling of the overall spending program, he also stated that for many items meeting the Victory goals would require a five-fold increase.[8]

In the succeeding section May, using Nathan's work, placed his translation of the Victory Program onto a financial basis and determined its feasibility in terms of national income accounts. In 1942 May stated that total national income would slightly exceed $100 billion and would not be much higher in 1943 if present plans were adhered to. But he strongly advocated scrapping present plans in favor of a maximum economic effort that would raise national income to $140 billion in 1943. He also pushed for an immediate increase of 1942 spending plans from $30 billion to $40 billion, and for an increase in military spending for the first six months of 1943 to $65 billion out of an annual income of more than $130 billion. In his conclusion, May stated, "Under such an effort our total defense production by September 30, 1943, would aggregate approximately $115 billion, or over 75 percent of the Victory Program."[9]

Despite these massive projected outlays, May was adamant that American consumers would feel only minimal effects on their standard of living. His analysis claimed that the increased spending on the Victory Program could be met without any substantial sacrifice by the American people. May claimed that consumer consumption would never fall below $60 billion a year, and, although the availability of durable goods would be curtailed, there would be an abundance of food, clothing, furniture, and services.[10]

Virtually every bit of production needed to fight the war was to be paid for out of increases to national income. While many households would have to postpone the purchase of a new car or refrigerator, the availability of most other consumer items actually increased. In fact, the amount of GDP spent by consumers for their own use increased throughout the war, and by 1945 it far exceeded what consumers spent in 1941.[11]

Real consumption per capita rose sharply in 1940 and 1941 before dropping slightly in 1942. It rose again in 1943, however, and by 1944 personal civilian consumption was at an all-time high.[12] While there were some bottlenecks in items such as housing (particularly in locations where new war industries were springing up) and certain edible commodities (especially sugar and butter), the often-told tales of personal sacrifice to help win the war are largely myth. Furthermore, because expensive durable goods were actually in short supply and household income was rising throughout the war, circumstances (and stark memories of the Depression) encouraged consumers to save large amounts of personal income—much of it in war bonds. This huge savings pool coupled with pent-up consumer demand for durable consumer items was what would propel America's vast postwar economic expansion.

May's report did not end there. It went on to lay out in depth the feasibility of the Victory Program in relation to raw materials, labor supply, and industrial facilities. While each of these components of feasibility is important, an in-depth analysis of each would divert us from the main point: that the economy could support only a certain level of production growth regardless of the increasing availability of labor, raw materials, and facilities.[13] When the great disputes over feasibility took place, they were almost all fought in financial and national income terms.

In essence, May's report plainly stated that if America were committed to a Victory Program capable of winning a global war then the military procurement officials were not asking nearly enough of American industry. Although May listed a number of specific areas that required production increases ranging as high as five times military estimates, his overall plan called for doubling the overall scope of military orders to date. Unfortunately, he did not deliver his report until three days before Pearl Harbor, too late to affect the tidal wave of production demands about to descend on industry.

Furthermore, it was obviously not possible in 1941 to foretell the nature and duration of America's participation in the war. Whatever May's study implied as necessary in monthly or quarterly scheduling over the two-year production period, it was exceedingly hypothetical. Thus, while the date set assumed for planning purposes a start of an all-out offensive against the Axis powers in 1943, this timing was extremely uncertain since it had no foundation in any strategic decisions. This lack of a firm time schedule, of course, had been one of the chief stumbling blocks in the development of usable requirements totals all along. Still, although the requirements under the Victory Program were more complete than any other statements had been thus far in the run-up to war, they were also enormous by any previous standard. For the two-year period outlined in the beginning of the program, the total projected outlay was close to $90 billion more than Congress had yet authorized.[14]

The unique value of the Anglo-American Consolidated Statement in pointing up basic problems now became apparent. With this programming document in hand, and despite some uncertainty about its ingredients or premises, production chiefs had a comprehensive base for its plans. This was fundamental to increasing output because industrialists could not appraise demand or expand production facilities intelligently without objectives laid out far in advance of actual production schedules. Moreover, fiscal policy also depended on knowledge of the future program since Congress could only provide continuing large funding authorizations on the basis of demonstrated real future requirements. In addition, the setting of manpower goals in terms of how many people would be in uniform and how many would remain behind to enable production goals to be met relied completely on the establishment of production objectives. Similar considerations applied to the expansion of raw material production, as well as to importing and stockpiling programs. Finally, appraisal of the program for internal balance could only begin when the national authorities had stated the totals for major components of all facets of the Victory Program.

Thus, the balance sheet was a mirror of production policy. Working with it, during the months and years that followed, lent progressively more substance to the previously amorphous conception of an all-out effort. It facilitated the interpretation of data and provided a means of measuring actual munitions production against a number of significant yardsticks—requirements for defeat of the Axis, maximum production possible under complete mobilization, and the like.[15]

In summary, when May forwarded his memorandum to Nelson in December 1941, the production schedules for all defense items represented a financial commitment of $27 billion in 1942 and $34 billion in 1943. Both May and—after being convinced—Nathan believed that these totals could be reasonably increased to $40 billion–$45 billion for 1942 and $60 billion–$65 billion for 1943 without unduly stressing the American economy or denying the consumer crucial goods or services.[16] Still, all of this rested on estimates and assumptions. No one in the government or in the military had yet sat down and formulated firm production schedules based on real wartime requirements. This was about to change, out of suddenly urgent necessity.

The Japanese attack on Pearl Harbor brought an end to the period of speculation and forcefully demonstrated the desperate need to start basing war production on a strategy to win the war. The time had come to make real and serious plans, but as yet there was still no consensus on how to do it.

On 9 December President Roosevelt conducted a White House meeting with thirteen men representing all the war production agencies, the men who would have responsibility for implementing whatever grand plan they might develop. Among those present were Donald Nelson (director of the Supply Priorities and Allocations Board [SPAB]), William Knudsen (director of the Office of Production Management [OPM]),[17] Robert Patterson (under secretary of war), Harry L. Hopkins (special assistant to the president), Henry L. Stimson (secretary of war), E. R. Stettinius Jr. (Lend-Lease administrator), and James F. Forrestal (under secretary of the Navy)—men whose points of view on war production were important and by no means unanimous.[18]

The meeting had no particular focus; the president had simply summoned his leading defense officials to ask, in effect, "What shall we do now?" Crucial differences of opinion immediately surfaced as to the adequacy of existing goals. While Nelson, depending on the analysis of May and Nathan, was optimistic concerning the achievement of a 1942 program (which seemed extraordinary by 1941 standards), Knudsen held that production could only reach 75 percent of what Nelson believed was possible. The meeting failed to resolve this basic difference in outlook, but instead turned to a general discussion of problems raised by the war. With the failure to reach a resolution, Nelson felt compelled to work with both May's and Knudsen's estimates simultaneously. Two days later, he wrote to the secretary of war for fresh information on the Army program and asked for totals of military requirements based on both conservative and liberal estimates of what industry could produce in all major product categories. Nelson and his assistants followed up in conversations with military representatives, where they pressed for higher goals, disregarding the position of Knudsen and his supporters. On Christmas Eve, May talked with Somervell—then assistant chief of staff, G-4 (supply)—and urged him to encourage his procurement officers to raise their sights.

Prime Minister Churchill and Lord Beaverbrook dramatically emphasized the same point when they visited Washington for the Arcadia Conferences, which took place from 22 December 1941 to 14 January 1942. In a meeting where leading American war production and military advisers were present, Beaverbrook pointed out that the United States had no experience in the level of losses its forces would incur in the coming Allied offensives. Moreover, he claimed that America had little conception of the productive facilities of the Axis powers or the number of Axis tanks its Army would have to contend with. He repeatedly emphasized that the United States needed to set its sights higher in planning for production of the necessary war materiel. He then called on the United States to plan for the production of forty-five thousand tanks in 1942 against Knudsen's estimate of thirty thousand.[19]

The British leaders' visit was fruitful not only in terms of the joint conversations on the prosecution of the war, but also for its missionary effect on those American officials still dubious or needing more convincing that an all-out effort would be necessary. Specifically, the British representatives made clear that the United States would have to greatly revise upward existing production objectives for 1942 and 1943. As Nelson's and Beaverbrook's statements reinforced one another, the president addressed himself to this problem.

Near the end of 1941, Roosevelt requested, through Hopkins, that Nelson prepare a list of production objectives he considered realistic for 1942. In turn, Nelson, using the Victory Program compilations as his basis and, with further advice from May and Nathan, came up with a list of fifty thousand completed aircraft, forty thousand tanks, 112 major combat ships, and 7 million tons of merchant shipping. In addition, he proposed that capacity should increase steadily so that by the end of 1942 the annual production rates should be sixty thousand tanks and eighty thousand planes. The objectives were high, but no more impressive than those suggested by Beaverbrook.[20]

Writing to the president at the same time, Beaverbrook pointed up the need for even higher output in certain categories. Roosevelt's reaction to these proposals was all that Nelson and his associates at SPAB could have hoped. On 5 January 1942 the president, writing to Knudsen and Sidney Hillman, associate director general of the OPM, directed the establishment of a munitions schedule that conformed approximately to Nelson's list. On the following day, though, when the president delivered his message to Congress on the same subject, Roosevelt revealed that even Nelson's goals, in his opinion, did not cover the need in the major categories.[21] The totals were now set at sixty thousand planes for 1942, and one hundred twenty-five thousand planes for 1943. He fixed the tank totals for the two years at forty-five thousand and seventy-five thousand, respectively. Some twenty thousand antiaircraft guns were to be turned out in 1942, and thirty-five thousand the following year. The merchant ship goals were perhaps the most startling of all: 8 million tons for 1942 and 20 million tons for 1943.[22] Nelson figured that Roosevelt's "must" items would cost between $52 billion and $55 billion, which was generally in line with what Nathan and May considered practicable.[23]

Unfortunately, the president's new "must" items were not the entire story. In fact, they were only the beginning. Because they were only a list of major end items, it fell to the services to design a balanced program around the "must" list. For instance, one hundred eighty-five thousand aircraft and eighty thousand tanks by themselves meant nothing. The aircraft needed airfields, maintenance and support sections, and munitions to shoot and drop. Tanks needed to be part of divisions, with artillery, engineers, infantry, and a host of other items for support. Moreover, the entire establishment required training bases, logistical depots, and the creation of an infrastructure to support modern mechanized warfare. All of this would have to be on top of Roosevelt's "must" items, which were already pushing what the experts on national income believed was the outside edge of the possible. Without taking into account the feasibility of the task, in February 1942 the Army added a further $62 billion (through 1943) in demands to the "must" items.[24]

Virtually in an instant, the president and the Army had thrown out years of analysis and months of careful planning. When Nathan and May added the cost of Roosevelt's "must" items to the Army's supply program, they immediately realized there was looming trouble and began working out the numbers needed to convince everyone else they were walking into a crisis. The civilian economists within OPM (soon to be WPB) understood that if the president held to his "must" items, then the entire production program would become unbalanced and impossible to complete. But in those panicked weeks and months after Pearl Harbor no one was listening to them. After all, Roosevelt had already told the nation, "Let no man say it cannot be done."

CHAPTER 8

The Great Feasibility Debate

★ ★ ★

On 19 February 1942, Nelson created the Planning Committee within the War Production Board (WPB) and gave it three problems to consider. First, it was to review the total munitions program in terms of the balance among its constituent parts—the relation of military requirements to essential civilian needs and to the total national economy. Once this was done, the Planning Committee was to examine the relationship between the shipping situation and the planned munitions program, and then examine the airplane program in terms of the feasibility of meeting the goal of sixty thousand planes for 1942.

Apparently, Nelson had not yet focused on the overall feasibility of the munitions program.[1] Instead, the effects the war would have on the civilian economy and whether plane production could be increased sufficiently to attain Roosevelt's goals consumed his interest. On the other hand, Nathan, the head of the Planning Committee, believed that the group's most important task was to ascertain whether the munitions program for 1942 and 1943 was achievable in the time allotted. In John Brigante's view, Nathan was alone in holding this view during the early meetings of the Planning Committee. According to Brigante, both Fred Searls and Thomas Blaisdell resisted Nathan on this point and urged that the committee focus on assessing the existing and prospective bottlenecks.[2] They supposedly claimed that, while this would not present the larger view of the production effort, it would get them off to an active start by addressing specific, tangible, and presumably solvable problems. The actual minutes of the first Planning Committee meeting tell a different story, however:

> There was general agreement that the war munitions program must be analyzed item by item, as well as in terms of its over-all relation to the total production of the country. The Chairman [Nathan] noted, as an example of the interrelationship of these two approaches, that the building of additional plants may be criticized on either of two grounds: (1) That they would raise the schedule of munitions production to an impossible percentage of the total national production, or (2) that the building of particular plants would be a waste of construction materials, as the specific raw materials or tools that would be required for operations of those plants would not be available. . . . The Chairman announced that he asked the Statistics Division [headed by Kuznets] to translate 1942 and 1943 military objectives into terms of raw materials, so that this analysis may be available to the Committee.[3]

Not only did all committee members agree that a comprehensive feasibility study was an important undertaking, but they also had Kuznets make a preliminary presentation of the matter. Kuznets duly appeared before the committee on 13 March 1942 and suggested that there were two alternative approaches to the process of appraising military objectives: "One [approach] is to arrive at a feasible military production estimate by determining the total production of finished articles of which the country is capable, and subtracting from this total the irreducible minimum of production required for civilian requirements. The second approach is to analyze qualitatively the specific military requirements as compared to the specific resources for production."

Kuznets argued that the overall quantitative approach should precede the categorical, qualitative analysis so the "outer limits of total military requirements" could be fixed. If those estimates proved to be infeasible when measured against the framework of total national productive capacity, they should be returned to the armed services for downward revision before attempting a quantitative analysis. A significant advantage of the quantitative approach was that "it makes possible a broad comparison of our war effort with that of other nations having longer experience with war production problems." However, "the measurement of the war effort by total percentage of one year's national income can be misleading if allowances are not made for the extent to which in any one year a nation is drawing on its accumulated stocks as distinguished from its current output."[4] Interestingly, Kuznets also pointed out to the committee, "If proper account were taken of German drafts on her own and conquered nations' stocks of goods, the percentage of German current output devoted to war production would be about 40 percent as contrasted to the 70 percent of German national income often attributed to war production."[5] At the end of this meeting, Kuznets' offer to complete a thorough feasibility study was accepted by the board.

Nathan, who kept abreast of Kuznets' ongoing work, informed the committee on 13 March that in order to meet the presently stated objectives of $75 billion of war production and expenditures for 1942, monthly expenditures for the year would have to average $6.25 billion dollars, and that, since the monthly expenditures were presently running at only $2.5 billion, this meant the rate of expenditure would have to rise to a level of $10 billion a month before the last quarter of the year to make up the difference. Because it was impossible to grow the economy efficiently to absorb this level of activity, the committee meeting ended by raising the possibility, for the first time, of cutting the munitions program by 25 percent. Nathan also broached for the first time the idea of creating a super-coordinating body that would combine oversight of military strategy and production activities. As envisioned by Nathan, this new body would examine strategic decisions in relation to production considerations and then determine the appropriate revisions of either.[6] Later, when Nathan had fleshed out this idea and presented it to Somervell, it had the same effect as waving a red flag in front of a bull and probably underpinned much of Somervell's resistance to entertaining arguments that feasibility constraints were restraining his procurement plans.

Nathan suggested to the committee that it inform Nelson that production objectives for 1942 and 1943 were unattainable and that it also propose to him that he advocate the establishment of a board "familiar with both the strategic and production factors, and authorize it to determine initially the reductions in specific objectives of the war munitions program that are necessary to impart feasibility and balance to the program."[7] The rest of the committee, however, convinced him to wait for Kuznets to deliver his full report before officially informing Nelson and asking him to act.

On 14 March Kuznets completed his report. Its findings, once presented to production experts outside the Planning Committee, proved unsettling. Based on the most optimistic projection of GDP growth, the most the military could hope for was a program consisting of $35 billion in expenditures for 1942. By adding in soft items such as food, the military could count on $50 billion in 1942 and $64 billion in 1943. Moreover, raw material shortages were already showing up and the present program for 1943 was completely out of line with expected supply. But this was not the end of the production program's problems. Machine tool assembly was already hopelessly behind and there was no hope that production would ever catch up to planned factory construction. Furthermore, basic civilian requirements placed a cap on what percentage of GDP was available for any particular year and limited the 1943 military program to $64 billion.[8]

In sum, Kuznets' analysis of all major criteria for judging the feasibility of the program concluded that the U.S. economy could not meet present total goals within the periods set.[9] With Kuznets' study in hand, the committee, with Stacy May in attendance, considered the feasibility question in much greater detail on 16 March and agreed to submit a formal recommendation to Nelson that he call for the government to reduce the total munitions production objectives. Afterwards, the committee discussed alternative methods of implementing its recommendations.

The committee then discussed Searls' proposal that the procurement officers be bypassed and that Nelson himself should undertake reductions after consultations with strategy representatives of the armed services. Blaisdell suggested that they refer the matter to the president so that Roosevelt could designate selected military and production authorities to cooperate in establishing a practicable set of overall objectives. Nathan recommended, though, and the others (including May) agreed that Nelson should send letters to the secretaries of War and the Navy, requesting them to designate individuals with authority to meet with WPB representatives to adjust the Victory Program objectives for 1942 and 1943.[10] In discussion, there was general agreement that the current estimates of the 1942 war munitions program must be cut by some 35 percent so that total expenditure on war munitions and war construction amounted to not more than approximately $40 billion.[11]

To accomplish this, Stacy May suggested revisions (see Table 8.1) to the 1942 objectives be made after careful scrutiny.[12]

Furthermore, May advocated that 1943 production objectives be limited to the rate of production achieved by December 1942, which he estimated would be $6 billion monthly. This meant that the government would cap 1943 military expenditures at $72 billion for 1943.[13] Others claimed this figure was optimistic and pushed for a number that would not inflate expectations for

Table 8.1 May's Production Revisions

	1942 Stated Objectives (billions)	**Proposed 1942 Objectives** (billions)
Total munitions:	$62.6	$42.6
Planes	9.2	9.2
Naval ships:	$4.8	$3.2
Merchant ships	1.8	1.8
Defense aid	3.1	2.0
Foreign orders	0.2	0.2
Ordnance, Army	15.6	9.2
Ordnance, Navy	3.7	2.4
Miscellaneous munitions, Navy	$1.2	$1.0
Miscellaneous munitions, Army	$7.5	$5.0
Industrial facilities	$6.5	$4.2
Other construction	$8.4	$4.0

the future beyond what they believed attainable but that still was within May's estimate. After much discussion they decided on a 1943 total of $60 billion. The $12 billion dollar gap between May's $72 billion estimate and the $60 billion limit that was reported to Nelson and through him to the Joint Chiefs of Staff (JCS) would subsequently allow the committee a lot of leeway in negotiations with the services. Thus, when the services balked at the extent of the cuts and later suggested a higher figure, May and Nathan felt free to appear magnanimous.

On 17 March Nathan sent Nelson an extensive list of recommendations, summarizing the committee's findings to date.[14] The letter proposed a number of specific reductions in 1942 objectives, including the stunning call for large reductions in the 1942 and 1943 munitions program. According to Nathan, it was imperative not only to cut munitions spending, but also to cease contracting for new production facilities and machine tools because capacity was already beginning to run ahead of the labor supply and raw material resources.

For a week after receiving the Planning Committee's recommendation, Nelson took no formal action. Then, on 24 March, he summoned his principal division heads for a conference to consider the entire problem. Participants included Sidney Hillman, W. H. Harrison, James Knowlson, May, Nathan, Blaisdell, and Ferdinand Eberstadt (then–executive director of the Army and Navy Munitions Board [ANMB]).[15] As a result of this conference, May drafted a letter for Nelson to send to the secretaries of War and the Navy stating, "Our production program cannot go forward effectively until we have decided upon objectives which require an all-out effort and are practical of accomplishment." The letter also requested that each secretary designate a representative to collaborate with the WPB in reviewing the war munitions program and arriving at specific requirements.[16] Two days later, Brigadier General Lucius Clay, one of the chief officers of the services of supply, was designated as the War Department's representative, and the committee assumed that the Navy would soon make a similar appointment. In Nathan's opinion, Clay appeared to sympathize with the Planning Committee's thoughts on feasibility—he had earlier suggested that the president's 6 January goal for tanks needed reduction. This, combined with the associated reduction in other ordnance items, would have reduced the cost of the 1942 objectives by $5 billion.[17]

Nelson finally met with Army representatives on 29 March. During the meeting Clay and Under Secretary of War Robert P. Patterson agreed that the 1942 and 1943 requirements were not feasible and that they needed to declare a moratorium on new construction until their staffs had carefully screened all requirements. Nelson had hoped that this recognition would lead the Army to reduce its production requirements in order to help in achieving the president's "must" items. He was discouraged, therefore, to find that the Army (the Navy did not send a representative to the meeting), despite agreeing that it could not attain its production goals, was not willing to reduce its supply program, taking the position that "its requirements were set to conform with the size of the President's end-product program, and that they could not be altered until the President initiated downward revision of his own goals."[18] So, rather than Nelson convincing the Army to reduce its goals, Patterson convinced Nelson that any reduction in the final product totals must start with a modification of the president's "must" program.

Accordingly, Stacy May drafted another letter for Nelson that went to the president on 30 March 1942. The letter reminded the president that in December 1941 he had been informed that the country could produce $40 billion in munitions in 1942 and another $60 billion in 1943. It went on to state that the Army, the Navy, and the Maritime Commission had already formulated programs far in excess of these numbers. Since the War Department was claiming it could not reduce its objectives without sacrificing vital equipment, the letter offered the president two options. He could either order that his "must" items be adhered to and the sacrifice of other items deemed vital by the military, or he could authorize the armed services to revise all objectives to within the bounds of feasibility, including those objectives directed by himself.[19]

Unfortunately, Nelson changed May's letter to read, "As you realize, I do not feel qualified to pass on the relative urgency of weapons desired by the Army. However, I have examined the production possibilities and must report that, in my judgment, it will not be possible to provide all of the items set forth in your list of objectives, and at the same time produce everything else now called for under the programs of the Army, the Navy, the Maritime Commission, and Defense Aid."[20]

While this letter served to announce the production predicament to the president, it did not ask for a decision. Given Roosevelt's predilection to ignoring issues—on the assumption that underlings would resolve most problems before he was forced to come down on one side or another—this letter allowed the president to postpone a decision. This standard Roosevelt management procedure often had an unfortunate consequence. Many issues that could have been resolved early with a word from Roosevelt festered until they had bloomed into a crisis where both sides were so locked in their positions that compromise was impossible. The feasibility of the Victory Program was such an issue.

Moreover, Nelson's new letter used as its starting point a letter Marshall had earlier sent to the president requesting that he allow the Army to substitute halftracks and self-propelled artillery for the "must" number of tanks. The president agreed to this request, but this did not amount to any actual reduction of total objectives—merely a reshuffling of them. Even taken together, Marshall's and Nelson's letters somehow failed to alert the president that a crisis was brewing requiring immediate and decisive action. Rather, from the president's perspective it appeared as if things were rolling along in a satisfactory fashion except for some tweaking that was needed on the margins. One reason for the president's failure to grasp the dimensions of the growing problems is that Nelson forwarded another note to the president on 1 April that the Planning Committee appears to have been unaware of. In this letter, Nelson asked Roosevelt to make some modifications to the production program, but then stated, "The proposed modification does not represent a decrease in production . . . it would meet all requests on hand and now foreseen for tanks and, at the same time, would provide the equipment for a balanced military force."[21]

Despite his apparently ambivalent position on feasibility, Nelson did follow up with Roosevelt in conversation, informing the president of the importance of reducing the total program for 1942 to approximately $40 billion. Roosevelt firmly refused to consider a reduction of his "must" objectives, but accepted that the services needed to reduce their objectives. Roosevelt merely gave his verbal approval to Nelson for a reduction in the Army's supply goals, however, and did not undertake to inform the services that the president expected them to make cuts (nor did Nelson ask him to do so). Given the contempt that Somervell and even Marshall were beginning to hold for Nelson, his ability to influence them was minimal. Without a direct order from Roosevelt, Nelson did not have the authority to force on the military any decision that they opposed.

Notwithstanding this, the Planning Committee believed the president was now in their camp. During its meeting on 6 April Nathan told the committee that Nelson had received the president's approval to reduce the munitions program by $5 billion in 1942. Furthermore, Nathan informed the group that Nelson had instructed them to meet with representatives to be designated by the War and Navy departments for this purpose. Nathan emphasized to the committee that they were not to determine specific individual cuts, but were simply to bring considerations of production feasibility to bear on the thinking of the Army and Navy representatives responsible for the revision of the program.[22]

There was now a fundamental weakness in the WPB position, and Searls saw it immediately. Although Nathan claimed that the president's approval of a reduction would be a sufficient wedge to get the services to move immediately, Searls foresaw a prolonged period of negotiations during which things would significantly worsen.[23] In the event, Searls was right, but he lost the immediate debate and the committee opted to pursue negotiations in good faith. In the upcoming weeks, the Army did reduce its supply program by about $4.5 billion, but the facilities and construction program, instead of being frozen as Under Secretary of War Patterson had agreed in late March, actually rose by $1.6 billion during April. As Nathan pointed out at a WPB meeting late in April, this meant that the total of munitions and construction objectives for 1942 was still, in his opinion, about $15 billion above the highest attainable level.[24]

By this time the idea of feasibility was meeting resistance from a growing number of agency heads and senior WPB members, who asserted, "the strategists decide what their requirements are, and our job is to get industry to fill those requirements."[25] Moreover, the bulk of the establishment still did not trust Kuznets', May's, and Nathan's opinions. The three men were most often viewed as a coterie of academic "long-hairs" with no hands-on experience in production, strategy, or war. Men who grew up watching production increase as greater amounts of capital (human, financial, and material) were added to the process did not easily accept theoretical studies such as "National Product in Wartime" as true caps to production possibilities. They plainly could not understand how the high goals established by the president could actually work to lower overall achievement.[26]

Somervell had not been lying idle during this period of negotiations. He was a big believer in establishing outsized goals as a way to motivate industry to aim high and achieve great things. He was supported in this by the president, who had seized on the outsized goals of the current Victory Program to spur America to action and clearly demonstrate to all the enormity of the effort that victory would require. Somervell did not view the present situation as a matter of feasibility. Rather, he thought increasing production shortfalls reflected a combination of WPB coddling of the civilian sector, poor administrative procedures by the WPB when it came to scheduling and setting priorities, and Nelson's basic unfitness for the task. Using his connections with Harry Hopkins, he convinced the president to go with his personal inclinations and to send a letter written by Somervell's staff to Nelson. The letter, dated 1 May 1942 and signed by the president, reaffirmed the War Munitions Program of 1942 and even increased some of the "must" items.[27] Moreover, the letter stated that the president's goals included all complementary weapons and other supplies required and insisted on an expedited expansion of the necessary construction and facilities. He followed up on this letter with one on 4 May asking Nelson to report to the president what was being done to speed up lagging production.[28]

Stymied in his attempt to bring runaway production objectives to heel, in early April Nathan convinced Nelson to establish a feasibility board. This board met several times, and on 21 April sent a report, signed by Kuznets, to Nathan, urging that a full-scale feasibility analysis be undertaken. Nelson approved, and from early May through July Kuznets and a small staff worked unceasingly on a comprehensive study of the feasibility of the entire Victory Program. While they conducted this study, the rest of the Planning Committee focused on short-term problems capable of rapid adjustment and repair. Nathan himself, however, spent his time educating the rest of the senior members of the WPB and any other government officials who would listen on the concept of feasibility. In much the same way that Monnet had tirelessly worked every available venue to advocate the establishment of super-sized production goals, Nathan now worked the WPB circuit and beyond it to explain why it was important to rein in those runaway goals. Overall, though, it appeared to the services and other government agencies that the WPB and the Planning Committee in particular had abandoned the feasibility question, when they were actually only waiting on the final Kuznets study before declaring bureaucratic war. Throughout this period production objectives continued to rise, while actual achievements fell farther behind.

On 12 August Kuznets delivered his feasibility report to the Planning Committee. It represented an extensive analysis, covering more than 140 pages, divided into four lengthy studies.[29] Since 1942 was more than half over, the study concentrated on the 1943 production program. The results of 1942 had to be accounted for, however, since the uncompleted portion would be carried into 1943, enlarging that part of the program even more.

The first section of the study emphasized the military production and construction sectors. This was fundamentally an analysis of recent GNP statistics, primarily divided between the military and civilian sectors of the economy. Here, Kuznets again reiterated his conviction that military production objectives were so massive that any attempt to carry them through would result in fewer rather than more finished products.[30]

Kuznets devoted the remainder of his report of his study to examining the other facets of feasibility. Summarizing these sets of findings, his study noted that for the remainder of 1942 and for 1943 there would be shortages in all important raw material categories that would seriously impede the total output. Moreover, Kuznets believed a substantial labor shortage would reveal itself by the end of 1943 unless strong measures were taken to move workers where they were critically needed. The main problem in his estimations was not a countrywide shortage of labor, but rather the immobility of many potential workers who lived far from the growing war production centers. Finally,

Kuznets drew attention to a shortage of machine tools available to equip new and converted factories.[31]

The key parts of Kuznets' study, however, were his overall estimates. On the basis of production rates and his calculated estimates of how fast the nation's GDP could grow, Kuznets found that 1942 munitions output would fall $15 billion short of its goal. In the event, he was off by only $1 billion, since actual output was $45 billion and not the $44 billion he estimated. Similarly, he found that the 1943 goal of $93 billion was at least 30 percent too high, and that the best that one could hope for was $75 billion. This $28 billion shortfall would increase to $33 billion if the 1942 shortfall was rolled over to 1943.[32]

According to Kuznets, the most important implication of his findings was the crucial requirement of establishing feasible goals since no satisfactory production scheduling procedures could ever be devised as long as overall objectives remained beyond the nation's capacity. Thus, Kuznets stated that the most pressing need was the development of "well-formulated and properly screened and tested objectives."[33] Going beyond pure economic analysis, he suggested to the committee that it would be impossible to establish such objectives unless the president created an authority "both amply informed and empowered, to set them."[34]

Here Kuznets was echoing Nathan's March proposal for the creation of a super-organization capable of coordinating both strategy and production. Because the military viewed strategy as its singular domain, this suggestion looked much as if the civilian production agencies were encroaching on the military's area of responsibility. It was a suggestion that uniformed military and General Somervell particularly would bitterly contest. In hindsight it was a remarkable piece of naiveté on Nathan's, Kuznets', and May's part to believe they could carry off this suggestion, particularly because they could refer to their own experience in vehemently opposing military attempts to gain greater control of production controls. The notion that the military would be any less resistant to a power grab in the opposite direction reveals a certain bureaucratic naiveté on the part of Committee members.

But according to Brigante, this is exactly what Kuznets appeared to recommend. Kuznets proposed that a supreme war production council be established in order to represent all the factors that he believed had to be taken into account in a well-formulated production program. According to Kuznets, a segregation of strategic, economic, and political factors was impossible, and no mechanism that called for separate application of them, with continuous shuttling among the agencies supposedly representing each, would really work.[35]

Kuznets advocated making this new body a permanent institution that would focus on broad questions of production strategy. In his vision, it also would include people responsible for military strategy, for production strategy in its broadest sense, and for social and political strategy. Considering that instituting any such proposal required the support of General Somervell, Kuznets made a major bureaucratic error by failing to include a representative from military procurement in this new oversight body. Finally, Kuznets wanted this body to have full authority over the Army, the Navy, and the Maritime Commission to be able to enforce its decisions on the broad outlines of any future production program. That Kuznets regarded the establishment of this group as crucial in importance was indicated by his closing statement: "Unless such a body is established . . . we are in grave danger of reducing materially the contribution that the productive system of this country can make to the war effort. We shall be threatened by continuous imbalance in output and by failure to obtain . . . the vast flow of munitions which we are capable of producing."[36]

Nelson approved Kuznets' study in late August, and noted that he thought the study was "remarkably well prepared" and a "magnificent analysis of our production program."[37] Nelson only commented on the portion of the report dealing with feasibility analysis, however, and remained silent about whether he concurred with the suggestion to create a "supreme war production council." Nathan and the rest of the committee interpreted this silence as approval, although the evidence says otherwise. Nelson had already opposed previous attempts to involve the Supply Priorities and Allocations Board (SPAB) and the WPB in strategy and often went out of his way to draw a clear line between board authorities and those of the military. In fact, he was at that time pushing a different proposal, out of another office, to ask the military to establish a "requirements committee" with which the WPB could coordinate information and activities. Moreover, since the Planning Committee's idea of a "supreme production council" appeared to bypass Somervell entirely in favor of direct access to the Joint Chiefs, it could not fail to garner the chiefs' intense hostility. Furthermore, this perceived slight made it easy for Somervell to discount the plan to which it was attached—namely, feasibility.

Although Nelson was at best equivocal on the idea of a "supreme production council," he ordered sixty copies of the study to be produced without modifications. Of these copies, three went directly to Somervell, Vice Admiral Robinson (head of Navy procurement), and Harry Hopkins. In a break with delivery protocols, Nathan personally delivered the three advance copies and included his own note with each.[38]

Only Somervell replied to the document, and his response was far from what the planners had hoped. Given that the data were, to his mind, so unreliable and the percentage so inconsequential, Somervell could not support any changes to the current production program. He was also put off by the fact that only a few months before the statisticians had advocated a large increase in production goals, and now that he had complied they were changing their tune and screaming for reductions. Somervell continued his reply with a point-by-point rebuttal of specific elements of Kuznets' proposal. If he had left it at that, there was a good chance that reasonable men still might have arrived at some compromise in a few weeks since the production system's failure to attain stated goals was becoming manifest to most observers. Somervell could not resist the urge to twist the knife, though, and ended his letter with a hand-grenade: "To me this is an inchoate mass of words. . . . I am not impressed with either the character or basis of the judgments expressed in the reports and recommend they be carefully hidden from the eyes of thoughtful men."[39]

At first, Nathan was reluctant to show the reply to Kuznets because the latter had spent most of the summer preparing the study. But Kuznets heard about it and after some prodding Nathan handed him a copy of the reply. Initially, Kuznets was angry, but then began to think Somervell's reply amusing. After all, Kuznets was already considered the world's foremost authority on national income statistics and accounts, and here was a man in uniform stating that his intellectual work should be kept from "the eyes of thoughtful men." The entire response played all too true to the stereotype of the military mind.[40]

Confident that his analysis was sound, Kuznets petitioned Nathan to prepare a draft counterresponse for delivery with Nathan's signature. With Nelson's consent, Nathan forwarded a reply to Somervell on 17 September 1942, not wasting any time on a shot across the bow. Rather, he opened with a broadside amidships: "In view of the gravity of the problem discussed in these documents, I hesitate to take your memorandum seriously." Remarkably, Nathan's rejection of Somervell's arguments became even more pointed after this blunt opening. He pointed out, for instance, "The fact that we once urged that the sights be raised is no reason for now adopting an ostrich-like attitude when goals are established that are above probability of achievement." After his own point-by-point refutation of Somervell's points, Nathan concluded with a blistering attack on Somervell's dismissal of Kuznets' estimates:

> I appreciate your frankness in stating that you are not impressed by the character or basis of judgments expressed in this report. Your conclu-

> sion . . . that these judgments be carefully hidden from the eyes of thoughtful men is a non-sequitur. Also, I am obliged to be frank with you in expressing my disappointment in your reply. The problems discussed are important and their intelligent consideration is urgent. The author of the documents is recognized nationally as one of the ablest and soundest authorities on our national economy and upon its ability to produce for peace or war. I think it would be most unwise to bar these problems, which have been given careful consideration by the staff and members of the Planning Committee, from people who have responsibility for the success of the war effort and the welfare of this country.[41]

Neither Somervell's memorandum nor Nathan's reply were couched in the language of diplomacy. In fact, they had clearly designed their letters as the opening salvos of a titanic bureaucratic struggle, which is how the media portrayed them.[42] Although both sides appeared to realize they were carrying their acrimony too far, the dispute was now out in the open and needed to be formally addressed. Nelson placed it on the agenda for the 6 October WPB meeting. Press coverage alerted the White House to the growing dispute, and Roosevelt's minions informed Nelson that the president wanted the problem resolved quickly, telling him that the meeting could not be rescheduled. Nathan was called to the White House to present a lengthy explanation of the feasibility study to Harry Hopkins and his aide Isador Lubin, who was also an assistant to the president and an expert statistician.[43] Finally, before the meeting, Nathan took the precaution of presenting and explaining the entire study to Leon Henderson, who fully concurred with its findings. Henderson, with his direct access to Roosevelt and his unparalleled ability to bulldoze those who stood in his way, proved a valuable ally in the coming struggle. The fact that Henderson had the reputation of being a vocal all-outer added credibility to his stand that the military would have to cut back on its requirements.

Somervell came armed with a letter from General Marshall to Nelson, dated 6 October.[44] The letter began by stating Marshall's belief that an effective and elaborate machinery for the guidance of the strategic effort already existed. Given that, Marshall did not believe that a joint committee consisting of an economist, a politician, and a person familiar with strategy but not with production would be an effective means of controlling the war effort. It concluded by declaring, "Lt. General Somervell is the designated representative of the War Department for the interpretation of strategy to the War Production Board."

In addition to securing this letter, Somervell had also prepared for the meeting by discussing the question with Under Secretary Patterson and Vice Admiral S. M. Robinson, both of whom were regular attendees of WPB meetings. He secured their approval of his position on the matter of feasibility. In the case of Robinson, his interest in the meeting's outcome was less than that of Somervell. No matter how the question would be resolved, Robinson was satisfied that the Navy's procurement programs would proceed on schedule.[45] Nevertheless, because of his close relationship to Somervell, he supported the latter's position. As for a "supreme production council," Robinson could see no advantage in its establishment, and therefore actively concurred in Somervell's desire to oppose this along with the feasibility findings of the Planning Committee.

Nathan's speech, given at the beginning of the meeting, contained little that was new to those present. He merely presented a summary of Kuznets' feasibility study and concluded with a plea for the creation of a joint production strategy body. Taking up where Nathan left off, Wayne Coy, assistant director of the Bureau of the Budget, inquired whether the Army and the Navy would admit that the 1942 program was too large to be feasible. Somervell replied that, whereas it was clearly necessary to utilize all means to achieve the program, it would be 90 percent complete by the end of the year, in contrast to the 81 percent that Nathan had estimated.

Somervell declared that he was "not so despondent" as those who believed they could not meet production goals, even if more-effective controls were instituted. He further claimed that the government could avoid existing and impending shortages in critical materials through more-intense efforts on the part of the producers. Finally, he emphasized that in the interest of providing for the needs of soldiers and sailors the nation should concentrate all of its efforts on increasing supply. According to Somervell, the work involved in the millions of recomputations necessary to reduce the requirements program was not worth the doubtful benefits it might provide.

At this point, Henderson, in answer to Somervell's remark that the use of dollar figures in the committee's report had not impressed him, commented that dollar and national income figures seemed to be "the best common denominators of capacity." Somervell replied that in his opinion it would be possible to reduce dollar costs by 10 percent from existing prices. He then continued his criticism of Nathan's report: "We already have the Combined Chiefs, Joint Chiefs, the Combined Production and Resources Board, the Munitions Assignments Board, the Army and Navy Munitions Board, and the War Production Board. What good would be a board composed of an economist, a politician, and a soldier who does not know production?"

Nathan then made clear that in his view the production authorities could not question strategy, but inquired whether the Joint Chiefs, for their part, had considered feasibility fully in establishing military requirements. With his letter from Marshall to Nelson spread before him, Somervell replied that the supply programs submitted to WPB adequately represented the material expressions of strategy. Furthermore, he saw no need for the board to concern itself with strategic considerations. When Coy inquired what steps the government should take if production fell below strategic requirements set by the chiefs of staff, Somervell answered that this would necessitate merely making changes in the supply programs presented to WPB for the following year.

Robinson then supported Somervell's position by asserting that the Army and Navy would be able to keep the production effort in balance and by expressing confidence that the entire program would henceforth be more effectively scheduled. Under Secretary of War Patterson took up the argument by stating his opposition to the creation of a new production-strategy board, but suggested that it would be beneficial to have WPB officials meet from time to time with the Joint Chiefs "for an exchange of attitudes"—the only conciliatory note voiced.

After a period when the military representatives dominated the meeting, a concerted attack on the armed services began. Lubin, acting for Hopkins, pointed out that failure to meet production schedules on time meant that the JCS would not have the munitions expected and that "some means of informing them should be provided." McNutt asserted that, despite repeated efforts, his War Manpower Commission had not been able to obtain reliable data on the manpower needs of the Army and Navy. He also denied the validity of Somervell's contention that there was sufficient coordination in the manpower situation and stated that Somervell had not made good on his earlier promise that the War Manpower Commission would be informed of the Army's needs. Nelson himself observed that the Army had not informed the WPB of the recently adopted proposal to increase the size of the Army and that such proposals vitally affected the general shortage of manpower.

Despite these criticisms, Somervell, Robinson, and Patterson seemed likely to prevail by default. Without a firm WPB decision, the Joint Chiefs could hardly be expected to lower goals then projected for 1942 and 1943. Thus it appeared that the discussion might end without any effective acceptance of Nathan's proposals. But during a brief lull in the proceedings, Henderson began to speak in a low voice, almost as though he was thinking aloud. The subject of his quasi-soliloquy was the figure set by Nathan as the maximum productive effort (munitions, construction, and nonmunitions expenditures) that the nation could achieve in 1943, and that Somervell and Patterson held to be insufficient for the conduct of the war. "The amount in question, 90 billion dollars, was interesting," said Henderson, "because it exceeded by far the value of our entire national product both for 1933 and 1934." Then, as if a great light were dawning, he said, in substance, "Maybe if we can't wage a war on 90 billions, we ought to get rid of our present Joint Chiefs, and find some who can."[46]

The meeting received this statement in dead silence, which allowed Henderson to turn to Somervell and proceed to make the most violent personal attack ever heard in a meeting of the WPB. He announced that he found himself disgusted with Somervell's repeated obstinacy, overbearing manner, and ignorance of production problems. He stated flatly his belief that Somervell had always padded his requirements, and that the general had no idea of the disastrous implications of infeasible goals. For a considerable period, Henderson gave vent to every grievance he had accumulated throughout the first year of the war.

Somervell was silent. During his numerous struggles with WPB and his frequent disagreements at Board meetings, no one had ever spoken to him in this fashion. Nor could Henderson resist one final thrust. When W. L. Batt, a WPB vice chair, attempted to assuage Henderson by pointing out that, after all, Somervell did not make the strategy, Henderson replied, "Ain't he got a letter?"[47]

After this the meeting, which had occupied more than twice the usual time, rapidly drew to a close. Patterson again recommended that the armed services be given whatever they requested. Coy and Somervell discussed the problems raised by the size of the Army, and Coy predicted that new augmentations of the munitions program would be forthcoming. Nelson, showing obvious embarrassment, stated his belief in maximum production, but warned that plans would have to support essential civilian activities, such as railroads. Finally, Stacy May stated that the nation could meet the program if it were redesigned to produce in fifteen months what had been scheduled for twelve months. Vice President Henry Wallace and Under Secretary of War Robert Patterson pointed out that they would have to inform the president promptly if any rescheduling affected the president's announced objectives. On this inconclusive note, the meeting ended.

Two days later the Planning Committee considered alternative means of securing revisions to the 1943 program. Anticipating further military objections to production cuts, Kuznets suggested an alternative way to sell the idea. Rather than tell the military they had to reduce requirements, Kuznets advocated that the committee inform the military that it could have everything it wanted, but at a new date. In a memorandum to the committee, he stated, "If we could, say that the objectives in many areas are to be pushed forward—say to the middle of 1944—and that production schedules for 1943 are to be reduced, we would perhaps encounter less opposition than if we insist on the reduction of the objectives proper."[48]

Furthermore, Stacy May, present by invitation at this meeting, urged abandonment of the proposal to form a super-production-strategy committee. In his opinion, this goal was impossible to achieve, and an emphasis on the importance of effective collaboration among existing military and production bodies should replace the proposal.[49]

The committee accepted both proposals and forwarded the recommendations to Nelson immediately prior to the next meeting of the WPB, set for 13 October. These two proposals had gone far toward making solutions to the feasibility program more palatable to both the military and to Somervell, in particular. First, as far as production went, the new proposals followed Somervell's own suggestion made during the 6 October meeting: if the nation could not meet production objectives he would be in favor of just adjusting the following year's schedules to finish the job.[50] Second, they removed from consideration the one idea Somervell found most loathsome in the committee's proposals: the creation of a new group that would bypass him and take away his position as the person who translated the Joint Chiefs' strategic plans into production plans.

As the Planning Committee was meeting, Somervell was having his own epiphany. The day after the 6 October meeting, Under Secretary of War Patterson, Somervell's boss for production-related matters, sent Somervell a memorandum basically telling him to accept the Planning Committee's stance on feasibility.[51] In his letter Patterson admitted that the production program was beyond the country's ability to fulfill, and that major cuts in the program would soon become necessary. He also said he foresaw that with so many programs (such as shipping and aircraft production) sacrosanct, most of the cuts would have to come from Army programs and possibly from the Navy's capital ship program.[52]

So by the 13 October WPB meeting both sides were ready to compromise. Nelson began the meeting by stating that the production goals for 1943 were not practicable. A long statement by Henderson stated his conviction that even the Planning Committee's more-feasible overall goals would be impossible to meet without substantial improvements in methods of production and scheduling. After some remarks by Nelson and Lubin that indicated that any further reductions to civilian-oriented production would damage the overall economic effort, Henderson again took up his cudgel. Since the president would not consider a reduction in his "must" items, it was necessary to cut the military supply program by about 50 percent.[53]

Although he had vehemently contested each of these points the preceding week, Somervell (along with Patterson and Robinson) kept silent throughout each of these presentations. After hearing that the WPB had abandoned the idea of a super-production-strategy committee and listening to proposals to roll 1943 production over into 1944, Somervell spoke up for the first time. After expressing general agreement with Mr. Henderson, Somervell stated that he was more optimistic regarding the management and control of the program. He then suggested that Nelson write a letter to the Joint Chiefs informing them the president's "must" program when coupled with their own objectives constituted a total too great to attain within the established limits. Somervell then stated it would be the responsibility of the JCS to determine, after consulting with the president, what action should be taken to bring the overall program within the limits of production feasibility.[54]

Both Patterson and Robinson then seconded Somervell's proposal, stating, "A letter needs to be sent to the Joint Chiefs outlining the difficulties discussed at the present meeting and suggesting that the program be reviewed from this viewpoint, since an early decision on this matter was urgent."[55] After some brief discussion, the meeting adjourned. Nathan immediately drafted a letter to the Joint Chiefs for Nelson to sign and deliver.

Upon receipt of Nelson's letter, the Joint Chiefs immediately began considering reduction proposals that would bring total objectives down to $80 billion. Nelson's letter and a proposed JCS reply were the primary topic of discussion at the Joint Chiefs meeting on 20 October.[56] After some debate the Joint Chiefs directed the Joint Staff planners to prepare a study indicating where reductions could best be applied to retain a balanced program and at the same time bring total requirements within production capability. The planners were directed to have this study ready for submission to the JCS no later than 10

November 1942.[57] A letter from the JCS, signed by Admiral Leahy, informing Nelson of this decision was sent the next day.[58]

By the end of November, the Joint Chiefs had completed their work, which led to a reduction for 1943 in the Navy program of $3 billion and the Army program of $9 billion.[59] Although the total JCS program was still $5 billion above what the Planning Committee thought feasible ($80 billion vs. $75 billion), May and Kuznets declared it was possible and Nathan agreed.[60]

After more than half a year of bureaucratic warfare, Nelson and his team had won. Their victory was not without personal costs, however. Nelson's handling of the issue, along with other squabbles with Somervell, had ruined his relations with the Joint Chiefs beyond repair, and they became increasingly antagonistic. While Roosevelt did not fire Nelson, the president gradually pushed him aside in the WPB and then made Nelson's position redundant with the appointment of Supreme Court Justice James Byrnes to the Office of War Mobilization, which eventually assumed most of WPB's coordination functions. Discouraged, Nelson left government service within the year.

The feasibility dispute also brought about the demise of the Planning Committee, which was demoted to a secondary position in early 1943 when Charles E. Wilson, then vice chair of WPB, reorganized the Planning Board. According to Brigante, Wilson's decision was greatly influenced by the antagonism Somervell and other military officials felt toward Nathan and the rest of the Planning Committee.[61] As a result of this reorganization, Nathan resigned and the other members followed his lead.

While Kuznets and May returned to academia, Nathan, along with Leon Henderson's top aide, David Ginsberg, enlisted.[62] Both had found themselves stunned by an article in a Virginia newspaper that claimed that thousands of Americans were dying while a couple of Jews (Nathan and Ginsberg) got paid for planning how best to send good Christian boys off to fight their war. Upon their arrival in boot camp, they saw a *Washington Post* article about their enlistment posted on a bulletin board inside the front gate. On it was scrawled in black grease pencil, "These sons-a-bitches arrive today." Later that day both men were cleaning out the latrines when Ginsberg commented that so far the Army was not treating them very well, to which Nathan retorted, "About as well as or better than they treated us in Washington."[63]

The effects of the 1943 reductions on military planning and future strategic operations were profound. In no small measure, these cuts decided when the invasion of northern Europe (D-day) would take place. Before examining how they did so, it is necessary to carefully analyze the positions of the Joint Chiefs, and in particular the position of General Marshall, in relation to the invasion. Marshall's stance on the invasion of Europe at the Casablanca Conference in January 1943 was decisively influenced by debates over feasibility in October and November 1942.

CHAPTER 9

Marshall's Commitment to a 1943 Invasion of Europe

★ ★ ★

In 2005 the Army Center for Military History published a volume on American military history that included the following statement: "At Casablanca [Conference, 12–23 January 1943], General Marshall made a last vigorous, but vain stand for a cross-channel operation in 1943."[1] *Once again, an "official" history perpetuated a myth that has no basis in fact, a tradition dating back to the first official histories of the war—popularly known as the Green Books. Ever since publication of* Strategic Planning for Coalition Warfare: 1943–1944, *many historians have accepted that, during the Casablanca Conference, Marshall opposed further operations in the Mediterranean and continued to push for a decisive invasion of northern Europe in 1943. According to Maurice Matloff's 1958 official history, "It was extremely important for the American and British leaders to decide on the "main plot." To support this view, Matloff quotes Marshall as stating, "Every diversion or side issue from the main plot, acts as a 'suction pump.'" After this, Matloff presents his own insight into Marshall's thoughts, and states, "It was Marshall's belief that in the diversion to TORCH [the invasion of North Africa] the United States and Great Britain had been 'abnormally fortunate.' He still favored a main British–American effort against Germany in the form of a cross-Channel operation aimed at northern France."*[2]

In a single paragraph the official historians captured their two main points: Marshall's revulsion to all diversions from the main effort and his desire for a cross-Channel operation in 1943. Unfortunately, this version of events has serious flaws. First, the Marshall quote was far from complete. The part the authors left out totally reverses the point they were trying to make. The minutes of the Casablanca Conference reveal that, immediately after making the "suction pump" remark, "He [Marshall] stated that the operations against Sicily appeared advantageous because of the excess number of troops in North Africa brought about by the splendid efforts of the British Eighth Army."[3]

Besides neglecting to inform their readers that Marshall was not adamantly opposed to further Mediterranean operations, the official historians categorically stated that Marshall was a strong advocate for a 1943 cross-Channel invasion.[4] This is most certainly wrong. By the time Marshall and the rest of the Joint Chiefs arrived in Casablanca, a 1943 invasion was no longer a serious option from their point of view. The Joint Chiefs' goal in Casablanca, therefore, was not to persuade the British to commit to a 1943 invasion, but rather to get their agreement to an invasion, with the exact date to be determined later.

That Marshall, at Casablanca, would strongly advocate a 1943 invasion is more a result of the extrapolation of his previous stance on the matter than a reflection of his thinking by late 1942. Before Operation Torch the evidence of Marshall's support for a cross-Channel invasion as soon as feasible is beyond doubt. Marshall was joined without reservation in this policy by the Joint Chiefs and the president. Moreover, the British chiefs of staff and Winston Churchill fully supported a decisive cross-Channel invasion. They did insist, however, that the Allies not launch it before preparations ensured a fair chance of success.[5]

As early as the Arcadia Conference, which ended in mid-January 1942, the Allies formally affirmed both the American-British-Canadian (ABC-1) Conference's (29 January–27 March 1941) identification of Germany as the primary enemy and that the most efficient means to defeat Germany was a continental invasion, although the route to that invasion was still open for debate. According to the conference minutes, the combined chiefs recognized that no large-scale offensive against Germany was possible, except for one on the Russian front. Although the chiefs kept open the possibility of a 1942 invasion in the event of a German collapse, they believed that the optimal time for a continental invasion would not arrive until 1943. The record further states that this invasion would be a prelude to a final assault on Germany itself, and went so far as to direct that the Victory Program "be such as to provide the means by which this can be carried out."[6]

After the Arcadia Conference, General Marshall ordered his planners to prepare a more detailed strategic plan focused on the decisive defeat of Germany. In response, by 1 April Brigadier General Eisenhower had completed the basic outline of this plan, which Marshall approved and sold to the president. The plan consisted of three major parts:

1. Bolero: The build-up of men and materiel in England for a cross-Channel invasion
2. Roundup: The actual invasion of northern France scheduled for 1943
3. Sledgehammer: A smaller invasion of as little as a half-dozen divisions to be carried out in 1942 in the event an imminent Soviet collapse necessitated a sacrifice to relieve pressure on the Soviets

After receiving the president's approval for the basic concept, Marshall flew to Britain with the president's friend and adviser Harry Hopkins to sell it to the British. After several days of consultations, Churchill agreed to a public pronouncement "that our two nations are resolved to march forward into Europe together in noble brotherhood of arms, in a great crusade for the liberation of the tormented people."[7] After this, both Marshall and Hopkins believed they had British support for a 1943 invasion, while Marshall turned his attention to Sledgehammer in 1942, which, in Marshall's opinion, the British had also accepted, if conditions were right.[8]

Soon after Marshall and Hopkins returned from London, Anglo-American conceptions for future operations began to diverge. Toward the end of May, Soviet Foreign Minister Vyacheslav Molotov first visited Britain and then the United States. While Molotov was in Britain, Churchill told him that a second front was a priority, but remained vague as to when it would prove possible. By the time he arrived in the United States, the Soviet foreign minister was ready to press for a more specific commitment, and he found a receptive audience. During a 30 May White House meeting, the president seemed committed to a 1942 cross-Channel invasion. After getting Marshall's assurance that developments were far enough along to assure Stalin that there would soon be a second front, Roosevelt authorized Molotov to inform the Soviet leader that he could expect a second front during that year.[9]

Even before this commitment, Marshall and the Joint Chiefs had begun focusing on the possibility of conducting Sledgehammer in 1942 with the intention of establishing a lodgement in the Cotentin or Brest peninsulas, which the Allies would reinforce by a more massive Roundup the following year. The president, who had earlier appeared supportive of Churchill's conception of a North Africa invasion, no longer supported such an operation and was fully supportive of a rapid Bolero build-up and launching Sledgehammer, sooner rather than later. That Sledgehammer was the president's prime focus became apparent when he was informed that his suggestion to redirect one and a half divisions and a thousand aircraft, that had been targeted for an early invasion of northern Europe, to the Pacific to shore up crumbling defenses would delay the Bolero build-up. The president's suggestion came up for discussion at a meeting of the Joint Chiefs on 4 May when Admiral King tried to have it both ways. King had prepared a memorandum in which he expressed agreement with the Army that there should be no undue delay in preparations for Bolero, but in which he said he did not agree that forces in the Pacific should be kept at a bare minimum. In his opinion, the problem of holding in the Pacific was as important as and more urgent than Bolero.[10]

After considerable discussion, the chiefs were unable to reconcile their differences. Consequently, they agreed to submit their divergent views to the president. After the meeting, King wrote a note to the president, pointing out, "Disastrous consequences would result if we are unable to hold the present position in the Pacific." He closed by telling the president, as "Important as Bolero may be, the Pacific problem is no less so, and certainly the more urgent."[11]

Despite King's impassioned pleas, Roosevelt's decision was a succinct, "I do not want BOLERO slowed down."[12]

By the end of May, the British were becoming animated over U.S. ambitions to invade the continent in 1942. Churchill, alarmed at the emphasis the U.S. chiefs of staff appeared to be placing on a possible cross-Channel operation in 1942, decided the time had come to cross the Atlantic to determine how matters stood. The situation in Africa was rapidly deteriorating as General Rommel advanced towards the British stronghold of Tobruk. The British chiefs were not eager to commit to a possible but doubtful operation on the European continent in the fall of 1942 that would use troops that were desperately needed in Egypt. At the same time, they believed that some form of invasion of North Africa might be extremely helpful. Moreover, British planners had not succeeded in developing what they considered an acceptable plan for Sledgehammer.[13]

Churchill spelled out his objections in a letter he delivered to the president when they met in Hyde Park, New York, in early June. In it, the prime minister first appeased Roosevelt by telling him that arrangements were proceeding apace to enable six or eight divisions to be landed on the coast of northern France in 1942. He then informed the president that, although preparations were ongoing, the British government was not in favor of undertaking a limited operation in 1942 if it was likely to lead to disaster. In support of this position, Churchill laid out some of the negative results of failure: "The French people would be exposed to Nazi vengeance, it would not help the Russians and would gravely delay the main operation in 1943." Churchill concluded by saying that the Allies should not make any substantial landing in France in 1942 unless they were going to stay there.[14]

Right or wrong, Churchill's arguments appealed to Roosevelt, who was always interested in reducing loss of life.[15] By the time the president and prime minister returned to Washington to continue discussions with their military staffs present, the president was half-convinced to scrap Sledgehammer and was beginning to look at North Africa as the first sphere of combat operations for American forces—an idea that had long appealed to him.

In the Washington talks with the British Imperial General Staff, General Alan Brooke opened the debate. According to Guyer's unpublished official history, Brooke announced the British chiefs had exhaustively examined the question of an early invasion but had not been able to discover any worthwhile objective commensurate with the risk. Brooke went on to inform the Americans that there were twenty-five German divisions in France against which the Allies, due to a lack of landing craft, could only hope to throw some six divisions. In sum, Brooke considered it unlikely that such a small invasion would cause the Germans to remove any forces from the Eastern Front, even if it did secure a small lodgement. It was quickly apparent that the British strongly opposed Sledgehammer, except of course, in an alternative concept as an operation to take advantage of a marked German weakening. General Brooke did reaffirm Bolero, but proposed that alternatives be considered in the event a cross-Channel operation later proved impracticable. Among these alternatives was the revival of Gymnast, the expedition against North Africa.[16]

The reaction of the American chiefs was visceral. King was utterly opposed to Gymnast taking place in 1942, which would open a "ninth front." He told the assembled group that the risks already taken in the Pacific to provide for Bolero had caused him great anxiety, and Gymnast would render the Pacific situation still more desperate by requiring an immediate withdrawal of naval forces from the Pacific for redeployment to the Atlantic. Marshall reiterated that opening another front would "achieve nothing" and that from the military point of view there was "no other logical course" but to concentrate on Bolero and drive ahead, while diverting only the minimum of forces elsewhere. Marshall emphasized that even the 1943 continental operation might be impossible unless the Allies devoted all efforts now to its preparation. To defeat the Germans, declared Marshall, "We must have overwhelming power, and North West Europe was the only front on which this overwhelming superiority was logistically possible."[17]

In private discussions with the president, the Joint Chiefs emphasized that Gymnast would seriously curtail reinforcements to the Middle East with possible disastrous consequences in that theater, since even a successful Gymnast operation could not give the support necessary to the British Middle East forces in sufficient time to be effective. Moreover, Gymnast would thin out naval concentrations in all other theaters, particularly in regards to aircraft carriers and escort vessels. What really upset the Joint Chiefs, however, was that Gymnast would markedly slow preparations for Bolero, particularly the accumulation in Britain of necessary aircraft, antiaircraft, and service units. The Joint Chiefs concluded by informing the president that it would be unwise to disperse available resources on a doubtful venture.

Whatever the president's attachment to a North African invasion might have been, the arguments of his chiefs convinced him to again support a 1942 invasion of northern Europe, both in public and in private discussions with Churchill. Ironically, the American debating success was probably due in large part to Churchill and his staff's preoccupation with the news that Tobruk had fallen to Rommel. This was a blow to Churchill because Tobruk had withstood a year-long siege the year before and the British took its rapid collapse this time as hard as the loss of Singapore in February 1942. When this thunderclap bulletin arrived, the conference rapidly shifted from debates over a cross-Channel invasion to determining how best and most rapidly to ship munitions to reinforce the crumbling British position in North Africa.

As Marshall made emergency plans to move hundreds of new Sherman tanks and modern aircraft to Egypt, he was content in the knowledge that this was a temporary diversion of resources now that the British had finally acquiesced in plans for a 1943 invasion. The full text of that agreement was brief. While it paid lip service to Gymnast it definitely focused everyone's attention on cross-Channel operations by ordering, "Plans and preparations for the BOLERO operation in 1943 on as large a scale as possible are to be pushed forward with all speed and energy." The agreement also continued to hold open the option for a 1942 invasion by calling for "the most resolute efforts to overcome the obvious dangers and difficulties of the enterprise. If a sound and sensible plan can be contrived, we should not hesitate to effect it." Despite the emphasis on as rapid a return to the continent as possible, the agreement did leave some hope for undertaking Gymnast, stating that "all possibilities of Operation GYMNAST will be explored carefully and conscientiously."[18] Since the agreement called offensive operations in 1942 essential while recognizing that such action on the continent was fraught with risk, the Gymnast option was set to grow in significance.

On 8 July, however, the British chiefs of staff dispatched a message to the U.S. Joint Chiefs that was to cause one of the most violent reactions of the Joint Chiefs of Staff (JCS) in the entire war. Referring to the June agreement, the British pointed to what they believed was an inconsistency in pressing on urgently with a full-scale Roundup in 1943, at the same time speeding preparations for a limited-scale Sledgehammer in 1942. Moreover, the British chiefs complained that mounting Sledgehammer meant the use of ocean-going shipping, which would entail a 0.75-million-ton loss of imports per annum to the British Isles. In conclusion, they pointed out that they and the prime minister considered the conditions necessary for Sledgehammer were "most unlikely" to occur. Regarding future operations, the war cabinet also laid down guiding principles. First, there would be no substantial landing in France in 1942 unless the Allies planned to stay. Second, there would be no landing in France unless the Germans were demolished by their failure against Russia.[19]

During the JCS meeting on 10 July, Marshall read the dispatch to his fellow chiefs and informed them that the prime minister had forwarded a similar note to the president, which concluded with a suggestion that the Americans reconsider Gymnast, while the British would consider undertaking Jupiter (Norway invasion). According to the JCS minutes, Marshall then read his comments on the British attitude, the gist of which was that Operation Gymnast would be expensive and ineffectual, and that it was impossible to carry out Sledgehammer or Roundup without full aggressive British support. If the British position must be accepted, he proposed that the United States should turn to the Pacific for decisive action against Japan. He added that this would tend to concentrate rather than scatter U.S. forces; that it would be highly popular throughout the United States, particularly on the West Coast; and that, second only to Bolero, it would be the operation that would have the greatest effect on relieving pressure on Russia. Admiral King expressed himself as being completely in agreement with General Marshall's proposal. Referring to Gymnast in particular, he said "that it was impossible to fulfil naval commitments in other theaters and at the same time provide the shipping and escorts which would be essential should that operation be undertaken."[20]

Marshall presented a draft of a memorandum for the president indicating the views of the U.S. chiefs. After some discussion and a few amendments, the chiefs signed and dispatched this memorandum to the president by air via officer courier. It stressed that execution of Operation Gymnast, even if found practicable, would definitely mean an end to Sledgehammer in 1942 and would curtail if not render impossible Bolero and Roundup for 1943. Furthermore, the chiefs contended that Gymnast would be indecisive, a major drain on resources, and would jeopardize America's position in the Pacific. The Joint Chiefs concluded by stating, "If the United States is to engage in any other operation than forceful, unswerving adherence to full BOLERO plans, we are definitely of the opinion that we should turn to the Pacific and strike decisively against Japan; in other words assume a defensive attitude against Germany, except for air operations, and use all available means in the Pacific."[21]

The president immediately called them to account. From Hyde Park, he responded "that he desired to have dispatched to him at once, by airplane, a comprehensive and detailed outline of the plans for redirecting the major effort of the United States to the war against Japan—including the effect of such a decision on the Soviet and Middle East fronts during the balance of 1942." Roosevelt also demanded definite plans for the remainder of 1942 and tentative plans for 1943. He did agree, however, that dispersions of forces should be avoided and that coordinated use of U.S. and British forces was essential. On the other hand, once again Roosevelt emphasized, "it is of highest importance that U.S. ground troops be brought into action against the enemy in 1942."[22]

Inasmuch as no one had foreseen any possibility of such a change of strategy, there were no detailed plans in Washington for major offensives in the Pacific. A hasty survey was made, however, and a paper drawn up outlining in general terms immediate adjustments that could be made. Roosevelt rejected these new proposals out of hand and made it clear he was not in favor of transferring the major effort to the Pacific. He referred to the proposal as a "red herring" and went so far as to suggest that "the record should be altered so that it would not appear in later years that we proposed what amounted to the abandonment of the British."[23]

Momentarily put off, Marshall came back to the matter with a vengeance when Roosevelt returned to Washington on 15 July. According to Sherwood, this was the one occasion that Marshall, whose patience had been exhausted by the off-again on-again status of the Second Front planning, strongly asserted that the United States forsake major operations in Europe in favor of an all-out offensive in the Pacific. Unsettled by this change of direction by his

Joint Chiefs, Roosevelt determined to settle the matter and cabled Churchill to inform him that Marshall, King, and Hopkins were leaving for London at once.[24]

Before sending the party off to London, the president issued detailed formal instructions to guide the conduct of negotiations. The final points of the letter formed the crux of the president's agenda. Here Roosevelt spelled out that he was unalterably opposed to an all-out effort in the Pacific against Japan. He reminded all concerned that the defeat of Japan would not defeat Germany, and that American concentration against Japan in 1942 or in 1943 would increase the chance of complete German domination of Europe and Africa. The president also asked his representatives to keep three cardinal principles in mind: speed of decision on plans; unity of plans; and attack combined with defense, but not defense alone. He concluded by stating that he expected U.S. ground forces to be engaged against the Germans in 1942, and finally that he wanted this matter settled within a week.

Under these instructions Marshall had lost politically before his mission even began, while Churchill prepared to exploit Marshall's weak hand.[25] According to Marshall's biographer, Churchill sensed that the president had given up the fight. Although he still supported Sledgehammer and Roundup, Roosevelt had let it be known weeks before that American forces had to be in action somewhere before the end of the year.[26] The British were certain they faced a divided delegation: "Hopkins is for operating in Africa, Marshall wants to operate in Europe, and King is determined to stick to the Pacific," Brooke wrote even before the party arrived.[27] If the British stood firm against the cross-Channel attack, there was no chance for Marshall to win.

In the event, the British did stand firm, while the unity of their American counterparts crumbled.

Throughout the debates over the launching of Operation Torch (the new code name for Gymnast), Marshall had told anyone who would listen that an Allied attack on North Africa would not only end any chance of conducting Sledgehammer in 1942, but also would make Roundup extremely unlikely for 1943. In a memo to General John Dill, British liaison to the Joint Staff, Marshall wrote that U.S. grand strategy held that only the minimum forces necessary to safeguard the country's vital interest should be diverted from operations against Germany. In Marshall's opinion, the decision for Torch violated that principle. Such a course meant that the Allies had accepted a defensive, encircling line of action for continental Europe except for air operations and blockade. He concluded his note by stating, "The requirements for the effective implementation of TORCH as now envisaged and agreed upon would, in my opinion, definitely preclude offensive operations against Germany."[28]

In a late July JCS meeting, however, both Marshall and Leahy brought King up short when he questioned the feasibility of Roundup in 1943. King claimed that Operation Torch would have the same results as Salonika during the last war, where the diversion of forces to a secondary effort had considerably weakened the main front.[29] Leahy responded, "We should not discount ROUNDUP entirely for 1943 and should prepare for the operation in the event the Germans were considerably weakened in their Russian campaign."[30] From this point forward, however, Marshall was beginning to have doubts about a cross-Channel invasion in 1943.

To sound out the Joint Chiefs as to their ideas for post-Torch strategic initiatives, the president convened a White House meeting on 25 November. Both the Joint Chiefs meeting minutes and Harry Hopkins' notes bear out one notable fact: Marshall never brought up the topic of a 1943 cross-Channel invasion.[31] In truth, his strategic conceptions at this point were definitely not anything that could be called a grand strategy. In fact, at the war's end Marshall admitted that the United States had not had a strategy at the time of the meeting, and did not really settle on one until after the Casablanca Conference.[32] According to the JCS minutes, the president and General Marshall discussed the possibilities for future operations. For a good portion of the meeting, the two men discussed various means of tempting Turkey into the war on the Allies' side, or, failing that, options for action in Turkey. It was not until toward the end of the meeting that the discussion turned to future operations in the Mediterranean. Marshall, rather than being adamant against such a diversion as might be expected based on his past positions, presented only lukewarm opposition. He believed that clearing the Mediterranean for sea traffic would require the occupation of Sicily, Sardinia, and Crete, and that careful consideration should be given to whether or not the large air and ground forces required for such a project could be justified in view of the results to be expected.[33]

By mid-December, however, Marshall had come up with another concept: rather than the massive Roundup he had previously envisioned for 1943, he proposed a smaller invasion of the Brest Peninsula.[34] This idea was considerably narrower in scope than anything Marshall had proposed before, and even as he stated it he understood that its prospects were not great. In fact, he ended up defending the proposal with the claim that the damage a Brest invasion would do to Germany's 1944 defensive prospects justified the possible annihilation of the invading force.[35] It was also a conception that was out of step with what his own Army planners were advocating.

On 11 December the Joint Strategic Survey Committee (JSSC), an organization Marshall set up under Lieutenant General Stanley Embick to plan long-term strategy, produced its first paper. In Embick's formulation, the earliest practicable date to conduct a strategic offensive directly against Germany was still 1943, but only on the assumption that the Allies would stand on the defensive in all other theaters. As a preliminary to this invasion, the JSSC advocated wearing down German strength by an integrated air offensive from bases in the United Kingdom and North Africa "on the largest possible scale." According to the JSSC, the major effort would go into building up forces in the United Kingdom, including transfers from North Africa, to launch a decisive offensive against Germany in 1943.[36]

This recommendation was directly at odds with what Army planners outside the JSSC were advocating. While they had not given up the idea that there must be a decisive campaign in northwestern Europe, they could not see how or when it could be launched. Resuming plans for Roundup in 1943 meant ignoring the fact that a decisive, large-scale cross-Channel operation was infeasible, as a matter of logistics, before mid-1944. Accelerating preparations for an invasion of Europe also meant sacrificing all the psychological and tangible advantages promised by Torch. It also meant disregarding the fact that large ground forces were still required in the Mediterranean to safeguard North Africa and the Middle East. In addition, the heavy losses incurred in 1942's Dieppe raid had made a strong impression on Army planners. Those planners thus accepted once more the indefinite postponement of Roundup.[37] Left out of Matloff's version is that by this time Army planners had received information on the level of cuts they would endure in munitions procurement as a result of the resolution of the feasibility dispute. The planners' change from advocating a 1943 invasion to advocating one in 1944 can be pinpointed almost to the day: the day they were told how severe the cuts would be. According to the "Determination of Army Supply Requirements," Army planners were officially notified on 15 December 1942 that the troop basis for 1943 would have to be cut in "order to bring production in line with new allowances." The new troop basis was not published until 1 February 1943. The fact that large cuts in expected 1943 force structure were on their way, however, was well known and became the basis for future plans.[38] When the JSSC prepared its strategic advice, it had no idea these cuts were on the way. It was also about this time that Marshall came to understand the implications that these cuts had for his own strategic concepts.[39]

The JCS discussed this report in closed session at their meeting of 15 December. Only four copies of the minutes were produced, all of which went to the members of the JSSC; none of them apparently survived the war.[40] During this meeting, Leahy took exception to many of the points in the JSSC study, particularly the idea of directing the entire strategic direction of the war toward Germany. He agreed that Germany was currently the principal concern, but he was not certain that it was the "primary enemy." Nor was he convinced that making the primary effort against Germany was "acceptable strategy."

King, on the other hand, was willing to accept Germany as the primary enemy, but he expressed concern at the offhand manner with which he perceived the chiefs were addressing the Pacific situation. He believed that there should be constant pressure applied against Japan to avoid postponing the end of that conflict indefinitely. He then urged that the chiefs determine a fixed percentage of war effort for the Pacific and suggested that the appropriate proportion would be 25 to 30 percent. When Marshall asked how one would arrive at a percentage of the total war effort, King replied that it was probably not possible to make an exact analysis. However, he believed a reasonable overall estimate would be that only 15 percent of the current war effort was going to the Pacific.[41] In effect, King was slyly putting forth a proposal for doubling the resources sent to the Pacific, a proposal that would surely kill any near-term prospects for a cross-Channel invasion.

Marshall agreed with King that continuous offensive operations in the Pacific were necessary to make progress.[42] Nevertheless, the major thrust of Marshall's remarks concerned the war against Germany. He showed little patience with operations based in North Africa, indicating that he believed landings in Sardinia or Sicily were just what the Germans themselves would recommend. Instead, he thought the Allies should build up strong forces in the British Isles as fast as possible and move against the Brest salient in spring 1943.[43]

In summary, Marshall headed to the Casablanca Conference in early January 1943 with the JCS severely divided as to courses of action for 1943, and with his own Army planners against a 1943 invasion. Most remarkable, there is no indication in the records that Marshall himself, by this time, actually supported an all-out invasion in 1943. His conception focused instead on a smaller lodgment on the isolated Brest Peninsula. Moreover, at the conference itself he barely mentioned even this reduced effort and was more than willing to concede any desires he may still have retained in favor of a 1943 cross-Channel invasion.

Casablanca Conference

According to an unpublished history of the JCS, "The British Chiefs of Staff had not changed their view, expressed in the pre-Casablanca interchanges on the question of a strategic concept, that a landing should be made in northern France in 1943 only in the event that Germany already showed definite signs of collapse. Early in the conference the U.S. *Chiefs resigned themselves to this and concentrated on the problem of which operations in the Mediterranean area would be most desirable*" (emphasis added).[44]

There in a nutshell is the Casablanca Conference. The JCS did not roll over at the behest of the British chiefs and their supposedly better-prepared staffs.[45] They had already decided to acquiesce to the British strategic viewpoint, as far as the Atlantic theater was concerned, before they even sat down for their first combined meetings. It is worth making a quick review of some of the key points of the JCS meeting at Casablanca, held in the days prior to the combined meetings.

As for Marshall's new pet idea—an invasion of Brest—General Mark Clark, Eisenhower's second in command for the successful North African invasion (Operation Torch), threw cold water on the plan almost immediately. According to the minutes of the first JCS meeting in North Africa, General Clark told the assembled chiefs that operations against the Brest Peninsula would be "very hazardous, require overwhelming air support, extensive naval support and immediate heavy follow up."[46]

Even Marshall took the opportunity to throw some ice water on his own plan. He told the other assembled chiefs that General Eisenhower had changed his viewpoint on the practicality of a European invasion as a result of his experiences to date in North Africa. In preconference conversations, Eisenhower had brought Marshall around to the idea that a successful invasion required that Roundup be organized on a much larger scale than previously envisioned. This meant that the invasion force would have to be double the size contemplated in any previous plan. More importantly, given lagging landing craft production, Marshall was disturbed over Eisenhower's belief that it would be unsound to count on more than one trip from the first wave's landing craft because only a very small proportion of them were likely to be available for a second trip.[47]

In fact, during the meeting Marshall only mentioned a cross-Channel attack one time, which was hardly a ringing endorsement of the plan. The following comes from the conference minutes:

> General Marshall said that we wanted to keep the German Army engaged with the Russian Army, and we wanted to make a landing on the Continent. Can we do that in time to support Russia in the summer? Will any other operation destroy our ability to make a Continental landing our main objective? We must insure that it does not. If we do Sicily we might not have the means to do anything on the Continent before October. We must determine what must be done to support Russia this summer. If it is essential that we attack, we must determine where. Everything now building up in the United Kingdom is composed of raw troops, which, however, are better than previous unseasoned troops.[48]

When the Joint Chiefs met with the president, Marshall not only failed to convince Roosevelt that an invasion of Europe was the best next strategic move, he often seemed to be trying to do the opposite by spelling out the difficulties. During meetings with the president, Marshall pointed out that he agreed with Lord Mountbatten and General Clark that there must be a long period of training before any attempt could be made to land against determined resistance. Moreover, Marshall stressed the British point that the rail net in Europe permitted the movement of seven divisions a day from east to west, which would enable the Germans to rapidly reinforce their northern European defenses. Startlingly, Marshall also told Roosevelt that there would be an excess of troops available in North Africa when the Axis powers had been expelled and "this is one of the chief reasons Operation Husky [the invasion of Sicily] appears to be attractive." When the president asked how many American divisions were currently in England, Marshall had to concede there was only one. However, he told the president he was hopeful that there would be six more by the following summer.[49] Finally, Marshall quoted Eisenhower's belief that an invasion of the continent would require a minimum of twelve divisions, which he admitted was double all previous estimates.[50]

Despite the claims of official historians that Marshall went to Casablanca determined to fight one more battle for Roundup in 1943, the evidence suggests no such thing. Even with his own president, Marshall listed the only factors weighing against the invasion without ever examining any benefit that a proposed 1943 cross-Channel invasion would possess. By the time the American chiefs had finished with the president and turned to meet their British counterparts, they were fighting a rearguard action to ensure that Roundup was still on the table for 1944.

Had Marshall strongly backed a cross-Channel invasion for 1943 at Casablanca, as the official historians contended, there were several instances during the meeting where Marshall remained silent when, if he had still been advocating a 1943 invasion, he most definitely would have been on his feet. For instance, at one point Sir Alan Brooke stated that with the limited ground forces available he did not believe that the Allies could muster a sufficient threat to northern France to force the Germans to divert much from the Eastern Front. To this Marshall made no rejoinder. When Brooke continued that the Germans still had sufficient strength to overwhelm us on the ground or perhaps hem us in to such an extent that any expansion of the bridgehead would be impossible, Marshall remained silent. Marshall even let slide by without comment a statement by one of the American chiefs, Hap Arnold, to the effect that based on discussions so far it looked very much as though no continental operations on any scale were in prospect before spring 1944. Arnold even went so far as to include the suspension of any further consideration of the small invasion of Brest without attracting Marshall's ire. Finally, when Admiral King said it was necessary to accept that the Allies could do nothing in France before April 1944, Marshall failed to protest.[51]

What the Allied chiefs did agree on was a firm commitment to land substantial forces on the north coast of France in 1944, and Marshall seemed content with that result. If, as the evidence indicates, Marshall was in agreement with a 1944 cross-Channel invasion date, one still has to explain what turned his mind from his previous fixation on reentering the European continent at the earliest possible date. Earlier in the war Marshall had pushed hard for an invasion in 1942, long before American forces were even remotely capable of such a feat. When that failed, he pushed strongly for a 1943 invasion. But by November 1942 he was at best lukewarm to the idea, and by the end of the year he appears to have given up on a 1943 invasion entirely. Prior to November 1942 Marshall fought tooth-and-nail against anything he perceived as a diversion from that goal to the point of threatening to divert the entire war effort to the Pacific if his plans for a rapid invasion of Europe were not adhered to. In all of this, he had the full support, if somewhat grudgingly given, of the Joint Chiefs.

Sometime between Torch and the Casablanca Conference, however, Marshall abandoned his single-minded crusade for a second front in 1943 and supported a major post-Torch diversion of resources to further Mediterranean operations. In this, too, the remainder of the Joint Chiefs joined him. The Americans were not overawed or overwhelmed by superior British negotiating skills or staff procedures, as historians have often suggested they were. Rather, they had simply changed their minds about the wisdom of a major 1943 invasion, though they do appear to have been more than a bit reticent about announcing their change of heart and thereby admitting that British strategists had been right from the beginning.

But why the change of heart? Part of the answer is that after Torch the American chiefs had sobered up to just how difficult a contested landing in northern France against a determined enemy might be. Eisenhower's doubling of what he considered the minimum number of divisions necessary for a successful invasion had shocked Marshall, as evidenced by his comments on the new requirement for twelve divisions as a minimum several times during the Casablanca Conference and again when meeting separately with the president. Running over second-rate Vichy French divisions had cost the American combat forces involved a surprising number of casualties; how much worse would it be facing the battle-hardened Wehrmacht?

Even more important, though, was that just about the time of Torch, the production agencies had informed the Joint Chiefs that they were not going to provide nearly the amount of munitions the chiefs were expecting to equip the Army's formations. Moreover, Marshall discovered that virtually all these cuts were going to fall on the Army while the Navy and air forces would escape almost unscathed. In fact, the day after Torch, Marshall sent a bitter memo to the president over troop estimates for 1943 in which he informed Roosevelt that this would cause a reduction of fourteen transportable divisions in 1943, and that such a reduction would preclude any chance of a 1943 cross-Chanel invasion.[52] Though this reduction turned out to be a misunderstanding that was eventually straightened out after a flurry of notes between Marshall and Roosevelt, Marshall still would face 1943 with significantly fewer divisions than he had assumed, because the production lines simply could not produce enough equipment.

CHAPTER 10

Why Marshall Changed His Mind

★ ★ ★

Questions remain. Why did Marshall hold onto his hope of a major 1943 invasion, and what caused his rapid position reversal? A presentation given by a staff officer who served on the Joint Staff's logistics planning section gives the short answer to these questions: "The very date of the landing in Normandy was based on studies of the availability of resources."[1] *In essence, when Marshall learned that the force he expected to have on hand in June or July of 1943 would not be available until June of 1944, the decision was made for him. Even a man as determined as Marshall could see that an invasion was impossible if the forces required did not exist.*

The second question is, Why did it take Marshall so long to come to this conclusion? The blame must fall squarely on Somervell's shoulders.[2] Either because he was absolutely convinced the civilian production experts were wrong, or possibly because he, like almost every other Army officer, never wanted to disappoint Marshall, Somervell failed to provide his boss with any indication of looming production problems. Even when shortfalls in 1942 production were becoming obvious, Somervell continued to present Marshall with optimistic reports.

As late as 24 August 1942, Somervell approved an estimate for Army strength that Marshall forwarded to the other Joint Chiefs. It stated, "This plan provides for a ground Army of 111 combat divisions and an air force of

224 combat groups with a total mobilization of 7 and a half million men by December 31, 1943. This is a modest establishment as compared with the actual and potential armies of our enemies. . . . This force represents an increase over the full 1942 Army in the amount of 37 division and 109 air groups."[3] Admiral King opposed this Army estimate because he believed the Army should grow only at the rate the Navy could move it and sustain it overseas.[4] This argument reached Roosevelt's ears, and the president ordered Marshall and King to take "a fresh and realistic look at 1943 over-all requirements from a strategic point of view. This implies that certain assumptions must be made on the estimated requirements for the United States forces of all types in the various probable theaters of war, by number and general composition, are determined."[5]

As a result of this memorandum, Marshall requested that Somervell reexamine the 1943 mobilization plan and report back to him on whether it was feasible. Somervell had his staff undertake this project at the same time Kuznets was delivering his final feasibility report to the Planning Committee. By mid-September, Somervell's analysis was complete; he then confirmed to Marshall that the strength of the Army to be mobilized by the end of 1943 had been "tentatively established" at approximately 7.5 million, adding, "The composition and strength of this force has been primarily dictated by our proposed strategic operational plans, which in turn have been integrated with the all important factors of available shipping and production forecasts of the required munitions."[6]

Somervell made this last statement having already read and replied to Kuznets' feasibility study. He thus was fully aware that the civilian production experts did not believe the Army's 1943 plans were achievable. Disregarding their views, he continued by stating, "The latest production analysis indicates that the objectives of the Army Supply Program for 1943 will be met . . . I feel confident that adequate munitions will be available to meet the full operational requirements for that portion of the total 1943 Army destined for overseas or for the defense of the Continental United States." Somervell concluded by recommending that "*no change be made at this time in the Army Supply Program, which represents the munitions required to sustain the planned operations of the Army of 7,500,000 men by 31 December 1943*" (emphasis added).[7]

So, a full two weeks after Kuznets had informed Somervell that U.S. industry could not meet the 1943 munitions objectives and less than a month before he would have to reverse his position and admit the Planning Committee was right, Somervell was telling Marshall that the Army could have everything planned for in 1943. Even more inexplicably, even after Somervell had conceded the Planning Committee's arguments, he could not bring himself to give the bad news to Marshall.

Instead, he continued to insist that the civilians were wrong and that Marshall could still get what he wanted. In a memorandum to Marshall dated 30 October 1942, Somervell related that Nelson and his statisticians believed this dollar amount was impossible to achieve. Somervell then attacked this position by claiming that because actual production costs to date were less than estimated, the discrepancy between what the Army programmed and what the statisticians said was possible was not that great. He continued by questioning the validity of comparing requirements on a dollar basis and claimed that the real production choke point was a lack of raw materials. For this, Somervell blamed the War Production Board (WPB). Remarkably, he supported his arguments by claiming that Leon Henderson shared his opinion: that U.S. output could be materially increased by better management. He then blamed the WPB's failure to properly allocate materials as the greatest single cause of mismanagement. Somervell finally concluded that the current Army program would be met because he expected, "a marked improvement both in management and in the vigor with which the production of raw materials would be handled."[8]

Here, Somervell had grossly misstated Henderson's position, while at the same time demonstrating either that he still did not understand the statistical concepts that underpinned the feasibility study or that he was willing to take advantage of Marshall's lack of education in this regard to paint a rosy picture of the production program he knew was not true. Which case is true cannot be known, although other documentation in Somervell's papers indicate that he fully understood how all requirements could be translated in dollar values. He even used this method within his own office to explain requirements to logistics officers. Whatever the truth, it was still a remarkable memorandum to send to Marshall while the Joint Chiefs of Staff (JCS) planners were already hard at work reducing munitions requirements. In fact, only ten days later the JCS planners would inform Marshall that they would have to cut his Army supply program by more than 20 percent.

The net result of this reduction of military objectives was that the Army reduced its 111-division goal for 1943 to 100 divisions. Moreover, the Army immediately cancelled the organization of fourteen divisions that Marshall had counted on being available by June 1943.[9] Even this reduction (along with a reduction in the strength of units already organized) was not sufficient to make sure newly organized divisions could be properly equipped. As a result, in January 1943 the Army slowed the activation schedules for many of its planned divisions. For instance, it deferred three divisions planned for activation in May, June, and August 1943 to the last months of 1943.[10]

In summary, without even taking into account shipping constraints or the drain of units sent to the Pacific and other operational theaters, the production experts had forced the Army to cut by more than half the number of troops Marshall thought would be in the United Kingdom by June 1943. This reduction occurred at the same time Marshall was beginning his preparations for Casablanca. Thus, the Army's chief of staff had no choice but to postpone his plans to invade northern Europe in 1943 for at least a year—not because of any change in the strategic situation or in his own ideas of how to win the war, but because the economists had forced him to do so.

APPENDIX 1

The Feasibility Concept

★ ★ ★

As Robert Nathan socialized the idea of feasibility within various policy circles, he asked Simon Kuznets to prepare an in-depth memorandum he could leave with people that further developed the concepts, a memorandum he often presented in outline form in conversation. Since these concepts were the underlying basis for the "great feasibility dispute of 1942" it is profitable to outline them as understood by the disputes' participants. Below is a digest version of Kuznets' memorandum to Nathan on feasibility.[1]

1. The Concept of Feasibility

The feasibility of a set of production goals is far from an unequivocal concept. It is important to distinguish the different variants and raise the question as to which concept of feasibility we wish to be guided by.

Three variants may be employed:

A. We may ask what production goals are feasible under conditions as they exist now or are definitely and securely in view. This, for our purposes, is the concept of minimum feasibility since it measures potential output without taking into account the intensification of the war production effort that may be expected. If applied, it would tell us what military or other production can be expected under a set-up identical with the present and including changes only insofar as they have already been enacted.

B. We may ask what production goals are feasible with an all-out effort, the latter developing not in an ideal situation but with human inertia, frailties, ignorance, selfish interests, etc., exercising a retarding effect. This concept of realistic maximum feasibility would yield an approximation to output to be produced under conditions in which an increasingly all-out effort encounters various resistances that might be expected.

C. Finally, we may ask what production goals are feasible under ideal conditions—i.e., under conditions in which every member of the community devotes himself whole-heartedly to the war effort in complete disregard of private interests, and in which such devotion is most intelligently and effectively applied.

2. Why Worry about Feasibility

The basic reason why feasibility is considered is that *an attempt to attain goals that are unattainable is likely to result in a situation which, for practical purposes, is worse than trying to attain more moderate but feasible goals. An attempt to secure unattainable goals is likely to result in an unbalanced performance in the sense that facilities will be built for which there will not be enough raw materials; that semi-finished products will be produced which it will be impossible to finish; and that finished products will be produced for which indispensable complements will be lacking* [emphasis in original]. If this criterion of balance were the only consideration, the best thing to do would be to set minimum goals. But, on the other hand, goals set will determine the magnitude of the productive effort eventually attained. Setting the goals low may, therefore, assure a fully balanced performance in that all equipment and inter-related final products will be turned out at a rate permitting their full use. But, the balance will be secured at a level of production far short of one that could be attained. *The real problem in determining feasibility is therefore to set your goals as high as possible, compatible with the attainment of a balance that is needed to assure usability of equipment and final products* [emphasis in original].

This reasoning can now be applied to a choice among the three concepts of feasibility defined above. If the criterion of balance is paramount it will be safest to apply the minimum concept of feasibility. But it obviously involves the sacrifice of possibly a substantial part of the production effort. The real choice is, therefore, one between the realistic maximum and the ideal maximum criteria of feasibility.

The advantage of using the former is that is permits the setting of goals with fair expectation of balance in the results. Even this inference must be qualified since uncertainties attach to the forecast of what an all-out effort can attain in the face of various obstacles. Both the effort and the obstacles are intangibles; and fluctuations in the fortunes of war and various other unforecastable elements may introduce a sizeable error in the total estimated to be feasible. On the other hand, this concept of feasibility lacks the advantages of the ideal maximum in that it may not set the goals high enough. In particular, it omits the possible influence on the realized productive effort of the incentives provided by maximum goals.

This important point can be made more specific. Let us assume that a realistic consideration of what an all-out effort in the production in munitions can attain in the face of the usual type of difficulties involves the consumption of X million tons of copper. With X million tons needed for military production, T million tons may be left for non-military consumption. The goal thus set does not recognize the possible influence on the demand for or allocation of raw material or the setting of a higher goal for military production. If a higher goal were set, let us say one that would require X plus A million tons for military production, and a shortage developed, the pressure of that demand might make it possible.

A. To divert to military production not the full amount of X plus A, but perhaps X plus one-half of A
B. To force a revision of specifications by which a larger total of finished military equipment would be turned out with A million tons of copper.

In the realistic situation in which the diversion of economic activities to war production occurs, the setting of higher goals for military production is an important factor in accelerating diversion toward the war effort; and the setting of low goals may quite effectively retard our war effort. It may be argued that the slowness with which the various restrictive mechanisms have been applied to civilian consumption in this and other countries and the delay that has occurred in the conversion of a number of industries that are potentially important for military production have been due largely to delay in formulating high enough goals for military objectives.

We face then the question as to how to retain the advantages of high levels of objectives as an important stimulus towards a greater war effort; and remove the disadvantages likely to arise if the high goals set are not realized and a lack of balance in the results appear.

3. Goals and Balances

The answer to this question lies in a better definition of what production goals really should be. The formulation of what it is that agencies concerned with the war effort are trying to achieve is the paramount task, and one that has to be carried through before any planning can be undertaken.

Production goals are statements of what final products are needed, when they are needed, and where they are needed. The what, when, and where cannot be disassociated from each other. But, if we can fix the when and where, the question of what can be answered in several ways, ways directly determined by the problem of feasibility and balance.

I see no reason why the authorities concerned with formulating the needs for military production should not be asked to formulate them with specific time objectives (and specific place objectives in cases where transportation may be an important problem). Further, there is no reason in the world why quantities needed at specified dates and places should not be determined for a minimum program, an intermediate program and a maximum program. The problem of balance is one that can best be solved by this differentiation among goals at various levels.

This suggestion may seem to run into two difficulties. The first is that the existence of several sets of goals, of which some are materially lower than others, may have a depressing effect upon the war effort in that people might be too easily satisfied by the attainment of minimum goals. In other words, the incentive towards a maximum effort might be lost if any set of goals short of the maximum is at all formulated. This, however, seems to be an organizational problem which should not be too difficult to solve.

There is no reason why the various bases for action, such as appropriations from Congress, plans and schedules for production, etc., should not be worked out for the maximum goals. There is no reason why the restrictive mechanisms intended to shut off non-military production should not be brought into operation in order to attain maximum goals. In short, there is no reason why the whole effort should not be organized in such a way as to permit the attainment of maximum goals if they are at all attainable. Only one difference should be permitted as compared with the situation that would prevail were we to have a single set of maximum goals; the scheduling of the productive effort should be such that if the maximum goals proved unattainable, the composition of the output of military items during any significant period of time would still be balanced.

The possibility of this happy result is denied by a second objection that might be made to the suggestion of distinguishing sets of goals. It will be claimed that the suggestion does not solve the problem since for a number of items in the military production program planning has to be done far in advance; unless commitment for the higher goals is made at the very beginning, the possibility of attaining them may have to be given up from the start.

It will be argued, for example, that if the maximum goals call for the production of X thousand heavy bombers, whereas the minimum goals call for the production of X minus A heavy bombers, unless facilities are planned in advance for the production of the differential amount of A bombers, you are not likely to get them. On the other hand, if you do commit yourself to this high goal in the way of new facilities, you run the danger of imbalance associated with setting goals that are impossible of attainment.

An answer to this problem lies in a more careful consideration of the goals. All goals, whether minimum, intermediate, or high, should presumably be attained as quickly as possible. But the minimum goals should be the more pressing ones; further extension beyond these minima should comprise components in military production the need for which is less pressing. If this is the case, then the problem of planning of facilities or of complements may be at least partly solved by saying that:

A. All efforts are to be directed to the most prompt realization of minimum goals.
B. Such efforts imply maximum utilization of all resources not yet engaged upon the satisfaction of minimum goals.
C. All commitments to new facilities can be accepted only if they are needed for or do not interfere with the satisfaction of minimum goals. A similar set of criteria can then be applied to the planning of such net additions to minimum goals as would convert these into intermediate goals; and, similarly, with the still further additions that would convert

> intermediate into maximum goals. Thus the whole question can be resolved in terms of planning specific as to amounts, types, dates, and places; and formulated in terms of basic preferences or priorities.

This will place a difficult task upon the agencies concerned with formulating military production goals and requirements. And it may be granted that no exact formulation of this type, without a substantial margin of error, is feasible. Yet, I don't see how we can plan without having such blueprints at hand; and it seems extremely important to urge the need for such blueprints and the utmost value of efforts directed towards securing them.

4. Work on Feasibility

In the past the analysis of feasibility developed in the Statistics Division was concerned with raising our sights—i.e., with demonstrating the possibility of much higher goals of military production. These resulting estimates had the advantage of being both fairly reasonable approximations of what could be done towards intensification of the war effort. It may seem rather fanciful, but all estimates concerning objectives have that tendency; within certain limits they exercise an effect that tends to make them come true.

Recently, the analysis of feasibility has been employed to suggest a need for limiting military objectives rather than extending them. And if the results of the analysis are taken seriously, they will eventually result in the restriction of the military program and hence of military production. The danger is that they may be restricted to levels below ones that might have been attained were the original goals left at a high level. Granted that the problem of balance is exceedingly important, there are several basic difficulties in our analysis of feasibility that would lead me to urge that a call for reduction of a single set of goals be immediately replaced by a call for several sets of goals of the type indicated in the preceding section.

Our feasibility analysis rests upon four types of approaches:

A. The over-all analysis in terms of national income or gross national product and its apportionment
B. The raw materials
C. The industrial facilities
D. The labor supply.

All of these approaches are couched in rough and general terms. This means that our feasibility tests may not be critical enough insofar as they do not deal with the problem of specific shapes, forms, skills, types, sizes, etc. On the other hand, other defects might yield too pessimistic a picture. Of these, the basic defect is that our analysis is almost always couched in terms of conditions as of a given date and place, and therefore does not allow enough for the possible adjustment and dynamics of the situation under conditions of an all-out effort. *In our over-all approach, we guide ourselves largely by either: the expected size of the national product and the maximum share of it that could be devoted to military production, or the current rates of total outlay of military production and the realistic expectations of their possible rise* [emphasis in original].

Either way of attacking the problem yields results subject to wide margins of error. In the first approach the all-important problem of unit costs enters, with the margin of error in it alone as high as 10 to 20 percent. If one adds the uncertainty in the forecast of the total national product (which may be in error on the negative as well as on the positive side) one does not feel too sure about conclusions that may be derived on this basis. Similarly, the extrapolation of monthly out-lays or volumes of output is based largely upon hunches. True, the analysis by both of these approaches may prove quite accurate as a forecast of the volume of output that could be attained. There is considerable inertia in the movement of the national product and in its distribution among various components so that one can gauge with some degree of reliability the range of its change over the near future.

The translation into raw materials raises a number of questions that crucially affect the results. The specifications used are not firm, our bills of materials may be in error, our estimates of civilian requirements are exceedingly vague, our measures of supply pay inadequate attention to existing inventories. On all of these counts shortages today may disappear tomorrow, because of change in the specifications, because actual consumption of raw materials in military production may turn out to be much lower than estimated, because the civilian requirements are cut under pressure.

Here again our analysis is of considerable value in suggesting the existence of a problem. Yet, it would be dangerous to use its results as an unequivocal measure of the existence of an insoluble problem; and we have tended to use them in this way in asking for a review of military requirements.

The analysis in terms of industrial facilities yields even less firm results. Estimated requirements for industrial facilities do not take sufficient account of conversion possibilities; of the inadequate spread of work among firms; of the possibility of raising rates of utilization of already available equipment.

Except for specific bottlenecks, the industrial facility problem cannot by the nature of the case be crucial. We have a large stock of industrial facilities which, on short hours, has turned out a huge national product. Presumably an increase in the intensity of utilization by raising the number of shifts, etc., can serve to raise enormously the productive performance of our complex of industrial facilities. True, there are some special cases, particularly those where facilities have always been operating around the clock, in which we may encounter serious bottlenecks that cannot be easily broken because of shortage of time. But certainly our analysis of the industrial facilities has never reached the point of demonstrating a case beyond doubt for the restriction of a set of final military objectives such as the one given for 1942 or for 1943.

The analysis of labor supply has always been in fairly rough terms. It has been based too much upon a general ratio between the additional dollar value of military production and increase in employment required. It also seems to me that the estimates of maximum labor force available were firm only in terms of the institutional framework of today.

In sum: our feasibility analysis has not been without value. It served to point out the problems that were likely to be created if the programs and objectives were pursued under the present conditions of social organization, specification, labor organization, etc. But, while it served to indicate the existence of problems under the conditions, and thus to direct attention to the solution of these problems, it would be dangerous to use its results as proof of absolute impossibility. So long as the lack of feasibility demonstrated was relative rather than absolute, its results should not be used to force downward revisions of military objectives.

But they can be used directly as a basis for asking the authorities responsible for military requirements to formulate them in programs of different magnitude. In this formulation the maximum would be the largest amount that seems to be needed, compatible with military utilization possibilities. Quite obviously this maximum is not going to be infinitely large. The limitations of supply of human skill for the use of instruments of warfare will impose definite limitations upon what the armed services can call for in such a maximum. We should be careful not to add to these limitations other restraining factors that might have a depressing influence on the war effort.

5. Positive Steps

If the arguments above are at all valid, both the Statistics Division and the Planning Committee ought to consider immediately what type of military requirements are needed for the better organization of the war effort. Obviously these requirements should be specific with reference to type, amount, place, and time; and should distinguish especially those minimum goals that comprise the most pressing and the most indispensable items; from extensions that are of the lesser order of priority and still further extensions that might bring the program to its maximum. Clearly, requirements formulated are needed from one and every branch of the armed services, as well as from such other agencies as Lend-Lease and the Maritime Commission. The objectives or requirements should be stated not only in terms of physical units but in dollar values, with the dollar values based upon a recognizable basis of reckoning. Furthermore, these sets of requirements will be changing. Indeed! with the fluctuating fortunes of war, it would be suicidal to demand a rigidly fixed set of objectives. But given the changes (which should be kept within narrow limits), it should be the responsibility of the armed services to supply data not only on the changed requirements but also on the present commitments and schedules, so that at any given time a comparison of appropriations, requirements, commitments, and schedules can be made.

If the various sets of requirements are to be formulated and the feasibility of extensions and the needs for complementary parts and balances reviewed, we need a mechanism by which a continuous integration of results submitted by the various branches of the armed services could be attained with the information and planning for the national economy that are the responsibility of the WPB. It seems to be extremely wasteful for the armed services to prepare plans and formulate requirements without apparently much relevance to feasibility; and then for the WPB to come back with feasibility analysis that may make for further revisions of the military requirements program. What is needed is continuously inter-related planning on the part of both the armed services and related agencies on the one hand, and WPB, on the other.

What is needed is a continuously operating Resources and Requirements Planning Committee. Whether or not it can be established, I sincerely think that we should take the initiative in asking for formulation of production goals (or requirements) of a character quite different from the ones we have been getting; and that the task of planning for balance at different levels of total magnitude of attainment be imposed upon the agencies that are responsible for formulating the requirements.

APPENDIX 2

The First Feasibility Study (14 March 1942)[1]

★ ★ ★

PLANNING COMMITTEE DOCUMENT 31

March 14, 1942

Simon Kuznets

Feasibility of Military Production 1942–1943

Section I. Gross National Product and Military Production

National income for 1941 was estimated by the Department of Commerce at 94 1/2 billion dollars. This total, however, does not describe adequately the fund upon which we can draw for real resources for military production. It is too large in that it includes profits from revaluation of inventories to the tune of $3 billion; and excludes consumption of durable capital sustained in the process of production, which can be estimated (excluding depreciation of owner-occupied residences) at $8 1/2 billion. With further adjustments for special emergency and contingency reserves and bad debt allowances ($1 1/2 billion), gross national product for 1941 can be estimated at $101 1/2 billion, exclusive of net additions to governmental inventory of assets which may well amount to several billion.

Similar measures of gross national product for 1939 and 1940 are $80 and $86 1/2 billion respectively. In 1941 prices the rough totals of gross national product for the three years are then as follows:

Calendar Years	1939	1940	1941
Gross National Product in 1941 $ billions	86.0	92.1	101.5
Percentage Increase from Year to Year*		7.1	10.2

* The increase would be substantially greater if we included additions to governmental assets.

What increase, if any, may be expected in gross national products as between 1941 and 1942? The answer can only be guessed at. I believe that we shall not be over pessimistic if we assume that the rise in gross national product from 1941 to 1942 will equal the percentage rise from 1940 to 1941. True, there will be a substantial rise in government outlay on military production and a drive to expand the volume of the latter. But, on the other hand, there are restrictive factors that did not operate in 1941: (a) Shortages of critical materials; (b) time and efficiency loss in conversion from peace time to war uses of large blocks of industrial facilities; (c) Shortage of skilled labor and dilution of skill.

If then we allow: (1) an addition to gross national product of 1941 of about $5 billion representing net additions to such government assets as structures, military equipment, lend-lease, stockpile, etc. (additions in excess of deficits); (2) an increase from 1941 to 1942 of between 10 to 15 percent—we obtain an estimate for 1942 of gross national product ranging from $116.7 to $122.5 billion (as compared with $106.5 in 1941). Let us accept a rough figure of $120 (in 1941 prices) in further discussion.

How much of the gross national product can take the form of military production (of hard items) and construction? The answer depends upon the resources available for such production; and these can be surmised by studying the composition of the gross national product in 1941. According to the estimates of the Department of Commerce, the gross value of durable consumers goods in 1942 amounted to $11.2 billion, of producers' durable commodities to $14.0 billion. However, these values include distributive costs. The proportion of the distributive costs in consumers' durable amounted to 40 percent of the final value product and in producers' goods to 15 percent. For construction, the adjustment for distributive costs is not made since construction values in the military program are likely to include distribution charges of dealers in construction materials. Excluding distributive costs, the total output in 1941 of durable commodities and construction amounted, therefore, to $29 billion. This total excludes, however, the value product of Government arsenals and shipyards for which I have no estimates at present.

The more inclusive total, which should probably be in the neighborhood of $30 billion, measures the production in the economic system of the type of goods that are ordinarily included under munitions and military construction (possibly excepting certain types of semi-durable goods included in such tables of military requirements as exclude pay, subsistence and agricultural foreign exports). How much of hard military production the productive resources that turned out these $30 billion in 1941 can produce in 1942 is a moot question. Even if we could assume that these resources would be transferred completely to military production and construction, there would still be a question of their yield in war use as over and against yield in peace uses. The complex of raw materials, machinery and labor used to produce a truck, a locomotive or a typewriter may, when employed (with some adjustments) to turn out a tank or torpedo parts, yield a higher or lower gross value of finished product. The raw materials may be used more or less economically; the machinery may find, upon conversion more or less productive use; labor may be applied more or less efficiently. These changes in productivity are not clearly taken into account in the usual assumption of constant price level; the changes are not in prices of identical goods, but in the technical conditions of production that make labor, machinery and sometimes even raw materials not quite comparable as between civilian use and use for war production. And while the possible differences in the yield of complexes of productive factors as between peace and war uses tend to be kept within limits (under assumption of constant prices) by the continuity and identity of these factors in the process of transition, there may be sizeable differences nevertheless.

Until our study of the unit costs of military products has gone much further than it did so far, we shall not be in a position to deal with the problems even by rough approximation. I shall proceed, therefore, on the assumption that $1 billion worth of peacetime goods turned out by these resources in 1941 may be expected to be replaced by $1 billion worth of military goods in 1942. This assumption may underestimate the possibility of military production measured in dollar values, perhaps by as much as 10 or 20 percent; but also overestimate the possibilities of full conversion.

If we assume that durable goods and construction will form the same proportion of the gross national product in 1942 as they have in 1941, i.e., about 30 percent, the possible output of such durable goods and construction in 1942 becomes roughly $36 billion (in 1941 prices.) This assumption is, however, on the low side, since the pressure for increase will be channelled primarily into augmenting the production of hard items. It is, perhaps, more reasonable to assume that if the total gross national product increases (amounting to $13.5 billion) the major part, say $10 billion will be additions to output of durable goods and construction. On this, more reasonable assumption, the gross value (excluding distributive costs) of durable goods and construction may amount in 1942 to $40 billion (in 1941 prices).

But of this total we must allow some part for peace time durable commodities and construction (consumers' durable, producers' durable and civilian construction). The minimum allowance that can be made here is for $5 billion of civilian goods (1/3 of consumers' durable in 1941, 1/4 of producers' equipment, 1/3 of private construction). This would leave a residue for the production of hard military items of some $35 billion in 1942. The range of error in this estimate is such that the true value may well lie anywhere between $30 and $40 billion (in 1941 prices).

The estimate above refers to hard military production exclusively. It makes no allowances for pay and subsistence; for the non-munitions parts of military requirements; in short, for any items in the war expenditures that represent goods classifiable as perishable or semi-durable commodities. How large these excluded items may be, I have no basis for stating now. But if we assume them to be roughly about $10 billion in 1942 (excluding pay which is a transfer item rather than a draft upon real resources) the feasible expenditures lie somewhere between 40 and 50 billion dollars in 1941 prices. This addition to hard production can safely be made because demand for military items of perishable or semi-durable type can be well satisfied with the productive resources of the country.

A total war outlay of $40 to $50 billion would amount to a diversion from the gross national product of 34 to 42 percent. The experience of other countries would seem to suggest that this percentage is fairly close to the ratios obtained in countries that have had a longer history in war production. Armament expenditures in Great Britain and Germany in 1941 amounted to about 45 percent of the gross national product; they were at about 35 percent in Canada while the ratio in Japan was not much over 30 percent. However, these figures should be checked further to see whether or not the ratios are comparable. (They are not insofar as they include pay.)

The situation for 1943 can be foreseen only with great difficulties, since it depends in large part on the developments in 1942 which, in turn, are subject to uncertainty. If in 1942 we do add to our industrial facilities to the sum of $7 billion; if our conversion experience shows that a considerable part of the presently existing equipment can be used for war purposes it may well prove that the increase in the gross national production in 1943 over 1942 equal the percentage increase from 1940 to 1941 (used above to apply to the change from 1941 to 1942.) On this rather rough assumption, gross national product for 1943 would amount to about $135 billion in 1941 prices.

If we again allow for an increase from 1942 to 1943 in output of durable commodities and construction equal to most of the increase in gross national product (say $12 billion out of the $15); and a minimum of $5 billion for civilian durable goods and construction—the possible hard military production in 1943 would amount to $47 billion. The range of error again is such that the true value may be between $42 and $52 billion. Adding to it $15 billion for subsistence and soft items, we obtain a range of war outlays in 1943 of $57 to $67 billion (in 1941 prices). This total would amount to between 43 and 50 percent of the gross national product.

My own impression is that these estimates are on the optimistic side, unless the unit cost consideration should be given more weight than I am ready to give it now. The present rate of total war outlay, including both hard and soft items, is somewhat over $2.5 billion per month. To attain a total outlay in 1942 of between $40 and $50 billion, the rate of monthly outlay by the end of the year should amount to between $5 and $6 billion. If such a rate is possible and could be maintained in 1943, we would presumably have a total outlay in 1943 of between $60 and $70 billion. But if we assume the outside limit of total war outlay in 1943 to be say $60 billion, it is unreasonable to expect that this rate will be reached as early as December 1942. As a matter of fact, it may well be that the curve of war outlay will be rising more steeply after the first half of 1942 than during the first 6 months. This means that our estimates for 1942, if not for 1943, are likely to be on the high side.

Section II. The Raw Materials Situation

Estimates of the raw material contents of the new set of military requirements were prepared by B. Fox. The military requirements used are described as follows:

1. Aircraft based on the 8-I program adjusted upwards by 25 percent approximately at the level of the President's objectives.
2. Army other than aircraft—G-4 objectives as of February 11, 1942.
3. Navy estimates are the more recent ones to run through June, 1943 and extended through the rest of the calendar of 1943.
4. Maritime Commission Requirements based upon 8,000,000 tons in '42 and 10,000,000 in 1943.
5. Army-Navy construction with materials included only where construction requirements are large.

No allowance is made in the tables that I am discussing here for: (a) materials in industrial facilities; (b) essential civilian and indirect military requirements. These are to be supplied by Fox today and will be enclosed with his memo.

On the basis of this incomplete picture of essential needs, the situation for 1942 is as follows: A definite shortage is expected in rubber, nickel, TNT and smokeless powder and military requirements are so close to total new supply as to suggest critical shortages in aluminum, vanadium, wool and toluol. Also, the copper situation is likely to be very tight even in 1942.

As for 1943, the war munitions program as presently designed seems to be impossible from the standpoint of raw material supply. The demand for copper alone runs over 3,000,000 tons, whereas the supply is only 2.2 million tons. Significant shortages appear also in zinc, nickel, rubber, wool, toluol, ammonium, nitrate, and smokeless powder. Even for such basic metals as steel and aluminum, in which the new supply for 1943 is still in excess of the military requirements, the demand on the part of essential civilian uses and indirect military is likely to produce an acute shortage.

Two comments are in order about the raw materials picture. First, the comparison is in terms of raw materials before any fabrication and it is quite possible that a lack or shortage of raw material taken in ingot form may still not solve the situation, insofar as facilities for various semi-fabricated shapes and products may prove insufficient to supply the demand. Second, the fact that shortages are so striking in 1943 is of bearing not only upon the 1943 program but also upon that for 1942. I assume that there is some relation between the requirements worked out for 1942 and for 1943. This should certainly be true of the needs for industrial facilities and military construction in 1942 since they are presumably designed to facilitate production in 1943; and it should be true of other items in the requirements program insofar as there should be correlation among the various parts, both at a given moment of time and over time. If this be true, the impossibility of carrying through the program set for 1943 should lead to a careful reconsideration of the requirements also for 1942.

Section III. The Problem of Industrial Facilities

The translation of military requirements into industrial facilities is much more difficult than the translation either into the raw materials or into needs for labor. One cannot add machine hours as easily as one can add the raw material contents or the labor hours needed to produce the variety of items that enter our military requirements. Even if one had for each military item the machine hours needed on various types of machines we would still face a difficult problem of how these hours are to be added and the total number of machine facilities derived. But, as a matter of fact, we don't have information on machine hours needed in the production of any but a few military items. One must, therefore, recur to other methods. Before summarizing the results of two experiments I would like to present a few general considerations.

The question: how much military production in addition to essential civilian and direct military, can be turned out with the industrial facilities now available, has two distinct aspects: The first, we may designate the aspect of specific use. Many of our industrial facilities are special purpose instruments and the attempt to increase the proportion of total output devoted to military items may run up against the difficulty that with the large body of industrial machinery in place there may be a shortage of special purpose instruments needed for military production. If this were not the case, if the specific use aspect of the industrial facilities problem could be completely neglected, then its second aspect would provide a basis for optimism. If one could disregard this problem of specific use, if one could proceed on the assumption that industrial facilities can be shifted freely from one use to another, the situation would be very simple indeed. We could then say that, as far as the facilities side of the picture is concerned, there should be no difficulty in attaining huge magnitudes of military production. In peace time, industrial facilities which, with but a few exceptions, were working on a short schedule of hours, produced as much as $30 to $40 billion of durable goods. If we wanted to operate each machine, or each item of industrial machinery or each press, etc. etc., the full number of hours a week that it can be operated consistent with keeping the machine intact and in good condition, the output possible under such conditions could obviously be two or three times as great as the output turned out under normal conditions of peace time. With the problem thus formulated the bottleneck would be in the imported raw materials or in labor, essentially in labor. For, given the huge facilities and domestic availability of raw materials, we could solve the problem of domestic raw materials, the bottleneck would be labor.

But the difficulty, of course, is that the specific use aspect of the problem of industrial facilities cannot be neglected; or rather could be neglected if we had more time at our disposal.

But time being costly, the limits of military production are set by the availability of special purpose machinery needed. The resulting question of feasibility has been explored in two studies, both relating to machine tools narrowly defined, i.e., excluding presses, bending machines and other types of metal working machinery.

The first study was prepared by Norman J. Meiklejohn and gauges the need for new tools, both domestic and foreign. The domestic part of the story is based upon ANMB estimates of requirements, which in turn assemble the needs for new machine tools as presented by the various branches of the armed services, including the Maritime Commission. With few exceptions these estimates are based upon military requirements lower than the most recent set of such requirements evaluated in Homer Jones' tables. For example, for the Navy Bureau of Ships they are based on the funds available for facilities for 1942. For the various ordnance types, either Navy or Army, they are based on the War Munitions Program, in some cases adjusted to production possibility. The tank and combat vehicles division estimate is based on 45,000 tanks in 1942. With a single exception of the Maritime Commission, whose machine tool requirements are very minor, the estimates are based on a program of military requirements substantially lower than that envisioned in our most recent set-up for 1942. Foreign demand is also a minimum, being based upon allotments rather than upon requirements. Of the $1.7 billion of total need, $1.55 billion are domestic and 0.54 billion are for export.

The estimates that I am quoting are, therefore, minimum and will be revised sharply upwards in a new set to be transmitted to the Army-Navy Munitions Board by April 1, 1942. As they stand at present, the total requirements for the machine tools for the 11 months of 1942 (from February 15 to

December 31) amount to 256 thousands units and $1.7 billion. On the basis of the units and the rates of production during December 1941 and January 1942 it would take 13 months to turn out these tools. But on the basis of value, the picture is much blacker. It would take about 20 months to supply these requirements at the rates of shipments in December and January. Granted that the value of the machine tool needs is exaggerated by being based upon a somewhat higher price level than is implicit in the shipments value. Yet, a substantial part of the difference in unit cost is due to the fact that the units in the requirements are more heavily weighted by complex types of tools than are the current shipments. If so, the time needed to satisfy these needs on the basis of current shipments would lie somewhere between 13 and 20 months; and even allowing a marked growth in output of machine tools there will be a close race between the minimum requirements and the feasible production of new tools in 1942. If one takes into account that no allowance is made for essential civilian and indirect military demands, it seems obvious that even on the basis of the present requirements, new tools could not be produced to an extent sufficient to satisfy these requirements. When they are revised on the basis of an increased military program, the needs for new machine tools will significantly exceed production possibilities.

Of course, one may say that some of these needs can be satisfied out of the stock of used tools, either in the hands of dealers or in the hands of such firms as are not employing them in the production of critical items. But I doubt that this source is of much importance unless our conversion process and especially the process of spreading military production over a wider area of our productive system is greatly accelerated. These tools are needed because for the special needs of military production there are not enough specific tools available. It is hardly likely that they would be present in great quantities either in the hands of used dealers or in the hands of industries ordinarily engaged in peace time output. Only a very intensive attempt to "explode" the military products into parts that could be fitted into ordinary peace time facilities would contribute significantly to the alleviation of a shortage of new machine tools.

One might also add that the comparison of requirements and current shipment rates for specific types of tools (on the basis of units) reveals in quite a number of them a shortage so great that, at shipment rates during the past two months, it would take over 2 years to provide the units required in 1942. Of the 62 types of tools, there are 21 for which the number of months necessary to produce needed amounts at the December–January rate of shipments adds up to more than 24.

Another approach to the industrial facilities problem is through the analysis of the commitments already made or likely to be made with the appropriated funds, an analysis prepared at my request by Matthew Rose. The following facts emerge: the total program for war industrial facilities as of February 28, including both projects under commitment and the program for which funds are available (but for which contracts have not yet been awarded) amounted to $18.7 billion, including provision for privately financed industrial facilities under certificates for necessity, at the rate of $150 million per month through June 1942. The Federal funds part amounts to $15.6 billion, of which $0.6 were completed by end of 1941. Completed projects under British funds amounted to $0.2 billion. And total private—was estimated at $2.9 billion, with $1.0 billion completed by end of 1913.

There was accordingly, a total of facilities still under way or yet to be committed of some $16.9 billion as of the beginning of 1942. Knowing the ratio of the value of machine tools to total value of facilities; the expected completion dates; the rates of completion by class of facility, Rose could estimate deliveries of machine tools (in dollars) required during 1942 for equipment. This needed total came out to be $1.28 billion. If we assume that monthly deliveries of new tools in this country rise from $85 million in January 1942 (their recorded level, exclusive of presses etc.) to $169 million in December 1942 (the rise more or less along a straight line), total deliveries in 1942 would amount to $1.52 billion. But of this almost a quarter should go to satisfy foreign requirements (about $380 million); which leaves a domestic new supply of only $1.14 billion, or slightly short of the new tool needs for facilities that are expected to be completed during 1942. The disturbing aspect of these calculations is that the deficit, which could be roughly estimated by months, is concentrated heavily in the early part of the year; that a doubling of the monthly rate of machine tool shipments during 1942 may be rather too much to expect from the machine tool industry; and that the estimates take no account of needs for new tools that may arise on the part of plants engaged in military production that do not apply for certificates of necessities, nor finance their extension by government funds. The needs of such plants for replacement are just as important perhaps as the need to equip the new facilities.

Section IV. The Labor Supply

The discussion above has already suggested that next to foreign raw materials that cannot be easily replaced, the supply of labor is the most fundamental factor in evaluating the feasibility of a huge production program. Given an unlimited supply of labor and the existence within a country of all essential raw materials, it should be possible within a comparatively brief period of time to produce the necessary end products, even if it requires a preliminary period of construction of new facilities or of production of new equipment. It is for this reason, I believe, that in the countries that have been engaged in a prolonged war effort it is the shortage of crucial raw materials not available within the country and even more the shortage of labor that become the primary obstacle to arise in the pace of war and total output.

The evaluation of the military requirements program in terms of labor supply is, therefore, most important. And the results of such rough evaluation as were presented by Hinrichs appear to suggest that an outlay of $60 billion on military production and construction in 1942 is out of the realm of feasibility. This total would require by the end of 1942, a quarterly rate of expenditure of some $25 to $26 billion; and would call for employment in war production work of some 33 million workers. If one adds to it armed forces of somewhat over 5 million men, the total number engaged in the war effort would amount to 38 million. On the other hand, the minimum needed for civilian production and agriculture is 32 million (with about 40 million so employed at present). The required total working force by the end of 1942 (including the men in the armed forces) would amount then to 70 million. According to Hinrichs, we can count on a maximum labor force of only 60 million. The 1942 program is, therefore, beyond the bounds of the possible labor supply.

According to Hinrichs, the program for 1943 is even more impossible, in terms of the labor supply involved. It would call for an employment of 37 million workers in war production alone; and with the addition of 8 to 9 million men in the armed forces, would call for the absorption of 45 to 46 million men in the war effort. If we add to it the minimum employment needed for civilian production and agriculture (of 32 million), and the necessary cushion for float unemployment, (of some 2 to 3 million), the total requirement is for a labor force of over 80 million men and women. According to Hinrichs, it is unreasonable to expect such an enormous working force. On the other hand, to quote his letter: "The Victory Program would require $16 billion expenditures in the last quarter of 1943. This will require 20 million workers on defense production. We can create an adequate labor force to carry this burden. It is about the job that we did in mobilizing the labor force in 1918." On this calculation, (i.e. the old Victory program) the demands in the last quarter of 1943 would be for: 20 million in war production, 9 million in the armed forces, 32 million on civilian and agriculture, unemployed float of 2 million—a total of 61 million. At present there are about 51 million people employed in all types of work or in the armed forces.

I would like to have the opportunity to study more closely Hinrichs' figures, and especially test them against the experience of other countries with a longer history of the war effort. But at the present juncture, I can only give you the gist of Hinrichs' conclusions. In terms of 1942, the maximum that his figures suggest would be somewhat over $45 billion; assuming a rate of $16 billion in the end of 1941 (and one of $8 billion in the first quarter of 1942), we would obtain an annual total (along a straight line) of some $148 billion in 1942. On the same basis, a maximum of $64 billion would be expected in 1943. All values here are of course, in 1941 prices.

APPENDIX 3

Wedemeyer's Victory Program[1]

★ ★ ★

Ultimate Requirements Study Estimate of Army Ground Forces

The specific operations necessary to accomplish the defeat of the Axis Powers cannot be predicted at this time. Irrespective of the nature and scope of these operations, we must prepare to fight Germany by actually coming to grips with and defeating her ground forces and definitely breaking her will to combat. Such requirement establishes the necessity for powerful ground elements, flexibly organized into task forces which are equipped and trained to do their respective jobs. The Germans and their associates with between 11 and 12 million men under arms, now have approximately 300 divisions fully equipped and splendidly trained. It is estimated that they can have by 1943 a total of 400 divisions available in the European Theatre.

The important influence of the air Army in modern combat has been irrefutably established. The degree of success attained by sea and ground forces will be determined by the effective and timely employment of air supporting units and the successful conduct of strategical missions. No major military operation in any theatre will succeed without air superiority, or at least air superiority disputed. The necessity for a strong sea force, consisting principally of fast cruisers, destroyers, aircraft carriers, torpedo boats, and submarines, continues in spite of the increased fighting potential of the air arm. Employment of enemy air units has not yet deprived naval vessels of their vital role on the high seas, but has greatly accelerated methods and changed the technique in their equipment. It appears that the success of naval operations, assuming air support, will still be determined by sound strategic concepts and adroit leadership. A sea blockade will not accomplish an economic strangulation or military defeat of Germany. Nor will air operations alone bring victory. Air and sea forces will make important contributions but effective and adequate ground forces must be available to close with and destroy the enemy within his citadel.

3. It is therefore imperative that we create the productive capacity to provide equipment for the following:

   A. Appropriate forces distributed for the defense of the United States, outlying possessions, and bases selected to facilitate the defense of the country and the Western Hemisphere.
   B. Task Forces which can effectively conduct military operations, primarily in the European Theatre, as well as in the Western Hemisphere and in other strategically important areas.
   C. The military forces of associates and friendly Powers committed to the policy of opposing Nazi aggression. Quantities to be limited only by our own strategic requirements and the ability of the friendly Powers to use the equipment effectively.

4. A sound approach to the problem of determining appropriate military means requires careful consideration of WHERE, HOW, and WHEN they will be employed to defeat our potential enemies and to assist our associates.

   A. WHERE. Accepting the premise that we must come to grips with the enemy ground forces, our principal theatre of war is Central Europe. Possible subsidiary theatres include Africa, the Near East, the Iberian Peninsula, the Scandinavian Peninsula and the Far East; however, the operations in those theatres must be so conducted as to facilitate the decisive employment of Allied forces in Central Europe.
   B. HOW. The combined and carefully coordinated operations of our military forces, in collaboration with associated Powers, must accomplish the following:
      (1) The surface and subsurface vessels of the Axis and associated Powers must be swept from the seas, particularly in the Atlantic and water areas contiguous to Europe.

(2) Overwhelming air superiority must be accomplished.

(3) The economic and industrial life of Germany must be rendered ineffective through the continuous disruption and destruction of lines of communication, ports, and industrial facilities, and by the interception of raw materials.

(4) The combat effectiveness of the German military forces must be greatly reduced by over-extension, dispersion, shortage of materiel, including fuel, and a deterioration of the Home Front. Popular support of the war by the peoples of the Axis Powers must be weakened and their confidence shattered by subversive activities, propaganda, deprivation, the destruction wrought, and chaos created.

(5) Existing military bases (the British Isles and the Near East) must be maintained. Additional bases, which encircle and close in on the Nazi citadel, must be established in order to facilitate air operations designed to shatter the German industrial and economic life. Such bases may also provide feasible points of departure for the combined operations of ground and air forces. In disposing of our forces, we must guard against dispersion of means in operations that do not make timely and effective contributions to the accomplishment of our main task, the defeat of Germany.

(6) The commitment of our forces must conform to our accepted broad strategic concept of active (offensive) operations in one theatre (European), and concurrently, passive (defensive) operations in the other (Pacific).

C. WHEN. The following factors with regard to the time element are important in determining the production capacity necessary to realize our national objectives:

(1) The lag between plan and execution is considerable. Past experience indicates that from eighteen months to two years are required.

(2) How many months will Germany require to defeat Russia, to reconstitute her forces subsequent to Russia's defeat and to exploit to any perceptible degree the vast resources of Russia? It is believed that Germany will occupy Russian territory west of the general line; White Sea, Moscow, Volga River (all inclusive) by July 1, 1942, and that, militarily, Russia will be substantially impo-

tent subsequent to that date. Thereafter, Germany will "Coventry" all industrial areas, lines of communications and sources of raw materials east of the line indicated, unless a drastic Nazi treaty is accepted by Russia. Germany will probably require a full year to bring order out of chaos in the conquered areas, so that it will be July 1, 1943, before she will largely profit economically by her "drive to the east." The maintenance of huge armies of occupation has become unnecessary. By totally disarming the conquered people, maintaining splendidly organized intelligence and communications nets, and employing strategically located, highly mobile forces (parachute, air-borne, mechanized, and motorized), Germany may control the occupied areas with relatively small forces, thus releasing the bulk of the military for other tasks. Obviously, our war effort time-table, covering the production of munitions, the creation of trained military forces, and the increase of transportation facilities (air, ground, and sea), is strongly influenced by events transpiring in the Russian theatre.

(3) We are confronted by two possibilities: first, a rapidly accelerated all-out effort with a view to conducting decisive, offensive operations against the enemy before he can liquidate or recoup from his struggle with Russia; second, a long drawn-out war of attrition. Under our present production schedule, we will soon have adequate military means to defend our outlying possessions and bases and to provide for the security of the Western Hemisphere, but we will not be able to provide sufficient appropriate forces for timely offensive action in the principal theatre of operations. The urgency for positive action exists, particularly while the enemy is contained militarily in Russia. It would strongly contribute to the early and decisive defeat of the Axis Powers, if the Allied forces could seize and firmly establish military bases from which immediate air and subsequent ground and air operations might be undertaken.

(4) The United States is approaching its task in a logical manner, but the production of materiel must be greatly accelerated to permit its accomplishment. At present, the bulk of our production has to be devoted to the support of Great Britain and associates, rendering it impracticable for us to undertake offensive commit-

ments. But time is of the essence and the longer we delay effective offensive operations against the Axis, the more difficult will become the attainment of victory. It is mandatory that we reach an early appreciation of our stupendous task, and gain the wholehearted support of the entire country in the production of trained men, ships, munitions, and ample reserves. Otherwise, we will be confronted in the not distant future by a Germany strongly entrenched economically, supported by newly acquired sources of vital supplies and industries, with her military forces operating on interior lines, and in a position of hegemony in Europe which will be comparatively easy to defend and maintain.

(5) The time by which production can reach the levels defined by our national objectives is highly speculative. July 1, 1943, has been established as the earliest date on which the equipment necessary to initiate and sustain our projected operations can be provided. The ability of industry to meet this requirement is contingent upon many intangibles; however, the program can be definitely accomplished, in fact, greatly exceeded, if the industrial potential of the country is fully exploited. The urgency of speed and the desirability of employing our present great economic and industrial advantage over our potential enemies cannot be overemphasized.

4. Strategic Employment of Ground Forces

A. The future alignment of Powers and their respective combat capacities cannot be accurately predicted. In order to arrive at a plausible basis from which to determine our future requirements, the following assumptions pertaining to the world situation as of July 1, 1943, are made:

(1) Russia is substantially impotent militarily in Europe. Resistance in Siberia, to include the Maritime Provinces, probably continuing.

(2) The Axis military strength is materially weakened through economic blockade; by losses in the Russian campaign; by British air and sea operations; by the inability to exploit quickly the extensively sabotaged Russian industries and raw materials; by lowered morale of the people.

(3) The military forces of Japan are fully involved with or contained by campaigns against a somewhat strengthened China, by the

Russian forces in the Far East Maritime Provinces, or by the threat of United States–British military and economic reprisals.

(4) Great Britain and associates have increased their fighting forces by creating and equipping additional combat units.

(5) The French will probably continue their passive collaboration with Germany.

(6) Control of the Mediterranean Theatre, including North Africa and the Near East, remains disputed.

(7) The United States is an active belligerent and is collaborating in an all-out effort to defeat Germany.

B. If these assumptions are correct, or even reasonably sound, on July 1, 1943, there will be no military bases remaining in Allied hands, other than the United Kingdom, possibly the northern coast of Africa, and the Near East. The establishment of additional bases, for example, in the Iberian Peninsula, the Scandinavian Peninsula, and Northwest Africa, will be bitterly contested by the Axis. However, to bring about the ultimate defeat of Germany, those bases and others even more difficult to establish must be available to the Allies. Obviously, carefully planned action, involving appropriate sea, air, and ground units must be undertaken. Allied success is directly contingent upon the coordinated employment of overwhelming forces, surprise and mobility, supported by sufficient reserves in materiel and manpower to insure a succession of effective impulses throughout the operations.

C. Latest information pertaining to the potential industrial capacities and military strengths of the opposing Powers (excluding the U.S.), as of July 1, 1943, indicates that the Axis Powers will have about 400 divisions available in the European–Near East Theatre and the Allied Powers approximately 100 divisions. To accomplish the numerical superiority, about 2 to 1, usually considered necessary before undertaking offensive operations, the Allies would have to raise about 700 divisions. A force of 700 divisions with appropriate supporting and service troops would approximate 22 million men. If Great Britain and the United States should induct so many men for military service, added to the tremendous numbers already under arms, the economic and industrial effort, necessary to conduct the war, would be definitely imperiled.

D. It is believed that the enemy can be defeated without creating the numerical superiority indicated. Effective employment of modern air and ground fighting machines and a tight economic blockade may create conditions that will make the realization of the Allied War Aims perfectly feasible with numerically less fighting men. Another million men in Flanders would not have turned the tide of battle for France. If the French Army had had sufficient tanks and planes, and quantities of antitank and antiaircraft materiel, France might have remained a dominant power in Europe. In June 1941, when the Germans launched their invasion of Russia, they knew that their adversary was numerically superior and could maintain that superiority in spite of tremendous losses. They probably also knew that Stalin was creating a military force of great power, consisting primarily of effective modern fighting machines, and that if they delayed their "drive to the east" another year, Russia would possess armadas of air and ground machines which would not only render an offensive campaign impossible, but would make large demands upon the German military to secure her eastern frontier. The Crete campaign also presents illuminating evidence in favor of modern fighting means when opposed by superior numbers that are equipped with inappropriate means and are operating under World War I static tactical concepts. Approximately 17,000 Germans attacked and conquered the island which was defended by about 30,000 British.

E. Our broad concept of encircling and advancing step by step, with a view to closing in on Germany, will remain sound regardless of future developments in the European situation, for it envisages the only practical way in which military and economic pressure may be brought to bear effectively against Germany. The loss of potential bases of operation, presently available, would render the accomplishment of our strategic plans extremely difficult and costly. It is important, therefore, that the Allies take effective measures to hold the United Kingdom, the Middle East, and North African areas. Also the islands off the north-western coast of Africa should be denied to the enemy. Before undertaking operations in connection with the establishment of additional military bases, for example, in the Scandinavian Peninsula, the Iberian Peninsula, Africa, and the Low Countries, a careful survey of the areas of projected operations and a thorough examination of the enemy capabilities are mandatory. The unfortunate Norway campaign of 1940 is a glaring example of a total lack of appreciation of such realities on the part of those responsible for the British expedition. The Germans employed approximately 175,000 men, strongly supported by the Air Force, to conquer and secure their lodgment in Norway. Special Task Forces, including two mountain divisions and numerous parachute units, made effective contributions to the success of the operation. Having gained a foothold, the Germans quickly established themselves in order to hold their bases and to facilitate exploitation. The British Forces dispatched against Norway totaled about 24,000 men, with no mountain troops and with inadequate air supporting units. The failure of the British Expedition is directly attributable to insufficient and inappropriate means. If and when the situation indicates the feasibility of an Allied expedition, against Norway for example, powerful and appropriate means, especially trained and equipped for the task, must be provided. Large and effective reserves must be readily available to preclude dislodgement of the initial forces and to facilitate subsequent exploitation. A careful study of Norway, including the terrain and communications net, and a survey of possible enemy capabilities, indicate the necessity for mountain, infantry foot and motorized divisions, numerous parachute, tank, antitank, antiaircraft, and air-borne units. The force required for the entire operation may total several hundred thousand men. The execution of the plan would be predicated on sea and local air superiority. The size of this force may appear large. However, even though our enemy may not be strong initially in the area of projected operations, the mobility of modern fighting means will enable him to concentrate destructive forces against us with unprecedented speed and surprise effect. The foregoing considerations apply with equal emphasis to proposed forces for other theatres of operations. Careful studies, concerning the Scandinavian Peninsula, the Iberian Peninsula, the Near East, and Africa, have been made by the War Plans Division of the General Staff, and these studies made important contributions in the determination of the estimated Ground Forces (See Tab A). The enemy capabilities in those theatres in 1943 would obviously be conjecture. Task Forces consisting principally of armored and motorized divisions must be created for possible operations in North Africa, the Middle East, France, and the Low Countries. The exact strength and composition of the Task Forces, necessary to seize and maintain military bases, will be determined immediately prior to the operation. We can avoid the unfortunate disasters experienced by our potential allies in Norway, France, the Balkans, and in Crete by planning now and creating quickly the production capacity necessary to equip the ground forces recommended (Tab A). We must not suffer ignominious defeat and be expelled from the bases that we elect to establish. If the premises and assumptions made earlier in this study are appropriate and sound, additional strategically located bases are vital to the splendidly conceived plans of the Air Force and finally may serve as areas of departure for the combined operations of air and ground forces. The seizure, retention, and effective utilization of these bases is predicated on the successful operations of adequate sea, air, and ground forces.

5. Shipping was a bottleneck in the last war and again increased demands will be placed on all transportation facilities, particularly water, by constant troop movements and the expanded war industrial and economic effort. In order to transport and maintain effective forces in European areas, several million tons of shipping and adequate port facilities must be made available essentially for military service. To transport five million men with their modern air and mechanized equipment to European ports over a period of approximately one year would require about seven million tons of shipping or 1,000 ships. To maintain such a force in the theatre of operations would require about ten million tons of shipping or 1,500 ships. But it is highly improbable that the situation in Europe will develop in such a manner as to permit or to require operations involving the movement of so large a force across the Atlantic within the limited time of one year, even if the ship tonnage were available. The progressive building-up of large military forces in the theatre will probably extend over a period of at least two years. This progressive movement would greatly reduce the demands upon maritime shipping for essentially military purposes and further would extend the period of time for the augmentation of maritime shipping now available. The realization of our present national policies may require operations in distant theatres by military forces of unprecedented strength. It would be folly to create strong fighting forces without providing the transportation to move and maintain them in the contemplated theatres of operations. The maximum possible shipbuilding capacity of our country, coordinated of course with other essential demands upon industry and raw materials, must be exploited and continued in operation for the next several years.

6. The foregoing considerations clearly indicate the importance of creating a productive capacity in this country that will provide the most modern equipment designed to give mobility and destructive power to our striking forces. The forces that we now estimate as necessary to realize our national objectives and for which production capacity must be provided may not be adequate or appropriate. No one can predict the situation that will confront the United States in July 1943. We may require much larger forces than those indicated below, and correspondingly greater increased quantities of equipment. Emphasis has been placed on destructive power and mobility, with a view to offensive maneuvers in our principal theatre of operations (Europe). The forces deemed necessary to accomplish the role of ground units in the supreme effort to defeat our potential enemies total 5 Field Armies consisting of approximately 215 divisions (infantry, armored, motorized, air-borne, mountain, and cavalry) with appropriate supporting and service elements. The strategic concept outlined in this paper contemplates distribution of U.S. ground forces approximately as follows: (More specific data will be found in Tab A.)

Iceland	29,000
Scotland	11,000
England	41,000
Ireland	25,000
Hawaii	61,000
Puerto Rico	34,000
Panama	42,000
Alaska	29,000
Philippine Islands	25,000
Smaller Outlying Bases	32,000
Potential Task Forces	
First Army	775,000
Third Army	590,000
Fourth Army	710,000
Brazil	86,000
Colombia-Ecuador-Peru	37,000
TOTAL	**2,500,000**

Strategic Reserves for which production capacity must be established but whose activation, location, and training will be determined by developments in the international situation	3,000,000
Troops in the Zone of the Interior and Fixed Defense Units (Ground)	1,200,000
TOTAL GROUND FORCES	**6,700,000**

TAB A

The Ground Forces estimated as necessary to provide for the security of the U.S. outlying possessions, the Western Hemisphere, and to make available appropriate forces for projected military operations follow:

1. Units organized, fully equipped, and trained as soon as practicable:

A. Military Bases and Outlying Possessions.	
Newfoundland	5,690
Greenland	2,531
Caribbean Bases	40,199
Puerto Rico	34,757
Panama	42,614
Hawaii	61,337
Philippines	25,397
Alaska	28,823
Iceland	28,709
Bases in British Isles	76,160
TOTAL	**346,217**

B. Potential Task Forces

Brazil	
1 Army Corps (1 Div. foot, 1 Div. Air-Borne)	42,392
2 Artillery Battalions Pack	1,804
1 Cavalry Regiment	1,591
5 Parachute Battalions	2,590
1 Antiaircraft Regiment and 2 Medium Battalions	3,619
2 Aircraft Warning Regiments	2,600
2 Tank Battalions (Light)	1,086
3 Anti-Tank Battalions	2,100
Services	28,864
Total	**86,646**
Colombia-Ecuador-Peru	
1 Division	15,245
2 Artillery Battalions	1,400
3 Parachute Battalions	1,554
1 Antiaircraft Regiment and 2 Medium Battalions	3,619
2 Tank Battalions (Light)	1,086
1 Aircraft Warning Regiment	1,300
Services	13,035
Total	**37,239**
First Army	
1 Army of 3 Corps of 3 Divs. ea.	242,216
2 Armored Corps of 2 Amid Div. ea.	53,556
8 Divisions (4 Mtzd, 2 Mtn, 2 Abn)	108,516
5 Parachute Bns.	2,590
13 Artillery Bns. (4 heavy, 6 [105mm], 375mm How Pk)	9,906
20 Antiaircraft Regts and 10 extra Bus. 37mm	46,970

11 Tank Battalions (3 Medium and 5 Light)	4,839
12 Aircraft Warning Regts	15,600
10 Tank Destroyer Bns; and 10 Anti-Tank Bn (Gun)	14,000
Services (Ord., QM, Sig., Engr., Med.)	278,069
Total	**776,262**

Third Army

1 Army (3 Corps, 9 Divisions)	242,216
1 Armored Corps (2 Divisions)	26,778
2 Divisions Motorized	32,258
6 Artillery Battalions (Medium & Heavy)	4,300
1 Cavalry Corps and 2 H-Mecz Regiments	26,867
2 Air-Borne Divisions	20,000
5 Parachute Battalions	2,590
5 Antiaircraft Regiments and 3 Med. Bns.	12,166
3 Aircraft Warning Regiments	3,900
15 Tank Destroyers or Anti-Tank Battalions	10,500
Services	207,860
Total	**589,435**

Fourth Army

1 Army (3 Corps, 9 Divisions)	242,216
1 Armored Corps (2 Divisions)	25,394
4 Divisions, Motorized	64,516
8 Artillery Battalions (Med. or Heavy)	8,800
4 Divisions (2 Mountain, 2 Air-Borne)	44,000
2 Parachute Battalions	1,036
15 Antiaircraft Regiments and 10 Med. Bns.	37,345
8 Tank Battalions (Medium or Light)	4,839
6 Aircraft Warning Regiments	7,800

25 Tank Destroyers or Anti-Tank Battalions	17,500
Services	256,413
Total	**709,859**
TOTAL TASK FORCES	**2,199,441**

A. The troops considered necessary in the ground forces, i.e. organized, fully equipped and trained, for current and future employment as security forces in military bases and outlying possessions, and as striking forces in any theatre; follows:

Military Bases and Outlying Possessions	346,217
Potential Task Forces	2,199,441
TOTAL	**2,545,658**

2. Production capacity should be created to equip approximately 3 million for the reserve units indicated below. Activation, location and training of these units will depend upon the international situation.

A. Strategic Reserves.

2 Armies (10 Army Corps, 27 Divisions)
14 Armored Corps (53 Armored Divisions)
51 Divisions Motorized
115 Artillery Battalions (Pack Medium or Heavy)
9 Divisions (2 Cavalry, 6 Mountain)
3 Airborne
22 Parachute Battalions
129 Antiaircraft Regiments and 133 Medium Battalions
86 Tank Battalions (70 Medium, 6 Light, 10 Heavy)
29 Aircraft Warning Regiments
290 Tank Destroyer Battalions
262 Anti-Tank Battalions (Gun)

TOTAL: APPROXIMATELY 3,000,000

3. Ground troops required for the Zone of Interior and Fixed Defense Units 1,200,000

4. Recapitulation of Ground Forces

Military Bases and Outlying Possessions	346,217
Potential Task Forces	2,199,441
Zone of Interior—Fixed Defenses	1,200,000
TOTAL	**3,745,658**
Units in reserve to be activated when situation requires	3,000,000
TOTAL ARMY GROUND FORCES	**6,745,658**

5. Air Force requirements (details submitted in a separate study)

Air Force Combat	1,100,000
Zone of the Interior Service units	950,000
TOTAL AIR FORCE	**2,050,000**

6.

Army Ground Forces	6,745,658
Army Air Forces	2,050,000
TOTAL ARMY FORCES	**8,795,658**

APPENDIX 4

Nathan's 6 October Memorandum for War Production Board Meeting[1]

★ ★ ★

Planning Committee Document No. 205

The Problem of Program Determination

(Report by Robert R. Nathan to the War Production Board, presented at the meeting on 6 October 1942)

This discussion addresses itself to the need for reviewing the production program for this country in comparison with the country's productive capacity. Under the production program we include the objectives for munitions, war industrial facilities, war construction, civilian-type products needed for the armed forces and Lend-Lease, and the essential needs of the civilian economy. The set of claims upon resources that this over-all problem represents are then to be compared with the country's productive capacity, as it can be measured now and can be foreseen for the immediate future.

The reason for discussing now this adjustment of the program to capacity lies in the danger of production objectives substantially in excess of the limits of feasibility. In considering limits of capacity and resources, we assume that strenuous effort will be made to reduce civilian consumption to the essential minimum; to use materials, facilities, and labor in the most efficient manner;

to gear our economic and institutional habits to the pitch of intensity that is required in an all-out effort. But if, on assumptions of such intensive utilization of the economy for war production purposes, we still find the production program in excess of feasible limits, then there is real need for discussing how the program can be adjusted to the limit of capacity.

But perhaps we *should* have a program in excess of capacity. There is one major advantage in having a program too large—in that there is constant pressure for an all-out war effort. Perhaps the disadvantages, which have already made themselves felt, may have been a cheap price to have paid for the speed with which armament production has increased and with which the output of civilian goods, in competition with war goods, has declined. However, the amounts of critical materials and resources now being used for non-essential purposes are relatively slight and the advantage of having a program, well above feasibility now appears to be more than offset by its disadvantages. Further, with excess fabricating capacity in many areas, there will be continued pressure for conserving the use of critical materials; and this pressure need no longer come from an over-sized program.

What are the disadvantages of having an excessively large program? In the first place, it brings imbalance in production as among various end items and as between complementary items and components. The easier parts of the program will be fully achieved, and, unless tightly controlled, will run ahead of schedule or beyond objectives, at the expense of more difficult items. There is already evidence of this situation.

When the program is beyond attainment, it is impossible to avoid the development of excess fabricating capacity. Each procurement unit must establish facilities to achieve its objectives and the net result is bound to be idle or only partly utilized plants. Having some excess capacity may be useful as permitting greater flexibility in the program; but substantial excess capacity means wastage of materials and, even more important, may result in a serious morale situation among workers and management. Unless the program is now adjusted, we may be increasingly faced with the slowing down and closing of plants throughout the country.

A very important danger of an overly large program is the failure to meet the most important segments of the program. This is illustrated in the case of aircraft where the allocation of materials and of machine tools has not been adequate to meet the objectives. As long as the programs are determined through compromises made monthly or quarterly at the Requirements Committee level, it will be most difficult to avoid cutting the most important parts of the program as well as other parts. Not only aircraft agencies but also merchant shipbuilding units have complained about having their requirements reduced relative to what was necessary to meet the objectives.

A further disadvantage of an excess program is the lack of flexibility in items and categories. As new weapons, models, or designs are required on the basis of battle experience, it will be more difficult to obtain the earliest possible production unless there is some margin within the program. It is much easier to introduce new equipment when some specific other part of the program need not be eliminated to compensate for the item. To some degree the entire question of quality vs. quantity is tied up with the size of the program in relation to resources.

Also, when the program is in excess of feasibility, the work of the Requirements Committee must to some extent be based on compromise and its determinations become much more difficult. Similarly, the mechanisms for distributing materials, no matter how efficient, are likely to bog down when the demands are far in excess of supply.

Finally, when programs are not properly integrated with resources, it is impossible to engage in coordinating and integrating the production of the United States with that of other nations. Until the objectives of the United States are reviewed in relation to feasibility, the work of the Combined Production and Resources Board, as well as other combined boards, must of necessity be seriously restricted.

If such dangers of too large a program are real, the need for continuous check and adjustment is obvious. On the supply side we must continuously review our efforts to expand production and use of resources. On the requirements side we must continuously review the program and its adjustment in the light of strategy, production, and global considerations. At the conclusion of this report we should like to urge upon the War Production Board certain recommendations intended to provide a basis for a continuous check upon and adjustment of the production program.

But before doing so it would be well to indicate why we think the program as it now stands is above the levels of feasibility. In so doing we summarize and supplement the findings of Document 151 [Kuznets' original feasibility report] in its analysis of the income potential, of the raw materials situation, of the facilities problem, and of the manpower problem. But we would like to emphasize that the findings of the report are only an occasion to raise the broad problem of program determination and adjustment; and that the minutia of its analysis should not obscure the fundamental need for a continuous joint check of the program, both on the side of reviewing the supply effort and on the side of adjusting the objectives to reasonably forward expectations. We turn now to the findings of the report.

For the over-all productive capacity of the nation there is only one common denominator that can be handled expediently, and that is the total dollar value of production. As matters now stand the dollar value of the requirements for munitions and war construction in 1942 aggregate nearly 55 billion. Against this total we have produced in the first eight months of the year slightly less than $26 billion, leaving a balance of more than $28 billion for the remaining four months. The analysis indicates that this residual objective will not be attained by the end of the year by about $7 billion. When the program is broken down as between war construction, including industrial facilities, and munitions production, it appears that the objective for war construction (which is identical with schedules) will be attained. The entire deficit will appear in the munitions category for which the dollar value objective is $40 billion for 1942. A deficit of $7 billion will, therefore, mean a shortage of 17 1/2 percent of the year's goal in munitions.

For the year 1943 the present requirements for munitions and war construction are given in the report as $87 1/2 billion. There are indications already that this represents an understatement of the true requirements which may now be set at somewhat over $90 billion. If we carry over the 1942 deficiency into 1943 and add it to the objectives for that year, the total in war munitions and construction will range between $95 and $97 billion. If to the total are added such items as pay, subsistence, food for the British, and other miscellaneous expenditures, the total war outlay for 1943 will range close to $115 billion. We may now ask what are the prospects of this program being attained in 1943.

In the first half of 1942 war outlays were at an annual rate of $41 billion and total non-war expenditures at the rate of 107 1/2, showing gross national product of 148 1/2.[2] Consumers' outlay was at fairly high levels, although in terms of 1941 prices it was already below the average for 1941 (by some 5 percent).

We assume that by December 1942 war outlays will be at an annual rate of $78 billion, or 6.5 billion per month, of which 5.55 billion will be munitions and war construction, and a billion in non-munitions. If private gross capital formation—i.e., private gross investment—is cut down to $61 billion, consumers' outlay to $71 billion (i.e., over 10 percent from their level in the first half of 1942), and we allow $12 billion for non-war Government expenditures, the gross national product in December 1942 will be at the rate of $168 billion.

Let us see now what the program requires in 1943. War outlays are set at 115 billion, of which $97 billion are munitions and war construction and $18 billion are non-munitions. If we assume that private gross capital formation is cut down to $5 billion, non-war government expenditure to $1.0 [billion], and consumers outlay is set at 1932 levels, total non-war expenditures should be $67.8 billion and the gross national product for the year should be at $182.8 billion.

There are several aspects of the comparison between December 1942 and the requirements for 1943 that indicate the impossibility of obtaining a picture such as is shown in the third bar in the chart—viz, 1943 requirements.[3] First, in December 1942 war outlays would be at the rate of 6.5 billion. On the straight line progression the attainment of 1943 goals of $115 billion would call for total war expenditures by the end of 1943 of over $12 billion per month, a level that seems impossible (no rise in prices is assumed between 1942 and 1943). Second, if consumers' expenditures will not decline below the level indicated in December 1942—i.e., $71.5 billion—a cut to an annual tota1 of $52.8 billion implies, again on the arithmetic progression basis, that by the end of the year consumers' expenditures would have to be at a level of roughly $35 billion—i.e., over 30 percent below the 1932 consumption outlay. Finally, it is clear that the consumers' outlay, of which services form a very substantial part (between 35 and 40 percent), uses many resources that cannot be diverted to war production.

That the drastic contraction in consumers' outlay required to establish the level of $52.8 billion for 1943 is beyond attainment is shown by reference to the experience of other countries. On the basis of rough estimates available, it appears that in U.K. civilian consumption plus private gross investment declined from 1933 to 1941 by 18 percent, and from 1938 to 1942 by 20 percent (in constant prices). In Canada, the same total rose from 1938 to 1941 by 21 percent and then dropped from 1941 to 1942 by 10 percent. In Germany, rough data suggest a shrinkage in real volume of civilian consumption by about 40 percent from 1938 to 1942. But a decline required here from 1942 to 1943 (i.e., from $76 billion to $52.8 billion in consumers' outlay and from $87 billion to $57.8 billion for the total of consumers' outlay and private capital formation) means a decline of well over 30 percent in a single year. On the other hand, if we assume that the level of $52.8 billion for consumers' outlay and $5 billion for private capital formation is to be reached only in December 1943 (rather than represent averages for the year), gross national product in December 1943 would have to be at the annual rate of $215 billion.

This would represent a rise in gross national product of almost 30 percent in a single year—a feat much beyond attainment for an economy that has already absorbed most of its surplus resources.

Another approach to the 1943 picture might be secured by comparing the distribution of the gross national product here with countries that have had long experience and a long history of active war participation. For the first half of 1942 war outlays in the U.S. formed approximately 27 percent of the gross national product. At the December 1942 rates forecast the percentage rises to about 46 percent. For 1943 the set-up on the basis of requirements would mean that war outlays absorbed 63 percent of the gross national product; and for the December 1943 distribution needed to assure the 1943 total, the percentage of gross national product absorbed in war outlay would amount to 75. Yet in 1942 a similar ratio for U.K. was 44 percent; for Canada, 43 percent; and for Germany, 50 percent.

The Document indicated why we assume the goal of $75 billion for war munitions and construction as feasible. On this assumption the shortages over against cumulative goals of $97 billion will be $22 billion, or almost 30 percent of the feasible levels. If a somewhat greater reduction of consumers' outlay appears possible and a somewhat greater intensification of our war effort, the excess over the feasible levels might be cut down to 25 percent. Thus, on the basis of our analysis, the present program appears much higher than its feasible levels; and it is quite possible that with larger bottlenecks appearing in almost all areas of the economy we might fall considerably short of the levels that we characterize here as attainable.

If we turn now to raw materials we may look at the picture shown in the other chart with reference to supply and requirements for carbon steel, alloy steel, copper, and aluminum. In this chart the deficits are cumulative from the last quarter of 1942.[4] They show briefly that for carbon steel the cumulative excess of requirements over supply does not disappear until the last quarter of 1943; in IV—1942 it is close to 11 percent of total supply. In alloy steel the situation is much more critical in that the cumulative excess in supply grows through 1943; and the current excess ranges between 11 and 25 percent of the total supply throughout the first two quarters of 1943. Even a more critical situation exists in copper with the excess growing cumulatively to the end of 1943; and ranging on a current basis from 20 to 25 percent of supply. In aluminum the cumulative deficit disappears only by the fourth quarter of 1943.

Two aspects of this materials analysis must be emphasized. First, the estimates are in terms of ingots and, therefore, we must look to bottlenecks in certain shapes and forms. Thus, in aluminum it is not the ingot supply but the supply of certain types of extrusions and forgings that is critical. Second, the fact that the deficits are beginning to be offset for some metals in the second half of 1943 is of help only if we can assume that rates of utilization of facilities can be raised not only in accordance with schedules but also beyond so as to absorb the excess of supply over requirements and offset the cumulative deficits. The question of timing is the most important in judging the feasibility of the program since the program has no meaning except in connection with the time schedule which is attached to it. A delay in balance of supply and requirements in materials to the second half of 1943 means in essence the impossibility of doing the 1943 program, even regardless of those cumulative deficits that do not disappear by the end of 1943.

This element of timing is also exceedingly important in the analysis of facilities. Scarcity of statistical data and difficulties in measuring productivity of industrial facilities limits the analysis. Yet, even in this field, major limitations are indicated. Whereas for the entire eighteen-months period ending December 31, 1943, machine tool requirements are slightly below estimated capacity, there are a great many critical machine tools that will be short throughout the period and many others that will be in inadequate supply for most of the period. This is especially true for the high quality and special type tools. Further, it should be noted that many of the facilities now under way are substantially behind schedule. An analysis of a large sample of facilities indicates that scheduled completion dates for all facilities have been postponed for about 30 percent of all projects with an average delay of about three months. On projects that are nearly complete, over two-thirds are expected to be delayed in completion, with an average delay in excess of four months.

The question as to whether the war production program is feasible from the point of view of facilities can hardly be answered from an over-all analysis. The limitation imposed upon the program on the basis of facilities will be specific rather than general. It is also quite possible that other limiting factors will be more restrictive in character. In general, our conclusion is that for many facilities capacity has proven and will continue to be above expectations. Also, more facilities can be made available for war production through more intensive requisitioning. Finally, it may be possible to convert equipment for less essential war work to more essential war work. This again, however, is a matter of meeting specific bottlenecks very promptly. Despite all these favorable factors there still remains the problem of specific tools for specific purposes and these may continue to limit production in 1943, especially during the early part of the year.

The analysis of labor requirements has been made with the help of such independent forecasts of labor requirements as are available. Based upon a program of war production (munitions and construction) consistent with the feasible levels indicated above—i.e., the levels of roughly 45 to 47 billion in 1942 and 75 in 1943—there will be a deficiency of more than 4 million workers by the end of 1943 relative to the normal labor force. It should be emphasized that in arriving at these conclusions the estimates assume, a total armed strength of 7.6 million by 1943 (this figure being the lowest of those available on the base of authoritative sources). The estimates of the War Plans Division indicate requirements of nearly 3 million more than this total in all armed services by that date. On the basis of this higher figure the deficiency at the end of 1943, if compared with the normal labor force, will be more than 7 million. The potential reserve of labor beyond the normal force is very considerable, including women engaged in home work, persons attending school, older people who may be brought back to labor markets, and others. While the indicated deficiency may be overcome through mobilizing the potential labor force, serious labor mobilization problems will be encountered in accomplishing this task. Here again total analysis may under-state the sum of specific situations. There are certain to be major problems in specific occupations, industries, and geographic areas, serious impacts already being encountered in agriculture, in mining, and in lumber. Further shifts of major magnitude will be required if the manpower needs of the feasible program are to be met. In the metal and chemical industries the labor demand is expected to increase from slightly under 7 million in June 1942 to over 11 million in December 1943.

It thus appears from the data relating to labor as well as to those relating to other productive resources that a major challenge faces us in attaining the problem indicated as feasible above, let alone the achievement of the objectives on the present excessively large program.

Three aspects of this analysis must be borne in mind if a proper evaluation of the inferences is to be made. First, the analysis is in aggregate terms in a sense that it relates aggregate demand to aggregate supply. It should be emphasized that even if total supply and demand balance there is by no means assurance of feasibility for the various specific parts. In other words, specific bottlenecks in machine tools, in labor skills, in shapes and sizes of materials, may well render any conclusions drawn from an over-all analysis too optimistic. Secondly, it is believed that the supply estimates, especially for raw materials, are on the optimistic side and can be validated only under the most favorable circumstances. This again tends to make our conclusions perhaps too optimistic. Third, the requirements stated may also be on the low side because of the general tendency on the part of the various claimant agencies to raise their claims. As the nature of the war unfolds, programs always tend to increase, and it is probable that in the coming months, as battle experience is gained, new demands will greatly exceed reductions through obsolescence and other factors. These three aspects of the analysis, all of which tend to make its inferences as to feasibility perhaps too optimistic, must be taken into account in interpreting its conclusions.

It must be emphasized that the levels of feasibility which we set as desirable represent a marked expansion of war production and a fairly drastic contraction of civilian consumption. It is far from our mind to call for a reduction of a program just to make things easier for people concerned with the war production effort; or allow fat to grow upon the body of the civilian economy. And it is equally far from our mind to place the whole onus of adjustment upon the armed services. But we are honestly convinced that the situation calls for immediate steps in the way of a review of the program, a review which, along the lines indicated above, should be periodic and involve joint action by the agencies responsible for production and by those responsible for program planning.

Two recommendations flow from the discussion of the broad problem at issue—the specific details of the analysis only serving to emphasize the urgency of action. The first recommendation calls for much tighter production control and scheduling than have been accomplished to date. In some degree this suggestion is gratuitous because of the major attention now being given to this problem. It is our belief that theoretically a system of scheduling, production control, and distribution of materials could be evolved that would operate to yield the maximum of feasible war production irrespective of the size of the goals. In other words, it is possible to conceive a system of scheduling which would insure the maximum output of the most critical items, even though the objectives might be many times what might be accomplished. However, such a system cannot be developed practically until in the program the levels of importance, the "must" part and the "non-must" are clearly distinguished, and until the complexity and decentralization of our war effort have given place to greater simplicity and unity. As matters now stand every war agency, every branch, every section, and every procurement office must of necessity attempt to accomplish its total objective, irrespective of what other more important demands might come first. It isn't practical to introduce such a complete control so as to deny access to even the least scarce materials to the less essential until the more essential items are complete. As a result, unfinished items are bound to appear in a program that is considerably beyond what can be accomplished.

The second recommendation calls for a continuous review of the program so as to bring the objectives in line with feasibility, and feasibility to the highest level. It is obvious that the War Production Board is called upon to exercise its greatest effort in attaining maximum utilization of resources for purposes of war production. The analysis of feasibility summarized below suggests as feasible levels rates of production for 1943 that are greatly in excess of the present rates of production. These levels will not be attained unless we apply ourselves towards the maximum utilization of materials, facilities, and labor in the field of greatest need for them, that is in the field of production of fighting equipment and means of transportation to the fighting fronts. Perhaps in a few months successful efforts will show us that our present forecasts of feasible levels were too pessimistic. We sincerely hope that this will prove to be the case. At any rate it is part of our second recommendation that the War Production Board periodically review its estimates of feasibility so that beginning with the present base there will be continuous improvement in our estimates of the productive capacity of the nation.

The second part of this recommendation is that the agencies responsible for program planning review with the War Production Board periodically [review] their programs, taking account of the over-all demands that they represent upon the resources of the economy. The purpose of this periodic review is to adjust the program to productive capacity as the latter is best seen and forecast at the date of review. This joint analysis by the WPB, responsible for intensifying the productive effort of the nation, and by the agencies responsible for the formulation of the plans upon which the programs are based, should serve the purpose of formulating at periodic intervals the long-range program that is feasible and that can become the basic blue-print to direct the efforts of the productive system.

APPENDIX 5

General Somervell's Comments to War Production Board Proposals of 31 August 1942[1]

★ ★ ★

Memorandum for Mr. Nathan,
Chairman Planning Committee War Production Board:

1. In response to your memorandum of September 8, 1942, I have reviewed the memorandum of August 31, 1942 by Mr. Simon Kuznets on Principles of Program Formulation and Planning Committee Document No. 151 by the same author. In document No. 151 the author states:
2. That his data are subject to a wide margin of error. That on the basis of these data production goals and capacities are about:

Goals	Billions	Capacities
1942	$55	$45–$47
1943	87.4	$75–$80 differences ranging from about 10% to 20%.

3. That the real solution lies, of course, in the introduction and maintenance of a more careful system of scheduling and of production control. But whatever decision is made, the paramount task should still be that of better scheduling and production control rather than securing a more feasible set of production objectives.
4. I am in agreement that his data are unreliable. I am of the opinion that the variations between Mr. Kuznets' "probabilities" and production goals are not percentage wise enough to justify a wholesale change in goals. Only a few months ago this office was urged by your statisticians to increase the goals. I am in complete agreement as to the real solution as offered by Mr. Kuznets. I am in complete disagreement with your conclusion that Mr. Nelson cannot secure proper scheduling within "a reasonable time." His program as outlined to me will definitely provide for this and is susceptible of accomplishment.
5. Some observations on other sections of the reports may be of interest to you.
   A. Industrial facilities pages 9 and 10. The construction program calls for about $23 billion of which $17 billion are for strictly military objects such as camps, etc., powder factories, and other facilities having no civilian counterpart, leaving $6 billion for industrial facilities. Obviously these could not be reduced by $5 to $6 billion as stated in the report. There have been too many ex-cathedra remarks on the subject of cutting facilities and some of the action taken as a result has actually reduced production of vital articles and caused some of the "imbalances" to which reference is made.
   B. Direct military construction page 11. I do not know Mr. Kuznets' military background nor what weight should be given to his opinions on either the availability or suitability of existing structures for barracks, etc. The Department will welcome a list of structures that have been overlooked. The statement that there has been an inadequate screening of such projects will bear analysis on the basis of the list.
   C. Merchant ships page 11 and 12. This whole paragraph suggests an inadequate basis for the ship building program. If any subject has been thoroughly reviewed, it is the necessity for transports. It is little short of farcical to throw doubt on the size of this program and to suggest that it be "the first in the field of end-products to be subjected to critical scrutiny."

D. Naval vessels and airplanes. The Navy and air force [*sic*] will no doubt comment on these sections of the report.

E. Production Strategy and Military Strategy and the memoranda of August 31, 1942. To me this is an inchoate mass of words. To suggest that military members of the super-super board should have nothing to do with production shows a complete lack of understanding of the problem. I should much prefer to trust to proper decisions from the President, Mr. Nelson, and military personnel knowing something of production, than to this board of "economists and statisticians" with military men without any responsibility or knowledge of production to fill in the "missing link."

6. *I am not impressed with either the character or basis of the judgments expressed in the reports and recommend they be carefully hidden from the eyes of thoughtful men* (emphasis added).

APPENDIX 6

Simon Kuznets' Reply to Somervell's Comments on His Feasibility Proposal (Sent under Robert Nathan's Hand)[1]

★ ★ ★

Your memorandum of September 12 concerning Planning Committee Document No. 151, "Analysis of the Production Programs," and Document No. 157, "Principles of Program Determination," has been received and read with a great deal of interest. In view of the gravity of the problem discussed in these Documents, *I hesitate to take your memorandum seriously.* However, I shall attempt below to deal with it point-by-point.

Point 1 (reference to point 2-b in your memorandum). Your summary of Mr. Kuznets' dollar totals is correct. However, your conclusion from these figures that the variations are not percentage wise enough to justify a wholesale change in goals overlooks the explicit statement on page 4, Document 151, that if the unfilled objectives from 1942 are carried over into 1943 the program in 1943 appears to be at least 25 percent above the total that seems feasible.

Point 2 (reference to point 3 of your memorandum). Yes, about a year ago we did urge an increase in the goals. I am more convinced than ever that it was a good policy, especially toward overcoming the "business as usual" attitude. When we were urging that the sights be raised, we simultaneously suggested over-all objectives which we regarded as feasible. We never pressed for an independent set of claims unrelated to available resources. The fact that we once urged that the sights be raised is no reason for now adopting an ostrich-like attitude when goals are established that are above probability of achievement.

Point 3 (further reference to point 3 of your memorandum). In justification of our conclusion that we are not likely to have a proper scheduling within a reasonable time, I call your attention to the actual production records and schedules of recent months which indicate an intolerable unbalance in the production and scheduling by the Procurement Services of end items in relation to objectives, of complementary items in relation to each other, and of components in relation to end items. Attention has been called to this situation for some months by the Office of Progress Reports of the War Production Board.

Point 4 (further reference to point 3 of your memorandum). Mr. Kuznets qualified his estimates by indicating the margin of error to which they are subject—a practice customary in any thoughtful and well-considered analysis. The degree of unreliability in the estimates stems largely from both the limited quality and quantity of the data derived from your department and other primary sources. The data were the best available to the War Production Board. If you have any information beyond that which we have already received from your department which would enrich our knowledge of this problem, I would greatly appreciate your making it available to us. For two years we have been greatly handicapped in the analysis of problems within our purview by the difficulty of securing reliable data from the procurement agencies on raw material requirements.

Point 5 (reference to point 4-a of your memorandum). The industrial facilities referred to on pages 9 and 10 of Document 151 cover all productive plants, whereas under direct military construction we only include barracks, naval bases, and other non-industrial construction. Your point, therefore, that there is only a $6 billion program for industrial facilities rests upon a misconception of terms. We have and are continuing to over-extend ourselves in the building of fabricating facilities. The action already taken to cut facilities unfortunately held up some expansion of critical raw materials, thus further aggravating a serious imbalance which was then apparent. We shall probably be faced with idle industrial capacity because of lack of materials, mainly because sponsors of new fabricating facilities refused to be realistic.

Point 6 (reference to point 4-b of your memorandum). The comments with reference to direct military construction on page 11 of Planning Committee Document No. 151 referred to a report of a special committee set up by

Messrs. Nelson, Forrestal, and Patterson to review the construction and facilities program. As I recall, you were present in Mr. Patterson's office when this committee was set up and, I believe, a copy of the committee's report was provided to you. A very careful study of the mechanisms for screening projects led to the conclusion that such screening was inadequate. The committee recommended the creation of an authoritative Board to review all facilities, to which you objected.

Point 7 (reference to point 4-c of your memorandum). To our knowledge the War Production Board has never been given an adequate statement of the Armed Service requirements for merchant shipping extended over a period of time far enough into the future to provide the basis for a reasonably formulated merchant shipping program. If such statements are available, we shall greatly appreciate having them made available to us. Scattered information which we have been able to assemble indicates a serious deficiency of shipping space relative to what is needed to move a substantial portion of armament we are scheduled to produce.

Point 8 (reference to point 4-e of your memorandum). I regret that the memorandum of August 31, which spells out the significant problems in relation to objectives and production planning, was not phrased so as to be comprehensible to you. Mr. Kuznets, in Document 157, not only does not suggest that military members of the Board should have nothing to do with production problems, but, on the contrary, insists that they should concern themselves intimately with them. The point is that this Board should make possible joint consideration of strategic, production, and political problems in the broad sense, and that such problems be a matter of concern to every member of this Board, be they representatives of the military strategy groups or production organizations. There is at present no such body to arrive at an aggregate program, taking into account all of these factors. Apparently you have changed your mind since May 15, 1942, for on that date you wrote to Mr. Nelson proposing "a combined Resources Board . . . to include not only representation of War Production Board and the British Supply Ministry but also of the armed services of both countries. The board should consider all available resources and requirements in the light of known strategical objectives with a view to matching resources against requirements so as to best meet these objectives."

Point 9 (reference to point 5 of your memorandum). I appreciate your frankness in stating that you are not impressed by the character or basis of judgments expressed in this report. *Your conclusions from it, however, that these judgments be carefully hidden from the eyes of thoughtful men is a non-sequitur. Also, I am obliged to be frank with you in expressing my disappointment in your reply. The problems discussed are important and their intelligent consideration is urgent. The author of the Documents is recognized nationally as one of the ablest and soundest authorities on our national economy and upon its ability to produce for peace or war. I think it would be most unwise to bar these problems, which have been given careful consideration by the staff and members of the Planning Committee, from people who have responsibility for the success of the war effort and the welfare of this country.* (emphasis added)

The basic findings of the report have been overlooked in favor of minutiae, with the resulting failure in your memorandum to deal directly with the important problem of program determination, which you so clearly recognized in your memorandum of May 15. The problems of mobilizing our economy for war are so big as to demand that contributions made by intelligent and thoughtful men be met with the most earnest consideration, not only so that all relevant information can be brought to bear, but also so that the problems can be settled in a helpful atmosphere of mutual trust.

Perhaps only time can serve to bring into proper light the importance of this subject. But I am convinced that in the not-too-distant future thoughtful men will sit down together and work objectively on these problems. The Planning Committee and its staff will be glad to take part in such conferences at any time. In the meantime, we shall continue to work on the basis of our conviction that in mobilizing our national resources for a war effort of this magnitude we must be conscientiously forward looking and deal forthrightly and aggressively with major problems, before they become so critical that they disrupt our National effort. On the other hand, to engage in a "Round Robin" of critical correspondence would be a waste of time.

/s/ Robert R. Nathan
cc: Mr. Donald M. Nelson

APPENDIX 7

Letter from Robert P. Patterson (Under Secretary of War) to General Somervell, Post 6 October Feasibility Meeting[1]

★ ★ ★

Memorandum to General Somervell:

1. It seems probable that we will be told by WPB that the military production program now outlined for the year 1943 is considerably beyond the capacity of the nation to fulfill within the time objectives. The position of WPB will be that the military requirements (Army, Navy, and Maritime Commission) for 1943 would involve production of some $95 billion and that the maximum military production actually to be expected will not exceed $80 billion. These figures in dollars will be backed up with figures in raw materials and in manpower.
2. It is also likely that WPB will recommend or direct that the production objective for 1943 be reduced to a point within striking distance of estimated maximum production for that year. The figure specified as the aggregate limit of the military program is apt to be between $80 billion to $85 billion.
3. The WPB position, that production objectives ought not to be far in front of estimated maximum production, is believed to be sound as a general rule. Otherwise our scheduling of production cannot represent reality, and it is generally agreed that without realistic scheduling we will continue to suffer

from maldistribution of materials, thus cutting down the actual output of finished weapons.

4. If a cut in military production objectives is to be made, it will be borne by the Army and the Navy.[2] It is safe to say that with the shipping situation what it is, the program of the Maritime Commission will not be touched, and it is also plain enough that the program for expansion of production of raw materials will not be cut below its present size. The reductions to be made in the Army and Navy programs, in order that the total objectives for 1943 may be brought down to the limit set by WPB, will be for decision by the Joint Chiefs of Staff, presumably with approval of the President. The reduction will be governed by considerations of military strategy.
5. I should suppose, in the light of the most recent military developments, that no reduction in the aircraft program would be considered by the Joint Chiefs of Staff. Supposedly, no reduction in the program for escort vessels, for smaller naval craft, or for aircraft carriers would be ordered. The most likely places for reduction would be in larger naval vessels with distant completion dates, in Army coast defenses, and in antiaircraft guns to be located in our own cities. It may also be necessary to re-examine our ammunition program, to make sure that present requirements are in line with probable needs. Cuts in other programs will probably be rendered necessary, particularly in lines where considerable savings in copper and in alloy steel will be brought about.
6. I should like to discuss the foregoing with you and with General Clay.

/s/ Robert P. Patterson Under Secretary of War

APPENDIX 8

Minutes of War Production Board 6 October Meeting[1]

★ ★ ★

Production Board Meeting XXXIV
October 6, 1942

Present: Board Members, Alternates, and Staff

Mr. Donald M. Nelson, Chairman
Vice President Henry A. Wallace, Chairman, Board of Economic Warfare
Mr. Robert P. Patterson, Under Secretary of War, acting for Mr. Henry L. Stimson, Secretary of War
Rear Admiral S. M. Robinson, Chief of the Office of Procurement and Materiel, Navy Department, acting for Mr. Frank Knox, Secretary of the Navy
Mr. Jesse H. Jones, Secretary of Commerce
Lieutenant General William S. Knudsen, Director of Production, War Department
Mr. Isador Lubin, acting for Mr. Harry L. Hopkins, Special Assistant to the President supervising the Defense Aid Program
Mr. Leon Henderson, Administrator, Office of Price Administration
Mr. John Lord O'Brian, General Counsel, War Production Board
Mr. W. L. Batt, Vice Chairman, War Production Board

Mr. Ferdinand Eberstadt, Vice Chairman, War Production Board
Mr. Milton Katz, Solicitor, War Production Board
Mr. J. S. Knowlson, Vice Chairman, War Production Board
Mr. Charles E. Wilson, Vice Chairman, War Production Board
Mr. Ernest Kanzler, Director General for Operations, War Production Board
Mr. G. Lyle Belsley, Executive Secretary, War Production Board

By Invitation

Lieutenant General Brehon B. Somervell, Commanding General, Services of Supply, War Department
Rear Admiral H. L. Vickery, Vice Chairman, U. S. Maritime Commission
Brigadier General Oliver P. Echols, Assistant for Procurement Services, Office of Chief of Air Corps, War Department
Mr. Will Clayton, Assistant Secretary of Commerce
Mr. Paul V. McNutt, Chairman, War Manpower Commission
Lieutenant William A. Weber, Assistant to the Vice Chairman, U.S. Maritime Commission
Mr. Wayne Coy, Assistant Director, Bureau of the Budget
Mr. Donald R. Belcher, Assistant Chief in Charge of Planning and Statistics, Navy Department
Mr. A. I. Henderson, Deputy Director General for Industry Operations, War Production Board
Mr. Robert R. Nathan, Chairman, Planning Committee, War Production Board
Mr. Simon Kuznets, Chief, Program Analysis and Research Section, Planning Committee, War Production Board
Mr. Wilbur Nelson, Administrator, Mining Branch, War Production Board
Mr. Stacy May, Director, Statistics Division, War Production Board
Mr. Joseph L. Weiner, Deputy Director, Office of Civilian Supply, War Production Board
Mr. Thomas C. Blaisdell Jr., Member, Planning Committee, War Production Board
Mr. Fred Searle Jr., Member, Planning Committee, War Production Board
Mr. Frederick Roe, Assistant Executive Secretary, War Production Board

1. Gold Mining[2]
2. Feasibility of the War Production Program

In reviewing the development of the war production program, Mr. Nathan pointed out that appropriated funds increased during 1941 from 20 billion dollars in March to 50 billion dollars in June and to 80 billion dollars in December. After Pearl Harbor, the acceleration increased and by the middle of 1942, appropriated funds have mounted to approximately 225 billion dollars. The magnitude of the increase has, of course, created serious problems.

Mr. Nathan emphasized that in reviewing the feasibility of the war production program, the Planning Committee has assumed that: (1) the country must engage in an all-out war effort and do everything possible to attain maximum production of munitions; and (2) the civilian economy must be reduced to the lowest level consistent with the largest possible production of munitions.

He pointed out that an overly large program has the advantage of acting as an incentive to total production and heretofore it has compelled curtailment in civilian economy and conservation in war production. However, as far as metal consumption is concerned, most of the possible curtailment in the civilian economy already has been accomplished and there is not the continued need for the same degree of pressure in this direction as prevailed many months ago. Much pressure for conservation can now be expected from the fact that some plants will be operating below capacity. On the other hand, an overly large program has these disadvantages:

1. Creation of lack of balance in end items, complementary items, and components. This is already in evidence.
2. Creation of excess fabricating capacity. This results, in turn, in wastage of materials entering into construction and impairment of the morale of labor, and management as plants slow down and close down.
3. Failure to meet the objectives of the most important segments of the program while meeting less urgently needed items, relatively easy to produce. An outstanding example at present is the aircraft program which is not receiving all the machine tools and metals required to meet the objective; merchant shipbuilding is being similarly restricted.
4. Lack of flexibility with consequent difficulty in introducing new items whose needs are dictated by battle experience.

5. Increased difficulty in effectively controlling the flow and distribution of materials.
6. Inability to coordinate and integrate the production program of the United States with those of other nations.

Mr. Nathan pointed out that the study of the Planning Committee (1PB Document 146), although necessarily not precise as to every detail, does indicate some serious basic problems. Existing schedules for 1942 call for over 14 billion dollars of construction and over 40 billion dollars of munitions. It is currently estimated that the construction program (based on schedules) will be met, but that munitions production will fall short of schedules by 7 billion dollars, or 17 percent. Objectives call for munitions production to a value of 22 billion dollars during the last four months of 1942; it is estimated that only 15 billion dollars will be produced.

For 1943, objectives shown in the report call for war construction and munitions production of 87.5 billion dollars of present purchasing power. Recent reviews of these objectives indicate they underestimate the actual program by several billion dollars. If the deficiency in 1942 production were carried over to 1943, another 7 billion dollars would be added. In addition, present plans call for 18 billion dollars of non-munitions items such as pay, food, et cetera, so that the total outlay for war purposes in 1943 would have to aggregate 115 billion dollars, requiring average monthly expenditures of 9.5 billion dollars. Because total war expenditures in December 1942 are estimated at not over 6.5 billion dollars, expenditures in December 1943 would have to amount to well over 12 billion dollars to achieve this average. For war construction and munitions alone, expenditures next year would have to average 8 billion dollars per month. Since expenditures for these items in December 1942 are estimated at not over 5.5 billion dollars, they would have to rise to 10.5 billion dollars in December 1943.

Studies of the Planning Committee indicate that a rate of gross national output of about 148 billion dollars prevailed in the first half of 1942 and that a level of 168 billion dollars might be reached in December 1942. Admitting that comparisons of the national product of various countries are imperfect, Mr. Nathan pointed out that with total war expenditures of 115 billion dollars in 1943 and civilian outlays reduced to the 1932 level, gross national product would have to reach 183 billion dollars and war expenditures would amount to 63 percent of the total. The total might be accomplished, but the composition appears wholly impossible. To achieve this level of war expenditures for the year as a whole, monthly outlay would have to rise throughout the year to a level of 196 billion dollars in December 1943, of which war expenditures would represent 147 billion dollars. Consumer outlays would fall to the wholly untenable level of 35 billion dollars, or one-third below the 1932 figure. If the 1932 level of consumers' outlays were to prevail in December 1943, the gross national product would have to reach 213 billion dollars. This means war expenditures would absorb not less than 75 percent of the national product in December 1943, an impossible portion. This compares with 27 percent in the first half of 1942, and a likelihood of 46 percent in December 1942. It is estimated that 1942 war outlay in the United Kingdom will be 44 percent of that country's national product. For Canada, this figure is estimated at 43 percent and for Germany, 50 percent. Whether any economy can devote much more than one-half of its output to war production is extremely doubtful. The Planning Committee regards as an outside and all-out and stimulating objective a total of 75 billion dollars of munitions and war construction and 18 billion dollars of non-munitions expenditures in 1943.

Exhibiting charts on the supply and requirements of metals (Document 149), Mr. Nathan forecast that on the basis of present schedules, there would be a serious shortage of alloy steel and copper, which will increase cumulatively through 1943. He pointed out that the estimates in these charts reveal large deficits in the next two or three quarters in these metals and in carbon steel and aluminum and, therefore, indicate that scheduling of production has not been closely correlated with available supplies. He stated further that although the overall shortage of key metals is serious, it is even more severe when considered in specific shapes and sizes, such as aluminum extrusions and forgings. Moreover, supplies already had been estimated optimistically, especially in view of delays now being encountered in completing expansion projects.

Discussing the feasibility of the present war production program from the point of view of labor requirements, Mr. Nathan pointed out that analysis is complicated by lack of authoritative information on the proposed size of the Army. Assuming a total armed strength of 10 million by the end of 1943 and a war production during the year of 75 billion dollars, a labor deficiency by the end of 1943 of 7 million workers, relative to the normal labor force, is indicated. To achieve objectives, not what is feasible, would necessitate a steady rise in production to a rate in December 1943 of 126 billion dollars, which would call for an additional labor force of at least 7 million, making a total labor deficiency of 14 million, a gap that is probably impossible to fill. The potential reserve of labor in women, older people, and others is considerable, but while the overall shortage may be partially overcome, labor problems in specific occupations, industries, and areas are certain to be acute and prevent the attainment of present objectives. Mr. Lubin pointed out that if munitions production and war construction aggregate not more than 75 billion dollars in 1943, the labor supply probably would be adequate. Mr. Nathan again emphasized that the shortage in specific areas would be more serious than revealed by the overall analysis.

Examining the Feasibility

Examining the feasibility of the program in terms of available facilities, Mr. Nathan pointed out that the question can hardly be answered from an overall analysis, but inadequacies of facilities in specific areas are already indicated and will impose major limitations upon production. In machine tools, for example, critical items of high quality and special type tools will be in inadequate supply for most of the 18-month period ending December 1943. Scheduled completion dates for 30 percent of all facilities projects have been postponed by an average of 3 months. Even with the scarcity of statistical data on facilities, Mr. Nathan stated, it is clear that inadequacy of facilities will limit production in specific and important areas in 1943, especially during the early part of the year.

In concluding his presentation, Mr. Nathan urged the development of better scheduling and the provision of an administrative mechanism to combine strategy and production.

Mr. Weiner pointed out that if a national product of 183 billion dollars a year is feasible at all, it could be achieved only by moving large masses of the population into areas of intensive production. This would require substantial increases in housing, transportation, and other facilities which would absorb large amounts of materials and therefore restrict, for an extended period, the proportion of national product originally conceived for direct war expenditures, probably nullifying for the time being the benefits of the increase in output.

Mr. Coy inquired whether the Army and Navy admit that the present program is too large to be feasible. General Somervell replied that while the report of the Planning Committee demonstrates the absolute necessity of utilizing all possible means to achieve the program, he believes that 90 percent of the munitions program for 1942 will be completed by the end of the year, in contrast to only 70 percent as estimated by Mr. Nathan and, consequently, it will be necessary to carry over a smaller deficiency into 1943 than that estimated by Mr. Nathan. Moreover, excluding the deficiency to be carried over from 1942, the program next year is not materially larger than the Planning Committee estimated as feasible. General Somervell said he is not so despondent about the War Production Board as to feel that with more effective controls over the distribution or materials to be attained through the quota system of allocating materials to each agency, production goals cannot be met. Because of continuing changes in specifications which are being effected daily, it is unwise to assume that the supply of alloys will be inadequate. The amount of copper which can be saved through the substitution of steel cartridge and shell cases may well be larger than estimated. The production and fabrication of aluminum, too, may exceed expectations.

In General Somervell's opinion, requirements, which are the needs of the soldiers and sailors, should not be reduced, and all efforts must be concentrated on increasing supply. It would be most difficult, involving millions of recomputations, to reduce the requirements program or change the schedule prepared by the Joint Chiefs of Staff in any way, since all items in the program are important. Military requirements have been computed realistically, not theoretically; they have been fully coordinated.

To a comment by General Somervell that he was not impressed with the dollar figures in the Planning Committee report, Mr. Henderson replied that the dollar and national income figures seem to be the best common denominators of capacity. General Somervell predicted that it will be possible to reduce dollar costs by 10 percent from existing prices.

General Somervell saw no need for the creation of a new organization in which strategy and production possibilities could be correlated as recommended by Mr. Nathan. Already there are the Combined Chiefs of Staff, the Joint Chiefs of Staff, the Combined Production and Resources Board, the Munitions Assignments Board, the Army and Navy Munitions Board, and the War Production Board. He failed to see what benefit would be derived from a board composed of an economist, a politician, and a soldier who does not know production. Mr. Nathan emphasized that the production authorities should not and could not question strategy, but he inquired whether the Joint Chiefs of Staff, in establishing military requirements, had taken full account of feasibility.

General Somervell said the supply programs submitted to the War Production Board adequately represent the material expressions of strategy, and he saw no need for the Board concerning itself with strategic considerations. In reply to a question from Mr. Coy as to what steps should be taken if production falls below the strategic requirements set by the Chiefs of Staff, General Somervell stated that all that need be done is to change the supply programs presented to the Production Board.

Admiral Robinson stated that the Army and Navy will be able to keep the production program in balance and expressed confidence that the entire munitions program will be more effectively scheduled.

Mr. Patterson expressed the view that a body consisting of production and strategy authorities would not be more fruitful in adjusting the program than the existing mechanism, and he urged that no new agency be created for this purpose. However, he stated that it would be beneficial to have the officials of the War Production Board meet with the Joint Chiefs of Staff from time to time for an exchange of attitudes. Mr. Lubin pointed out that failure to meet the production schedules on time means that the Joint Chiefs of Staff will not have the munitions available in the time required by them, and the Joint Chiefs of Staff should be informed of this.

Mr. McNutt pointed out that despite repeated efforts, the War Manpower Commission has not been able to obtain reliable data on the manpower needs of the Army and Navy. He inquired of Admiral Robinson and Mr. Belcher whether they could inform him of the number of men which it is planned will be in the Navy at the end of 1943, but they were unable to give him this information. Mr. McNutt said that as far as manpower is concerned, the existing Boards referred to by General Somervell have not been fully coordinated. General Somervell promised Mr. McNutt that the War Manpower Commission would be informed of the Army's manpower needs. Mr. McNutt pointed out that already there is a serious general shortage of manpower and that the specific shortages are even more critical; although labor shortages exist in 35 areas, 500,000 workers are idle in New York City. The Chairman observed that the War Production Board had not been informed of the recent proposal to increase the size of the Army, although this proposal vitally affects the production program.

Mr. Henderson pointed out that he had been one of the first to advocate the largest possible military program, but that in order to meet the established program the nation has been forced to sacrifice expansion of certain basic materials such as steel and copper. In his opinion, it is most unlikely that the nation can support a war outlay in 1943 of more than 90 billion dollars, and he inquired whether such an outlay, involving a production of 90 million tons of steel and a supply of over 2,600,000 tons of copper, is not enough to defeat our enemies who have limited resources. Mr. Patterson pointed out that comparisons with our enemies have limited significance because we were forced to start our armament program at later date and, in addition, we now have to supply not only the needs of our own Armed Forces.

Mr. Coy inquired whether the size of the Army should not be determined by the probable supply of available equipment and whether the men who could not be fully supplied should not be retained in production. General Somervell replied that the size of the Army should not be determined by the availability of equipment and that it would be useful to train, even with partial equipment, all the men the Army can induct. Mr. Coy inquired as to the magnitude of probable future increases in the program. As recently as September 17, the President had indicated that he contemplates raising the 1943 airplane objective by 6,000 airplanes and 8,000 gliders, and Mr. Coy predicted that further additions to the munitions program would be made from time to time.

The Chairman stated that his policies and actions had been based on the strong conviction that the most the country can produce is the least with which it can be satisfied. Every effort must be made to obtain the maximum production, provided the program is not thrown out of balance. Giving effect to the recent proposal for augmentation, the airplane program alone would call for an expenditure of over 30 billion dollars in 1943, or 40 percent of what the Planning Committee regards as a feasible total for munitions and war production. A program of this magnitude is bound to impinge on other items and appropriate adjustments will have to be made. In addition, if essential civilian functions, such as transportation, communication, repairs, and maintenance, are curtailed too severely, it will be impossible to support the maximum war production program.

The Vice President pointed out that to accomplish a 115 billion dollar production program next year, it would be necessary to have a national product of 183 billion dollars and to cut consumers' expenditures progressively so that by the end of 1943 they will be at a rate 60 percent below the 1932 level. He asked if Mr. Jones thought that the public could be brought to accept such a reduction in consumer expenditures in any one year. Mr. Jones replied that in his opinion, the largest cut that could be imposed in one year is 25 percent.

Mr. Jones observed that if the munitions program were properly balanced, it would be more advisable to be two or three months behind schedule than to cut the program. Mr. May stated that the program could be met if it is redesigned to produce in 15 months what is now scheduled for 12 months. The

Vice President and Mr. Patterson pointed out that it is most important that the President be informed of any rescheduling that deferred accomplishment of presently stated objective.

Notes

★ ★ ★

Chapter 1. Economics and War

1. In recent years there have even been a number of excellent works that focus primarily on the logistical aspects of war: see Ian Malcolm Brown, *British Logistics on the Western Front: 1914–1919* (Westport, CT: Praeger Publishers, 1998); Martin van Creveld, *Supplying War: Logistics from Wallenstein to Patton* (Cambridge: Cambridge University Press, 2004); Donald W. Engels, *Alexander the Great and the Logistics of the Macedonian Army* (Berkeley: University of California Press, 1980); and John A. Lynn, *Feeding Mars: Logistics in Western Warfare from the Middle Ages to the Present* (Boulder, CO: Westview Press, 1994).
2. The term "dismal science" itself originated in Thomas Carlyle's essay "Occasional Discourse on the Negro Question," *Fraser's Magazine for Town and Country*, vol. XL, February 1849, 531. It states, "It is not a gay science like some we have heard of; no, a dreary, desolate, and indeed quite distressing one; what we might call the dismal science." http://cepa.newschool.edu/het/texts/carlyle/carlodnq.htm (accessed July 2008).
3. Thucydides, *The Landmark Thucydides: A Comprehensive Guide to the Peloponnesian War* (New York: Free Press, 1996), 415.
4. Glyn Davies, *A History of Money From Ancient Times to the Present Day* (Cardiff: University of Wales Press, 2002), 68.
5. T. A. Rickard, "The Mining of the Romans in Spain," *The Journal of Roman Studies* 18 (1928): 129–43.
6. G. Suetonius Tranquillus, *The Lives of the Twelve Caesars* (Oxford: Oxford University Press, 2001), xxi.

7. Tenny Frank, *An Economic Survey of Ancient Rome*, vol. I (Paterson, NJ: Pageant Books, 1959), 320–45. According to Frank, during the Civil War Caesar raised approximately HS600 million from requisitions of silver and gold from Spain. For perspective, the HS600 million revenue in 50 BC was equal to about 600 million grams of silver or some 6.4 million troy ounces of silver. This would be equivalent to about twenty-three thousand Athenian talents (829.5 ounces per talent). In other words, Caesar collected from Spain roughly twelve times the peak revenues of the Athenian Empire.
8. Frank, *An Economic Survey of Ancient Rome*, 355.
9. There have been several first-rate histories of the financial revolution that allowed the Pitts to finance both the wars against Napoleon and the previous Seven Years War, most notably John Brewer, *The Sinews of Power: War, Money and the English State, 1688–1783* (Cambridge, MA: Harvard University Press, 1989); Peter Mathias and Patrick O'Brien, "Taxation in Britain and France: 1715–1810: A Comparison of the Social and Economic Consequences of Taxes Collected for the Central Governments," *Journal of European Economic History* 5, no. 3 (1976): 601–50; Patrick O'Brien, "The Political Economy of British Taxation 1660–1815," *Economic History Review* 41, no. 1 (February 1998): 1–32; J. M. Sherwig, *Guineas and Gunpowder: British Foreign Aid in the Wars with France, 1793–1815* (Cambridge, MA: Harvard University Press, 1969); and J. F. Wright, "British Government Borrowing in Wartime, 1750–1815," *Economic History Review* 52, no. 2 (1999): 355–61. However, while all of these works shed important historical light on the economics of a state at war, they do little to illuminate how economics influenced military strategy and operations.
10. Adam Tooze, *Wages of Destruction* (London: Viking Press, 2006) is an important first step in telling this story.
11. This is a statement that Churchill made in his memoirs but that was probably stolen from Lord George Curzon, who reportedly used it in a cabinet meeting during World War I, according to R. L. Welch, "The Necessity for an Economic Basis of International Peace," *Annals of the American Academy of Political and Social Science* 108 (1923): 82–84.
12. Interest on *consols*, the primary British debt instrument of the Napoleonic Wars, continues to be paid by the U.K. government on a regular basis.
13. This fortress is also known as Juliustrum.
14. Benjamin M. Anderson, *Effects of the War on Money, Credit and Banking in France and the United States* (Oxford University Press, American Branch, 1919; and Washington, DC: Carnegie Endowment for International Peace, 1919): 6. The Germans began storing additional gold in the Reichsbank in 1912, but ceased collecting reserves at about $360 million when they apparently considered they had enough to finance a major war. In reality it was enough to pay for at best a single month of fighting in 1915. See also J. Laughlin, *Credit of Nations: A Study of the European War* (New York: Scribners, 1918), 202–5. Laughlin places the total of Spandau gold at $51 million and goes into great detail on Germany's (and other

European nations') financial preparation for war, noting, "The high regards for the efficacy of gold to be kept in a 'war chest,' although rather medieval and contrary to modern ideas of keeping money in productive uses, persisted in Germany."

15. According to Niall Ferguson, "The British revenue side was exceptionally robust: as a consequence of the reforming budgets of 1907 and 1909/10—which had a far more decisive fiscal outcome than the comparable German finance bill of 1913." See Ferguson, "Public Finance and National Security: The Domestic Origins of the First World War Revisited," *Past and Present* 142 (1994). For an excellent study of Allied finance during World War I, see Martin Horn, *Britain, France, and the Financing of the First World War* (Montreal: School of Policy Studies, Queen's University, 1993).
16. Laughlin, *Credit of Nations,* 133–89.
17. For an excellent analysis of the scope and consequences of this effort, see Kathleen Burk, *Britain, America and the Sinews of War, 1914–1918* (London: HarperCollins Publishers, 1985). Some of this analysis is also summarized in her new book, which is easier to obtain: *Old World, New World* (New York: Grove Press, 2007), 380–460.
18. N. F. Dreisziger, *Mobilization for Total War* (Waterloo, CA: Wilfrid Laurier University Press, 1981), 15–45. See also Kevin Stubs, *Race to the Front: The Material Foundations of Coalition Strategy in the Great War* (Westport, CT: Greenwood Press, 2002).
19. This is obviously not true of the early years of the war when Britain ran down its reserves and liquidated most of its overseas investments to pay for war materiel produced in the United States. Still, it must be noted that England had exhausted its own production capacity long before it had begun to run low on cash. Once Lend-Lease began and then after America entered the war, no Allied nation had to worry about funding—they all only had to worry about production resources.
20. Henry Stimson and McGeorge Bundy, *On Active Service in Peace and War* (New York: Hippocrene Books, 1971), 352.
21. This claim was repeated in the Twenty-eighth Annual Report of the Board of Governors of the Federal Reserve System, 1941, 7–8.
22. John Woolley and Gerhard Peters, *The American Presidency Project.* http://www.presidency.ucsb.edu/ws/?pid=16253 (accessed 1 October 2007).
23. Ibid.
24. Ibid. See also Donald Nelson, *Arsenal of Democracy: The Story of American War Production* (New York: Harcourt, Brace, 1946), 136.
25. As shown later, the statistical revolution that made advanced production planning and scheduling on a national scale possible was just a few years old; there might have been fewer than a dozen Americans who actually understood these tools and their capability for directing a total economic mobilization for war.

Chapter 2. Unmaking the Victory Program

1. An early copy of this document can be found in the Wedemeyer Papers, Box 76, Hoover Institution, Stanford University, Stanford, CA. It has been reprinted: Charles E. Kirkpatrick, *An Unknown Future and a Doubtful Present: Writing the Victory Plan of 1941* (Washington, DC: Center of Military History, U.S. Army, 1990). A copy of Wedemeyer's paper can be found in Appendix 3.
2. There is not a single copy to be found in any of the records of the OPM, the War Production Board (WPB), or FDR's War Files, nor is it mentioned in any of the early histories of these organizations or their successors. In short, there is no evidence that any civilian with a major role to play in military production was even aware it existed. Furthermore, although the Wedemeyer Papers indicate a copy was sent to Secretary of War Henry Stimson, no record of it can be found in any of Stimson's papers, and his only mention of Wedemeyer in his autobiography is in reference to operations in China. Moreover, there appears to be no copy of the document in General Brehon Somervell's (head of Army Supply Forces) papers or in the papers of Undersecretary of War Robert Patterson, who was responsible for all Army procurement.
3. Mark Watson, *Chief of Staff: Prewar Plans and Preparations* (Washington, DC: Army Center for Military History, Department of the Army, 1950), 331. After this it is impossible to trust any of the volumes of the Army's official histories when they discuss the Victory Program or Wedemeyer because every one of them, including Industrial College of the Armed Forces, *Industrial Mobilization for War: History of the War Production Board and Predecessor Agencies: 1940–1945* (Author, 1947), which might have been expected to confirm sources a bit better—reference Watson's chapter on the Victory Program as their primary and often sole source.
4. Watson, *Chief of Staff*, 338.
5. Albert C. Wedemeyer, *Wedemeyer Reports!* (New York: Henry Holt, 1958), 63–85.
6. Colonel Don H. Hampton (Interviewer), "Interview with General Albert C. Wedemeyer" (USAWC/USAMHI Senior Officer Oral History Program, 14 March 1984).
7. It should be noted that in a page-by-page review of the official minutes of the joint chiefs of Staff (National Archive, RG 218.2) the author did not find a single reference to Wedemeyer's program, nor did he find any mention of the Wedemeyer plan in any records of the meetings of the service chiefs prior to the establishment of the Joint Chiefs of Staff. Furthermore, there is no mention of General Wedemeyer in reference to the actual Victory Program in either General Marshall's papers (stored at the Marshall Research Library adjacent to Virginia Military Institute) or in the papers of his deputy, General Thomas Handy (stored at the Military History Institute, Carlisle, PA).

8. Kirkpatrick, *An Unknown Future and a Doubtful Present*, 2. In his bibliography, Kirkpatrick states, "few papers in the Franklin D. Roosevelt Library at Hyde Park, NY, relate to mobilization, in part because of President Roosevelt's habit of conducting business orally. There is little of relevance in his papers, or in those of Harry Hopkins [the president's chief advisor on war production matters], or Henry Morgenthau [Secretary of the Treasury]." The George C. Marshall Papers in the George C. Marshall Library (Lexington, VA) likewise contain little information pertinent to the Victory Plan. Albert C. Wedemeyer's personal papers, which focus on the later part of his career, are in the archives of the Hoover Institution, Stanford University, Stanford, CA. Documents pertaining to the Victory Plan in that collection also may be found in the records of the War Plans Division. They offer little information that reflects on the day-to-day development of the Victory Plan. It appears that Kirkpatrick's research clearly shows that the Wedemeyer plan did not make much of an impression on anyone responsible for strategic mobilization; however, he inexplicably refuses to come to that conclusion. Furthermore, a comparison of the Wedemeyer Papers pertaining to the Victory Program with those in the records of the War Plans Division (Record Group 165 in the National Archives) shows they are identical. It is not too much of a speculative leap to assume that Wedemeyer copied them at some point to add to his own files.
9. Kirkpatrick, *An Unknown Future and a Doubtful Present*.
10. "The Ultimate Requirements Study: Estimate of Ground Forces," Wedemeyer Papers. A full copy of Wedemeyer's so-called Victory Program can be found as an appendix of Kirkpatrick, *An Unknown Future and a Doubtful Present: Writing the Victory Plan of 1941*. The peak mobilization number can be found in U.S. Bureau of the Census, Current Population Series 25, Selected Manpower Statistics, 62–64.
11. Kirkpatrick, *An Unknown Future and a Doubtful Present*, 78.
12. A page-by-page search of the boxes relating to the Wedemeyer Plan (Boxes 76 and 77, consisting of twenty folders) did not have a single item detailing how he arrived at the 10 percent figure. Similarly, there was neither evidence of how he arrived at any of his other estimates nor any paper trail to indicate he ever sent inquiries for information to anyone else, as he often claimed.
13. Author's conversation with the Princeton Demographics Center's (now called The Office of Population Research at Princeton University) archivist Chang Y. Chung on 10 October 2007.
14. Again, there is no evidence in his papers of that research or the ensuing calculations ever being done.
15. Kurt A. Raaflaub and Nathan Rosenstein, *War and Society in the Ancient and Medieval Worlds: Asia, the Mediterranean, Europe, and Mesoamerica* (Cambridge: Cambridge University Press, 1999). Some historians furthering work first done by Gaetano de Sanctis

in 1907 have advocated a much higher military participation ratio during the Second Punic War. This is probably true, but the circumstances were extreme and Rome's economic condition was dire throughout the period (and was saved only by grain from Sicily and silver from Spain after Scipio's conquests).

16. Strategy World, "The Military Participation Ratio" (on The Strategy Page), http://www.strategypage.com/cic/docs/cic88b.asp (accessed 1 October 2007).
17. François Crouzet, "Wars, Blockades, and Economic Change in Europe, 1972–1815," *Journal of Economic History* 24, no. 4 (1964): 573–74; Peter Mathias and Sidney Pollard, *The Cambridge History of Europe*, vol. 8, *The Industrial Economies: The Development of Economic and Social Policies* (Cambridge: Cambridge University Press, 1989), 407–64; Larry Neal, "A Tale of Two Revolutions: International Capital Flows 1789–1819," *Bulletin of Economic Research* 43, no. 1 (1991): 57–92. On average, British payments to Prussia equalled about 7 percent of Prussian GDP during the period of the Napoleonic Wars and often exceeded 20 percent of Prussian government revenues during the war years.
18. David Chandler, *The Campaigns of Napoleon* (New York: Scribners, 1973).
19. Compiled by the Navy War College; data can be found at http://64.233.169.104/search?q=cache:QXMfpJ9fXeMJ:www.lib.lsu.edu/cwc/other/stats/warcost.htm+us+wars+military+participation&hl=en&ct=clnk&cd=1&gl=us (accessed 1 February 2008). These numbers are confirmed in a recent Congressional Research Staff study, "American War and Military Operations Casualties: List of Statistics." This report can be found at http://www.fas.org/sgp/crs/natsec/RL32492.pdf
20. An exhaustive search of the Wedemeyer Papers at the Hoover Institution did not turn up a single piece of evidence as to how he made any of his estimates.
21. There are some tables of allowances in the files, but, as will be seen, they are not Wedemeyer's work but instead are the work of officers in the Army G-4 (logistics) section, which was begun well before Wedemeyer undertook his study.
22. Watson, *Chief of Staff*, 337–40. In a footnote, Watson states that this section is based on his discussion on these points with General Wedemeyer in 1948. See Watson, fn. 33, p. 340.
23. One reason that the staff did not surmise the "immense reach, complexity, and importance" of Wedemeyer's work at the time is that it probably was not viewed as a tremendous effort until Wedemeyer announced it as so after the war. Also, it is important to remember that Watson based his account of this episode and Wedemeyer's role in the creation of the Victory Plan almost entirely on his personal discussions with Wedemeyer.
24. Lawrence Guyer, "The Joint Chiefs and the War Against Germany," unpublished manuscript.
25. Ibid., Section 2 (n.p.).
26. Ibid.

27. See also "The Determination of Army Supply Requirements," for further confirmation of this position. This report (available in archival material stored at the National Defense University Library) was a restricted study prepared in 1946 by order of General Somervell. This never-published document details the history of military production and supply from the perspective of the Army logistical agencies and is supported by two full volumes of original supporting documents.
28. As will be seen, the reason the G-4 could deliver estimates so quickly is that they had been preparing just such estimates for months under orders from Colonel James Burns, who was working as a special assistant to Roosevelt's closest adviser, Harry Hopkins. Burns also provided the G-4 with a rough estimate of the eventual size of the force to plan for, which was approved by General Marshall.
29. These estimates remained woefully short of the information the civilian planning agencies required, but they were the starting point from which the actual Victory Program was built by Stacy May (see Chapter 3).
30. A case can be made that Wedemeyer's final presentation was delayed by new requirements established in a 9 July 1941 letter from the president to the Joint Chiefs of Staff (see Chapter 3). However, the author believes the president's demands were exactly what Wedemeyer and Aurand started out to accomplish in the first place, and Aurand found no reason to update his submission based on the new requirements.
31. See Chapter 10.
32. "The Ultimate Requirements Study," Wedemeyer Papers (Box 76, Hoover Institution, Stanford University, Stanford, CA). See also Kirkpatrick, *An Unknown Future and a Doubtful Present*, 125, and Appendix 3, this volume.
33. Richard W. Stewart, *American Military History*, vol. 2, *The United States Army in a Global Era, 1917–2003* (Washington, DC: Department of the Army, 2005), 93.
34. As noted earlier, there is no evidence that any industrialist was aware that Wedemeyer's paper even existed in any of the key archives of the production agencies.
35. As a side note of possible interest: while going through the Wedemeyer Papers, the author found several minutes of meetings where the topic of discussion was the Victory Program (all of the meetings took place in mid to late 1942). At the beginning of each of these records is a typed list of everyone who attended: Wedemeyer is not listed on any of them, except where he had written his name on top of the others. It is surely unusual that someone would write himself in as a participant in meetings on his own record copy of the minutes, unless he was writing himself into the historical record.
36. As will be demonstrated later, the economists at the WPB knew in late 1941 almost exactly how many divisions the U.S. Army could build, transport, and maintain. They would have viewed Wedemeyer's estimates as fanciful.

37. Wedemeyer, *Wedemeyer Reports!*, 74. Once again there is no trace of this supposed coordination, which one would have expected to produce voluminous correspondence, in the Wedemeyer Papers.
38. Marshall, *The War Reports of General George C. Marshall*, The United States News, 1947:157–58. http://www.ibiblio.org/hyperwar/USA/COS-Biennial/COS-Biennial-3.html (accessed 1 October 2007).
39. Brehon Somervell, "Problems of Production in World War II," Industrial College of the United States Archives (speech given at Fort McNair, Washington, DC, 18 November 1948).
40. In the Wedemeyer Papers there are several copies of extensive tables of allowances with detailed figures written in. However, there is no evidence that these tables found their way to the production people. More important, the tables are estimates of what it would take to supply a 2 million– and 4 million–person army; as such, they appear to be the result of the work of the Quartermaster Corps and G-4 and were assembled by Colonel Henry Aurand, because General Marshall and Colonel James Burns (special assistant to presidential adviser Harry Hopkins) directed them to prepare exactly such estimates. Since they did not give any indication of when the military wanted the items delivered, the production experts would have found them useless for planning purposes (as they did with the tables delivered from the Quartermaster Corps, which are commented on by various production experts, but which the author was unable to find in the records). They may have provided the initial building blocks for the "Consolidated Balance Sheet" produced by Stacy May, about which there will be more discussion later in this narrative.
41. A further indication that Wedemeyer's estimates of total requirements were not expounded throughout the system.
42. Robert Sherwood, *Roosevelt and Hopkins: An Intimate History* (New York: Enigma Books, 2001), 133.
43. Ibid., 158.
44. Ibid., 280.
45. A detailed report on the topic ("The Army Industrial College and Mobilization Planning Between the Wars") can be found at http://stinet.dtic.mil/oai/oai?verb=getRecord&metadataPrefix=html&identifier=ADA276612 (accessed 1 October 2007). A complete account of the IMP and the effects of its scuttling can be found in R. Elberton Smith, *The Army and Economic Mobilization* (Washington, DC: Office of the Chief of Military History, 1959), 119–31.

Chapter 3. The Real Victory Program

1. This memo can be found in President Roosevelt's office safe, in the "safe file" at the FDR Library in Hyde Park, NY.

2. The exception is Louis Morton, who covered the development of Plan Dog in some detail. See Morton, *Command Decisions: Germany First: The Basic Concept of Allied Strategy in World War II* (Washington, DC: Center of Military History, 2000), 35; and Morton, *Strategy and Command: The First Two Years* (Washington, DC: Center of Military History, 1961), 81–84.
3. W. K. Hancock and M. M. Gowing, *British War Economy* (London: Her Majesty's Stationery Office, 1949), 384.
4. Plan Orange eventually was overtaken by the first four Rainbow plans, which in varying degrees kept Japan as the primary enemy (particularly for the Navy) while also addressing the need for hemispheric defense against the Germans. The story of U.S. war plan development is well told in Henry G. Gole, *The Road to Rainbow: Army Planning for Global War, 1934–1940* (Annapolis, MD: Naval Institute Press, 2003), and in Edward S. Miller, *War Plan Orange: The U.S. Strategy to Defeat Japan, 1897–1945* (Annapolis, MD: Naval Institute Press, 2007).
5. Guyer, "The Joint Chiefs and the War Against Germany," Section 2 (no page number). In a letter to Admiral Hart, Admiral Stark wrote, "As a start on this I sat down one early morning and drew up the twelve page rough estimate, working until two o'clock the next morning. . . . After I finished the rough notes, I then got together with my staff and we went at it day and night for about ten consecutive days. The product which no one claims is perfect is now in the hands of the President."
6. Mitchell Simpson, *Harold R. Stark: Architect of Victory. 1939–1945* (Columbia: University of South Carolina Press, 1989), 66.
7. Plan Dog Case File, FDR Library, Safe Files, Hyde Park, NY.
8. Morton, *Command Decisions*, 235.
9. Guyer, "The Joint Chiefs and the War Against Germany," Section 2 (no page number).
10. Ibid.
11. Ibid.
12. Plan Dog Case File, FDR Library, Safe Files; Hyde Park, NY.
13. Ibid.
14. Ibid.
15. According to Guyer's unpublished history, "The Joint Chiefs and the War Against Germany," the first drafts of this document had five choices: (1) War with Japan in which we have no allies. (2) War with Japan with the British Empire and the Netherlands as allies. (3) War with Japan in which Japan is aided by Italy and we have no allies. (4) War with Germany and Italy in which Japan would not be initially involved and in which we would be allied with the British. (5) Remaining out of the war and dedicating ourselves exclusively to building up our defense of the Western Hemisphere, plus continued materiel support to Britain.

16. Ibid.
17. According to Guyer in "The Joint Chiefs and the War Against Germany," "The Chief of Staff of the Army and the Chief of Naval Operations were therefore authorized to use these proposals as the basis for staff conversations with the British and for the future actions of the Army and Navy staffs."
18. Simpson, *Harold R. Stark*, 72.
19. "United States–British Staff Conversation Report, ABC-1, March 27, 1941," in Stephen Ross, *American War Plans* (Florence, KY: Routledge, 2004), 67–101.
20. Ibid., 68–69.
21. Joint Board Estimates of United States Over-All Production Requirements, FDR Library, Safe Files, Hyde Park, NY.
22. John E. Brigante, "The Feasibility Dispute: Determination of War Production Objectives for 1942–1943." An unpublished case study by the Committee on Public Administration Cases (1950), 23.
23. Joint Board Estimates of United States Over-All Production Requirements, FDR Library, Safe Files, Hyde Park, NY.
24. FDR Library, Safe Files, Hyde Park, NY.
25. Lawrence Guyer, "The Joint Chiefs and the War Against Germany," Section 2 (no page number).
26. See Chapter 2, 14–16.
27. The requirements tables that are located in the Wedemeyer Papers closely resemble the "Munitions Program of June 1940," another copy of which is in the National Archive's War Production Board Records (RG 179.2.1). These tables were prepared at the direction of Colonel James Burns, although they had been modified over the intervening year as new appropriations were approved by Congress.
28. *Time*, 1 June 1942. A copy can be found at http://www.time.com/time/magazine/article/0,9171,790519,00.html (accessed 1 October 2007).
29. Smith, *The Army and Economic Mobilization*, 130.
30. Industrial College of the Armed Forces, *Industrial Mobilization for War*, 130. It was while working on this committee that Burns both got to know the key production experts and to understand their requirements from the military in regards to planning documents.
31. Memo from Burns to Assistant Secretary of War Johnson outlining Knudsen's request, 9 April 1941, National Archives Miscellaneous Records, RG 179.2.5.
32. See the documentation included in the "The Determination of Army Supply Requirements" (National Defense University, Washington, DC) for copies of this report and much of the associated correspondence.
33. Watson, *Chief of Staff*, 174.
34. Ibid., 175.

35. As mentioned earlier, the report the president received on 11 September can be found in the FDR Library, Safe Files, Hyde Park, NY. A copy of the Wedemeyer Report is in Appendix 3, this volume.
36. The estimates in the Wedemeyer Papers were actually those that Colonel Burns ordered prepared based on his overall estimates. This work was begun in June 1940 and later was continued by Colonel Aurand. There is no indication that the massive army outlined in the Wedemeyer Papers was ever translated into an estimate of munitions requirements.
37. Brigante, "The Feasibility Dispute," 24. This appears to be the first time a table of allowance was delivered in full and was likely the expanded "Munitions Program of June 1940."
38. Robert Nathan, "GNP and Military Mobilization," *Journal of Evolutionary Economics* (April 1994), 12.
39. "The United States at War: Development and Administration of the War Program by the Federal Government." Prepared under the auspices of the Committee of War Administration by the War Records Section, Bureau of the Budget (June 1946), 80. This document can be found at http://www.ibiblio.org/hyperwar/ATO/Admin/WarProgram/.
40. SPAB began life as the National Defense Advisory Commission and was later to transition into the OPM. The history and complex evolution of the multitude of organizations created to manage the economic side of the war is well covered in Paul A. C. Koistinen's *Arsenal of World War II: The Political Economy of American Warfare, 1940–1945* (Lawrence: University Press of Kansas, 2004).
41. Nelson, *Arsenal of Democracy*, 129.
42. Industrial College of the Armed Forces, *Industrial Mobilization for War*, 134.
43. Nathan, "GNP and Military Mobilization," and Sherwood, *Roosevelt and Hopkins*. Monnet, of course, has received far more acclaim and recognition as the so-called Father of the European Union.
44. Nelson, *Arsenal of Democracy*, 130. This is Monnet's claim. In actuality, U.S. GDP was roughly three times the UK GDP in 1941, while installed production capacity was about four times the size of Britain's.
45. Nathan, "GNP and Military Mobilization," 9.
46. Sherwood, *Roosevelt and Hopkins*, 226.
47. There are various versions of this story with Donald Nelson and William Knudsen, among others, claiming credit for originating the term.
48. Nathan, "GNP and Military Mobilization," 9.
49. Nelson, *Arsenal of Democracy*, 129–31.
50. Speech given by Robert Nathan on 25 May 1950, Publication No. L50–144, "Appraisal of the War Production Board," Industrial War College of the Armed Forces Archives, Fort McNair, Washington, DC.
51. Nelson, *Arsenal of Democracy*, 131.

52. Speech to the Foreign Policy Association, "The Production Line of Defense," 25 October 1941. A copy is maintained in the Stacy May Papers at the University of Wyoming. (There is no file location available because these papers have not yet been professionally archived.)
53. According to the official history of the Civilian Production Agency this idea had already been discussed and agreed upon as early as 18 February 1941. By 8 March, Stacy May's team was already putting together a ledger of American requirements and capabilities. This document was to be the basis of the Anglo-American Consolidated Statement that May would assemble later in the year. See Industrial College of the Armed Forces, *Industrial Mobilization for War*, 134–36.
54. Industrial College of the Armed Forces, *Industrial Mobilization for War*, 132.
55. There is some dispute on the origin of this quote, with the majority attributing it to Oscar Wilde, who wrote in *The Canterville Ghost* (1906), "We have really everything in common with America nowadays except, of course, language." See http://www.gutenberg.org/etext/14522 (accessed 7 December 2009).
56. Hancock and Gowing, *British War Economy*, 385.
57. Ibid., 386.
58. Nelson, *Arsenal of Democracy*, 133.
59. Ibid., 385.
60. Ibid., 136.
61. Ibid., 133.
62. A 4 December 1941 memorandum from Stacy May to Donald Nelson called for the average of all military requirements to be doubled: Records of the Office of War Production, National Archives, RG 179.1. See Chapter 7, this volume, for a detailed analysis for the reasoning behind this memorandum.
63. Industrial College of the Armed Forces, *Industrial Mobilization for War*, 140.

Chapter 4. The Economist's War

1. Editorial, *New Republic*, 14 September 1945.
2. None of the major histories of World War II written in the past twenty years mentions Stacy May, Simon Kuznets, or Robert Nathan, all of whom made a contribution to victory that arguably was at least as great as the joint chiefs' contributions.
3. Herbert Stein, "Papers and Proceedings of the Ninety-Eighth Annual Meeting of the American Economic Association," *American Economic Review* 76, no. 2 (May 1986): 5.
4. John Kenneth Galbraith, *The National Accounts: Arrival and Impact, Reflections of America: Commemorating the Statistical Abstract Centennial*, U.S. Department of Commerce Publication Commemorating the Statistical Abstract (Washington, DC: Government Printing Office, 1980).

5. Hancock and Gowing, *British War Economy*, 105–6. The authors have this to say about Britain's international financial position: "The aggregate sum of past overseas investments was less in 1939 than it had been a generation earlier; if the nation's holdings of gold were larger, its holdings of useful foreign securities were considerably smaller."
6. According to economic historian Richard Gardner, British gold reserves in 1940 stood at $4 billion. By mid-1941 those reserves were exhausted. See Gardner, *Sterling-Dollar Diplomacy* (New York: Columbia University Press, 1969), 174. British buying power was severely eroded by the precipitous depreciation of Sterling. This fall started in 1938, and Sterling had lost a fifth of its value by the time France fell. This decline continued almost uninterrupted during 1941–42. For a thorough analysis of this topic, see August Maffry, "The Depreciation of the Pound Sterling," Finance Division, Bureau of Foreign and Domestic Commerce (1939), http://library.bea.gov/cdm4/document.php?CISOROOT=/SCB&CISOPTR=4285&REC=8&CISOSHOW=4280 (accessed 1 October 2007).
7. M. Tullius Cicero, *The Orations of Marcus Tullius Cicero*, transl. by C. D. Yonge (New York: Harper, 1903), 95. This quote may be an adaptation of the original, "First of all the sinews of war is money in abundance."
8. Some economists claim that the draft was in effect a form of commandeering; however, it is an arcane argument and will not be addressed here. Furthermore, the Germans and the Japanese did make use of commandeering of the resources of conquered territories to propel their economies. However, Axis economic policy is outside the scope of this work and most economic historians now state that Japan and Germany suffered a net economic negative in dealing with their satellites and conquered territories. For in-depth discussion of this subject, refer to Tooze, *Wages of Destruction*, and Mark Harrison, ed., *The Economics of World War II: Six Great Powers in International Comparison* (Cambridge: Cambridge University Press, 1998), and Alan S. Milward, *War, Economy and Society: 1939–1945* (Berkeley: University of California Press, 1977). The United States was not immune from using captured labor and other resources. In his final report on the war to Secretary of War Stimson, Marshall boasts about the use of 62,075,800 prisoner working days (equals about forty-five thousand full-time workers on an annual basis) to assist the war effort (Marshall, *The War Reports of General George C. Marshall*, 284). However, use of this and other captured resources still made up only an infinitesimal part of the American war effort.
9. Hugh Rockoff, in Harrison, *The Economics of World War II*, 109. This position was articulated by Secretary of the Treasury John W. Snyder in a December 1951 speech at the Industrial War College. Snyder was a former director of the office of War Mobilization and Reconversion and previously was in charge of the Defense Plant Corporation, which financed the construction of new wartime production facilities. Snyder's speech "The Role of the Federal Reserve in Financing War" can be found at http://www.ndu.edu/library/ic1/L46–101.pdf (accessed 1 October 2007). It should be noted that Maynard Keynes'

pamphlet, "Paying for the War" (1940) also advocated using taxes as the primary funding method, as did most other economists at the time. A large collection of these writings is archived on the website for the NBER and can be accessed at http://www.nber.org/nber-history/ (accessed 1 October 2007).

10. Secretary of the Treasury Snyder in a speech one year earlier than the one noted above to the Industrial War College, with the same title, "The Role of the Federal Reserve in Financing War," can be found at http://www.ndu.edu/library/ic1/L46–101.pdf (accessed 1 October 2007).
11. Every economist in government had witnessed the hyperinflation in Germany, which contributed to Hitler's rise, and hence each was predisposed to view hyperinflation as one of the worst economic disasters possible.
12. Milton Friedman and Ann Schwartz, *A Monetary History of the United States: 1867–1960* (Princeton, NJ: Princeton University Press, 1971), 546–50.
13. Milton Friedman and other economists blamed the rapid wartime expansion of the monetary stock on the immediate postwar spike in inflation. See Friedman and Schwartz, *A Monetary History of the United States*, 546–50.
14. Gerald White, *Billions for Defense: Government Finance by the Defense Plant Corporation During World War II* (Tuscaloosa: University of Alabama Press, 2005), 45.
15. For an excellent study, conducted in 1942, of the funding methods being considered by the government and an analysis of their likely effect on the economy, see "Alternatives in War Finance," Department of Commerce, October 1942, http://library.bea.gov/cdm4/document.php?CISOROOT=/SCB&CISOPTR=3443&REC=9&CISOSHOW=3435 (accessed 1 October 2007).
16. Interesting statistics and graphs showing the amount of money in circulation, the gold stock, and reserve bank credit throughout the war period can be found in *Federal Reserve Bulletins* from the war. All these reports and the statistics have been gathered in several volumes, which can be accessed at http://fraser.stlouisfed.org/publications/ (accessed 1 October 2007). A good synopsis of the financial situation of the United States can be found in Anna Youngman, "The Federal Reserve System in Wartime."
17. Charles Whittlesey, "The Banking System and War Finance," National Bureau of Economic Research, New York, Financial Research Program, "Our Economy at War," Occasional Paper, 8 February 1943, 29.
18. Ibid., 12.
19. *Federal Reserve Bulletin*, July 1942, 592.
20. Clark Warburton, "Monetary Policy in the United States in World War II," *American Journal of Economics and Sociology* 4, no. 3 (April 1945): 378.
21. Ibid.

22. According to Secretary of the Treasury Snyder ("The Role of the Federal Reserve in Financing War," 1951), of these 16,000 banks only 6,300 were members of the Federal Reserve System, although these 6,300 banks controlled more than 75 percent of U.S. financial assets.
23. Warburton, "Monetary Policy of the United States in World War II," 380.
24. For an excellent primer on debt monetization and its potential impact, see Daniel L. Thornton, "Monetizing the Debt," Federal Reserve Bank of St. Louis (1984). http://ideas.repec.org/a/fip/fedlrv/y1984idecp30-43nv.66no.10.html.
25. Rockoff, in Harrison, *The Economics of World War II*, 107.
26. As we have seen, the debt was issued but then was immediately repurchased from the banks by the Federal Reserve, which is how the United States creates (prints) money in its open market operations.
27. Rockoff, in Harrison, *The Economics of World War II*, 108. Freidman shows rather conclusively that the monetary stock continued to increase throughout the war. However, this is a reflection of the multiplier effect earlier government security purchases had coupled with an increased monetary velocity (concepts we will not belabor in this work).
28. Speech given by Thomas B. McCabe, Chair, Board of Governors of the Federal Reserve System, on the "The Role of the Federal Reserve in Wartime," to the Industrial War College, 10 January 1951.
29. Ibid.
30. The Treasury and the Federal Reserve agreed to hold the interest rate on long-term bonds at 2.5 percent, with a sliding scale for shorter-term notes, depending on their maturity. The pricing of bonds was a complex problem all through the war. For those interested in the complexities of the debt market during the war, the best place to start is Henry C. Murphy, *The National Debt in War and Transition* (New York: McGraw-Hill, 1950).
31. McCabe, "The Role of the Federal Reserve in Wartime."
32. Whittlesey, "The Banking System and War Finance," 18.
33. Nelson, *Arsenal of Democracy*, 212–38.
34. Alan Gropman, *The Big L: American Logistics in World War II* (Fort McNair, Washington, DC: National Defense University, 1997), 160.
35. See "Alternatives in War Finance."
36. For a more thorough discussion of taxation and debt in wartime, readers are referred to Murphy, *The National Debt in War and Transition*.
37. Harold G. Vatter, *The U.S. Economy in World War II* (New York: Columbia University Press, 1985), 111.
38. Elmus Wicker, "The World War II Policy of Fixing a Pattern of Interest Rates," *Journal of Finance* 24, no. 3 (June 1969): 449.
39. Youngman, "The Federal Reserve System in Wartime," 49–50.

40. "Twenty-eighth Annual Report of the Board of Governors of the Federal Reserve System," (1941): 7–8.
41. A relatively thorough reading of the literature of the time shows that economists had no doubt that the United States could raise almost unlimited amounts of money. What concerned them was what methods the government would adopt to stabilize this massive growth in the monetary base in order to stifle inflation.
42. For an excellent study on the Federal Reserve during World War II, see Edward C. Simmons, "Federal Reserve Policy and National Debt During the War Years," *Journal of Business of the University of Chicago* 20, no. 2 (April 1947): 84–95.
43. Author interview with Mary Nathan, 5 October 2007.
44. Minutes of the Statistical Committee, 26 February 1942, National Archives RG 179, Box 5.
45. Robert Fogel, "Simon Kuznets (a short biography)," National Bureau of Economic Research, New York, Working Paper 7787 (July 2000), 1. This paper can be found at http://www.nber.org/papers/W7787.pdf (accessed 1 October 2007).
46. Fogel, "Simon Kuznets," 2.
47. Ibid.
48. Bureau of Economic Analysis, "GDP: One of the Great Inventions of the 20th Century," Bureau of Economic Analysis (January 2000) *Survey of Current Business,* Washington, DC.
49. Robert W. Fogel, in a speech given before the Association of American Universities (Washington, DC, 17 April 2000).
50. Carol Carson, "The History of the United States National Income and Product Accounts: The Development of an Analytical Tool," *Review of Income and Wealth* 21, no. 2 (1975): 153–81.
51. Adolph C. Miller, "War Finance and Inflation," *Annals* (January 1918): 113–34.
52. Carson, "The History of the United States National Income and Product Accounts," 154.
53. Ibid., 155.
54. Senate Resolution 220, 72nd Congress, 1st Session, Congressional Record, LXXV, 12285.
55. Carson, "The History of the United States National Income and Product Accounts," 157.
56. Rosemary D. Marcuss and Richard E. Kane, "U.S. National Income and Product Statistics: Born in the Great Depression and World War II," *Survey of Current Business*, Bureau of Economic Analysis, Washington, DC (February 2007): 35.
57. U.S. Congress, Senate, National Income 1929–32, S. Doc. 124, 73rd Congress, 2nd Session, 1934.
58. Marcuss and Kane, "U.S. National Income and Product Statistics," 36.
59. Carson, "The History of the United States National Income and Product Accounts," 160.
60. Fogel, in a speech given before the Association of American Universities (Washington, DC, 17 April 2000).

61. *Survey of Current Business*, Bureau of Economic Analysis, Washington, DC (January 2000).
62. Paul Samuelson and William D. Nordhaus, *Economics* (New York: McGraw-Hill/Irwin, 2004), 74.
63. For those interested in the complete collection of Kuznets' original datasets, see Simon Kuznets, *National Income and Its Composition* (1941). Kuznets later updated his data and interpretation to account for the effects of war on the nation's economic structure and output; see Kuznets, *National Product in Wartime* (New York: National Bureau of Economic Research, 1946).
64. Marcuss and Kane, "U.S. National Income and Product Statistics," 37.
65. It remains to be seen how the ongoing financial crisis as of this writing in 2010 will alter this analysis.
66. Bureau of Economic Analysis, "GDP."
67. The Bureau of Economic Analysis has made all of these studies available in digital form at http://library.bea.gov/ (accessed 1 October 2007). This particular document can be accessed at http://library.bea.gov/cdm4/document.php?CISOROOT=/SCB&CISOPTR=3026&REC=6&CISOSHOW=3023 (accessed 1 October 2007).
68. FDR Message to Congress on Stimulating Recovery, 14 April 1938. This statement can be accessed at http://www.presidency.ucsb.edu/ws/print.php?pid=15626 (accessed 1 October 2007).
69. Annual Message to Congress (4 January 1939). This statement can be accessed at http://www.presidency.ucsb.edu/ws/index.php?pid=15684 (accessed 1 October 2007).
70. Marcuss and Kane, "U.S. National Income and Product Statistics," 36.
71. For a wartime analysis of the superiority of GNP calculations over other national income accounts in regards to managing a total mobilization for war, see War Expenditures and National Production, by Milton Gilbert, *Survey of Current Business*, Bureau of Economic Analysis, Washington, DC (March 1942). This report can be accessed at http://library.bea.gov/cdm4/document.php?CISOROOT=/SCB&CISOPTR=3130&REC=6&CISOSHOW=3122 (accessed 1 October 2007).
72. GNP statistics also were critical in fighting a concept first outlined by John Maynard Keynes, "The Inflationary Gap." In gist, this is the expected rate of inflation caused by increased cash flows chasing a reduced amount of goods. While this is an important economic consideration for the proper functioning of a wartime economy, it does not pertain to our topic of production as it affected U.S. military strategy and will not be dealt with in this work.
73. This statement always rankles those who lived through the war or were raised on stories of rubber drives and rationing. However, the statistics bear out the fact that, except for large consumer durables, most Americans had more of everything than they did in the years preceding the war. For some interesting statistics on U.S. per capita food and other consumer production during the war, see Harrison, *The Economics of World War II*,

85–94. For the efficacy of scrap drives and other economic initiatives based on consumer participation, see Professor Hugh Rockoff's unpublished paper "Getting in the Scrap: The Salvage Drives of World War II," which can be accessed at http://econpapers.repec.org/paper/rutrutres/200002.htm (accessed 1 October 2007). For studies conducted during and immediately after the war on consumer consumption and related items, see Milton Gilbert, "National Income and Product Statistics of the United States 1929–46," http://library.bea.gov/cdm4/document.php?CISOROOT=/SCB&CISOPTR=3197&REC=6&CISOSHOW=3141); "National Income and National Product in 1943" (issued by the Bureau of Domestic and Foreign Commerce—http://library.bea.gov/cdm4/document.php?CISOROOT=/SCB&CISOPTR=3231&REC=4&CISOSHOW=3220), and "Monthly Estimates of Total Consumer Expenditures 1935–42" by William C. Shelton (Department of Commerce—http://library.bea.gov/cdm4/document.php?CISOROOT=/SCB&CISOPTR=3327&REC=10&CISOSHOW=33190). All URLs are current as of 1 October 2007.

74. All wartime production, income, and spending statistics tracked by the Commerce Department were recently posted on the Bureau of Economic Analysis' website in the digital library (www.bea.gov).
75. In May's case he worked in his own section, rather independently of Nathan, but all of his statistical work was now in support of Nathan's requirements.

Chapter 5. The Production Organizations

1. Those who wish to delve deeply into the establishment and development of the production agencies should read Paul A. C. Koistinen's masterful work, *Arsenal of World War II.*
2. Alan L. Gropman, "Mobilizing U.S. Industry During World War II," McNair Paper No. 50, National Defense University, Washington, DC (1996), 31.
3. Nathan, "GNP and Military Mobilization," 6.
4. See page 26 for more information on this topic.
5. Nathan, "GNP and Military Mobilization," 6.
6. The story of how the government financed the construction of a large part of the munitions industry from 1941 forward is both interesting and complex. Those interested in knowing more are encouraged to read White's *Billions for Defense.*
7. Speech given by William Knudsen to the Industrial War College in 1946, "Problems in War Production," http://www.ndu.edu/library/ic1/L46–101.pdf (accessed 10 April 2009).
8. Nelson, *Arsenal of Democracy*, 227.
9. Ibid., 232.
10. Ibid., 233.
11. Nathan, "GNP and Military Mobilization," 6.
12. Henderson presentation to the Industrial War College, "Organization and Administrative Problems of the Price Administrator," April 1950, http://www.ndu.edu/library/ic1/L50–130.pdf.

13. Ibid.
14. Henderson presentation to the Industrial War College, "Price, Profit and Wage Control," May 1947, http://www.ndu.edu/library/ic1/L50–130.pdf (accessed 1 October 2008).
15. Edward Stettinius had been a senior officer at both General Motors and U.S. Steel before accepting Roosevelt's offer to become director of the OPM in 1940. He later took over the direction of Lend-Lease and ended his government service, late in the war, as secretary of state.
16. Henderson presentation to the Industrial War College, "Organization and Administrative Problems of the Price Administrator," April 1950, http://www.ndu.edu/library/ic1/L50–130.pdf (accessed 1 October 2008).
17. Henderson, "Price, Profit and Wage Control." Will Clayton is one of the great unsung heroes of World War II. Rising from humble origins, he became one of the richest men in America through commodities trading. He put all his trading talents to work for the government during the war, assembling a team of fifty professional traders who purchased almost the entire available global supply of every strategic material and thereby denied them to the Axis. After the war, he became the driving force behind the Marshall Plan.
18. Gropman, "Mobilizing U.S. Industry During World War II," 33.
19. After World War I, the Army and Navy had cooperated to build an IMP that was to go into effect as soon as war was declared. This plan was updated on a regular schedule and provided the basis for military planning for industrial mobilization. The plan was never instituted because it was wildly out of touch with industrial realities in 1941; due to the United States enacting increasing mobilization activities on an incremental basis as the roll to war began, there was no big-bang event that would have called for the plan's initiation. However, from Roosevelt's perspective, the most troublesome part of the plan was that it took all industrial activities out of civilian hands and placed them in the military's. This was something Roosevelt would never countenance.
20. "The United States at War."
21. Gropman, "Mobilizing U.S. Industry During World War II," 34.
22. Ibid.
23. Bureau of the Budget, The United States at War: Development and Administration of the War Program by the Federal Government (Washington, DC: U.S. GPO, 1946).
24. Franklin D. Roosevelt, *The Public Papers and Addresses of Franklin Roosevelt* (New York: Macmillan, 1941), 622–31.
25. "The United States at War."
26. Nelson, *Arsenal of Democracy*, 117.
27. Koistinen, *Arsenal of World War II*, 126.
28. Industrial College of the Armed Forces, *Industrial Mobilization for War* (1947), 98.
29. Ibid., 99.

30. Koistinen, *Arsenal of World War II,* 128.
31. Ibid., 130.
32. Ibid., 131.
33. Industrial College of the Armed Forces, *Industrial Mobilization for War* (1947), 103.
34. Ibid.
35. Author interview with David Ginsberg on 11 October 2007. David Ginsberg was Leon Henderson's deputy during this period and later was general counsel to the OPA. In later life he was a counselor to presidents Kennedy and Johnson, but during this period he was Henderson's right-hand man and was present for many of the meetings discussed in this work. As far as the author can determine, he is the last of the New Dealers still living at the time of writing and his insights into the personalities involved in these debates were invaluable.
36. Koistinen, *Arsenal of World War II,* 132.
37. Industrial College of the Armed Forces, *Industrial Mobilization for War* (1947), 103.
38. "He had long since become the foremost mass buyer in the United States. From 1928 through 1938 he bought merchandise that sold for $4,500,000,000—some 135,000 items, from tin cups to tractors, from diapers to tombstones" (*Time*, 24 February 1941).
39. Industrial College of the Armed Forces, *Industrial Mobilization for War* (1947), 113.
40. Gropman, "Mobilizing U.S. industry During World War II," 43
41. Koistinen, *Arsenal of World War II*, 182.
42. Nelson, *Arsenal of Democracy*, 171.
43. Koistinen, *Arsenal of World War II,* 183.
44. Gropman, "Mobilizing U.S. Industry During World War II," 44.
45. In mid-1942 the civilian production experts finally forced the military to agree to dismantle the priorities apparatus in favor of a new system called the Production Requirements Plan (PRP). The PRP turned into an administrative nightmare requiring more than twenty thousand bureaucrats to process the paperwork that industry was forced to forward on a quarterly basis. With production scheduling on the verge of seizing up, a simplified system, called the Controlled Materials Plan (CMP) was instituted in late 1942. The CMP controlled just three metals (copper, aluminum, and steel) and assumed all other materials required for war production would fall into proper alignment once these three crucial materials were controlled. This debate took place at the same time as the feasibility dispute, which is the focus of this work. For those interested in the details of this critical facet of production controls, see Christman, "Ferdinand Eberstadt and Economic Mobilization," unpublished doctoral dissertation, History Department, Ohio State University, 1971; Koistinen, *Arsenal of World War II*; David Novick, *Wartime Production Control* (New York: Da Capo Press, 1976); Smith, *The Army and Economic Mobilization*; and "The United States at War."

46. "The United States at War," 81.
47. Nathan, "GNP and Military Mobilization," 8.
48. Robert Nathan, "An Appraisal of the War Production Board," a speech presented to the Industrial War College (25 May 1950), http://www.ndu.edu/library/ic1/L50–130.pdf (accessed 30 November 2007).
49. Nathan, "GNP and Military Mobilization," 8.
50. Nelson, *Arsenal of Democracy*, 32.
51. Koistinen, *Arsenal of World War II*, 186.
52. George C. Herring, *Aid to Russia* (New York: Columbia University Press, 1973), 16–20.
53. Ibid.
54. Ibid.
55. Ibid.
56. Koistinen, *Arsenal of World War II,* 186.
57. Author interview with David Ginsberg on 11 October 2007.
58. Koistinen, *Arsenal of World War II,* 187.
59. "The United States at War," 80.
60. Donald Nelson to Henry L. Stimson, Frank Knox, E. S. Land, and E. R. Stettinius, 17 September 1941, National Archives, RG 179, Box 1 (179.2.1).
61. Based on this title, it is clear that this was a restatement of the work done by the Army's G-4 and Colonel Aurand. It cannot have been the Wedemeyer Plan or even some revised version of it because it did not lay out any of the equipment required for his notional force and was useless as a production planning document.
62. Industrial College of the Armed Forces, *Industrial Mobilization for War* (1947), 139.
63. "Army and Navy Estimate of United States Over-all Production Requirements," 11 September 1941. National Archives, Record Group 225.
64. Industrial College of the Armed Forces, *Industrial Mobilization for War* (1947), 140.
65. Ibid., 139.
66. Comments by Robert Nathan on Stacy May report of 4 December 1941, National Archives, Record Group 179, Box 1. Note: This was based on May's best guess of what was needed to fight a global war. After Pearl Harbor, the military would first double and then triple these requirements, pushing them far into the realm of the impossible.
67. Author interview with Patricia Bass, daughter of Stacy May on 9 October 2007.
68. Letter to author from Donald May, son of Stacy May (dated 12 October 2007). In the Stacy May papers (maintained at the University of Wyoming) there is one letter that May kept throughout the war years. It was the only one he kept out of hundreds he received from average citizens. May kept it close to him as a source of motivation. In part it read,

> What in the name of heaven do you Washington bureaucrats mean by *not* seeing that our boys have the needed arms, guns, machine guns, rifles, they need. I am

sick at heart to think that we are asking them to fight well-equipped German devils without the equipment they need. I ask what the hell is the use of building a 3,000,000-man army if they don't have guns and ammunition. I ask you if you are going to go out there with them to watch them be slaughtered. Oh no, you will sit here and watch them go. You will read about the war in the papers while our boys die by the millions because some lunk-heads in Washington can't do their jobs.

Chapter 6. The War Production Board and Two Wars

1. Elliot Janeway, *The Struggle for Survival* (New Haven: Yale University Press, 1951), 220.
2. Thomas Fleming, *The New Dealer's War: FDR and War Within World War II* (New York: Basic Books, 2002), 410.
3. Norman Beasley, *Knudsen: A Biography* (New York: Whittlesey House, 1947), 130.
4. Ibid., 240.
5. Janeway, *The Struggle for Survival*, 226.
6. Executive Order 9024, 16 January 1942, National Archives, Record Group 179.2.1. Emphasis added.
7. When the author began researching this work, the first book he read on the period was Nelson's autobiography (*Arsenal of Democracy*) and he developed a natural sympathy for the man and a respect for his accomplishments. It took many months of further research for the author to understand that Nelson, despite many admirable qualities, was not the right man to fight the battles necessary to make sure war production was accomplished with maximum efficiency.
8. Janeway, *The Struggle for Survival*, 226.
9. "The United States at War," 107.
10. Industrial College of the Armed Forces, *Industrial Mobilization for War* (1947), 213.
11. War Production Board, General Administrative Order 2–23, 16 March 1942, National Archives, Record Group 179.2.1. Also discussed in Industrial College of the Armed Forces, *Industrial Mobilization for War* (1947), 213.
12. The Truman Committee was established by then–Senator Harry Truman to study and spot waste, fraud, and abuse within the national preparedness administration. The Roosevelt administration initially feared the committee would hurt war morale, and, according to Fleming, in *The New Dealer's War* (101), Under Secretary of War Robert Patterson wrote to the president declaring it was "in the public interest" to suspend the committee. Truman wrote a letter to FDR saying that the committee was "100 percent behind the administration" and that it had no intention of criticizing the military conduct of the war. By the end of the war, the committee was reported to have saved the taxpayers at least $15 billion, at a time when a billion dollars was still considered a significant sum of money by the United States government.

13. 77th Cong., 1st sess., Special Senate Committee investigating the National Defense Program, Hearings, pt. 12, 5089, 21 April 1942.
14. Nelson clearly thought that this was an area that civilian authorities were not competent enough to delve into, despite the fact that most of this work was done by civilians within the Army and Navy organizations.
15. Nelson, *Arsenal of Democracy*, 194–205.
16. Herman Sommers, *OWMR: Presidential Agency* (Cambridge, MA: Havard University Press, 1950), 73–75.
17. Author's interview with David Ginsberg on 11 October 2007. Mr. Ginsberg stated that Roosevelt had called him to his office in early 1941, while he was general counsel for OPA, and told him to gather a team of lawyers to analyze what laws would be required to manage industrial production in the event of war, and to have that team prepare the proper legislation for an immediate vote in the event of war. Mr. Ginsberg claims that virtually all of this work was completed by the middle of the year.
18. The IMP was written and updated by the Industrial War College throughout the 1930s, with the final update prepared in 1939. Their fundamental premise was that the military would assume control of U.S. production on M-Day (Mobilization Day, or the day war was declared). Due to industrial mobilization's rolling start from 1939 on and Roosevelt's strong desire to keep the control of the civilian economy out of the military's control, the plan was never instituted. For more information, refer to *Mobilization: The U.S. Army in World War II* (Washington, DC, 1990).
19. "The United States at War," 111.
20. Koistinen, *Arsenal of World War II*, 209.
21. These reorganizations have been covered in depth in several important works. For the Army, refer to *The Organization and Role of the Army Service Forces* by John D. Millett (Washington, DC: Office of the Chief of Military History, Department of the Army, 1954). The Navy story is told in Robert H. Connery's *The Navy and the Industrial Mobilization in World War II* (Princeton, NJ: Princeton University Press, 1951), while the story of the WPB organization is explained best in Koistinen's *Arsenal of World War II.* These organizations are big topics in and of themselves, but this work will focus on the parts and personalities that had the most influence on the great feasibility debates of late 1942.
22. "The United States at War," 109.
23. Christman, "Ferdinand Eberstadt and Economic Mobilization."
24. Industrial College of the Armed Forces, *Industrial Mobilization for War* (1947), 238.
25. Brigante, "The Feasibility Dispute."
26. Nelson, *Arsenal of Democracy*, 204–5. See also Industrial College of the Armed Forces, *Industrial Mobilization for War* (1947), 237.

27. General Administrative Orders No. 11, 3 March 1942. A copy of this document is reproduced in the Minutes of the Planning Committee, National Archives, RG 179.1 (Box 1).
28. War Production Board, Minutes of the Planning Committee, 26 February 1942, 3, National Archives, RG 179.1 (Box 1).
29. *Time*, 9 February 1942, http://www.time.com/time/magazine/article/0,9171,777568–1,00.html (accessed 1 October 2007).
30. Industrial College of the Armed Forces, *Industrial Mobilization for War* (1947), 240.
31. Ibid.
32. Millett, *The Organization and Role of the Army Service Forces*, 32. Most of those with a stake in the debate had been following developments for several months and knew that Marshall was just being polite. As the rest of this story will show, the big fights had already been fought, and Marshall was going forward despite whatever comments might be returned at this late date. By the time Marshall asked for comments, he had already secured the approval of Secretary of War Stimson, with a draft copy of the reorganization at the White House for the president to review.
33. Frederick S. Haydon, "War Department Reorganization, August 1941—March 1942 (Part I)," *Military Affairs* 16, no. 1 (Spring 1952): 12–29. This article, along with Part II, "War Department Reorganization, August 1941—March 1942 (Part II)," *Military Affairs* 16, no. 3 (Autumn 1952): 97–114, provides an excellent short history of the Army reorganization.
34. Haydon, "War Department Reorganization (Part I)," 17.
35. Ibid., 18.
36. Ray S. Cline, *The War Department: Washington Command Post: The Operations Division*, (Washington, DC, 1951), 70–71. See particularly the notes on interview with General Gerow (p. 77 and p. 79).
37. Haydon, "War Department Reorganization (Part I)," 19.
38. Ibid., 20.
39. The complete memorandum along with a late draft of the Harrison memorandum can be found in the National Archives, Record Group 165.8 (Records of the War Plans Division (1910–1942).
40. Haydon, "War Department Reorganization (Part I)," 28
41. Haydon, "War Department Reorganization (Part II)," 98.
42. Ibid., 99.
43. Testimony of Colonel William K. Harrison before Senate Military Affairs Committee, 6 March 1942, in Hearing before the Committee on Military Affairs, United States Senate, 77th Congress, 2nd Session, on S.2092, "A Bill to Establish a Department of Defense Coordination and Control," 13.
44. Haydon, "War Department Reorganization (Part II)," 99.
45. General Embick's role in determining U.S. war strategy will be seen below in Chapter 9 where we deal with Marshall's commitment to a 1943 invasion of northern Europe.

46. The full report of the Roberts Commission (77th Congress, 2nd Session, Document 159) can be accessed at http://www.ibiblio.org/pha/pha/roberts/roberts.html (accessed 1 November 2007).
47. Haydon, "War Department Reorganization (Part II)," 106.
48. For a short study of the command techniques of many of the top commanders of U.S. forces in World War II see Jim Lacey, "Soldiering and Sensitivity," *Military History Magazine* (January 2008): 58–62.
49. Otto L. Nelson Jr., *National Security and the General Staff* (Washington, DC: Infantry Journal Press, 1946), 356–60.
50. Minutes of the Opening Session, Special Committee, Reorganization of the War Department, 16 February 1942, WDCSA 020, 1942 (War Department Reorganization). These minutes were not distributed or filed but are reproduced in Nelson, *Arsenal of Democracy*, 356–60.
51. Haydon, "War Department Reorganization (Part II)," 112. This letter was delivered on 27 February 1942.
52. Ibid.
53. Ibid., 113.
54. Cline, *Washington Command Post*, 92.
55. This may be one of the few times General Arnold is referred to as genial. As one subordinate who worked closely with him said, "He pushed everyone relentlessly, he demanded, he cajoled, he was both sly and totally unreasonable. By demanding the impossible he worked miracles. His idea of administering a program was to think of something that needed doing and to tell someone to do it. No one ever stayed around to disappoint him twice" (James Lacey, "Senistivity for Generals," *Military History Magazine*, March 2008). As for Somervell being soft-spoken, this is a gross mischaracterization of the man.
56. "Streamlining the Army," *Time*, 9 March 1942.
57. From this point forward this work will use the more common name: Army Service Forces (ASF).
58. Millett, *The Organization and Role of the Army Service Forces*, 39. Millett's work remains the best history of the Army Service Forces and its accomplishments during the war. See also Gropman, *The Big L*; and G. Ruppenthal, *Logistical Support of the Armies*, vols. 1 and 2 (Washington, DC: Department of the Army, 1953). For a version that details more of Somervell's direct impact see John Kennedy Ohl, *Supplying the Troops: General Somervell and American Logistics in World War II* (DeKalb: Northern Illinois University Press, 1994).
59. Ohl, *Supplying the Troops*, 4.
60. Harry Yoshpe, "Organization for Production Control in World War II," 1946. This monograph was commissioned by the Army Industrial College and never published. A copy is on file in the archival section of the National Defense University Library, Washington, DC. Another copy scanned into pdf format is in the possession of the author. This ninety-four–

page monograph gives a detailed breakdown of the Army's productive organization from 1939 through 1945.

61. Ibid., 19.
62. Cline, *Washington Command Post,* 93.
63. "Memorandum to the Staff of the Under Secretary of War," 10 March 1942, as quoted in Yoshpe, "Organization for Production Control in World War II," 20.
64. Millett, *The Organization and Role of the Army Service Forces,* 39. General McNarney in testimony to Congress said that although Somervell would have two bosses, each would be for a different purpose. Although it violated good management practices, it was the "best practical solution."
65. Koistinen's *Arsenal of World War II,* 336–38, offers a more sympathetic picture of Nelson and the forces he had to contend with than is given below.
66. John Lord O'Brian, "Oral History Project," Columbia University, New York, 548–51. Quoted Christman, "Ferdinand Eberstadt and Economic Mobilization," 89–91.
67. Author interview with David Ginsberg on 11 October 2007.
68. Ibid.
69. Ibid.
70. Janeway, *The Struggle for Survival,* 239.
71. Millett, *The Organization and Role of the Army Service Forces,* 7.
72. Charles Murphy, "Somervell of the SOS," *Life,* 8 March 1942, 86.
73. *New Republic,* 13 April 1942, 487.
74. Aurand, it will be remembered, was the true author of the Army's portion of the Victory Program.
75. Nathan, "GNP and Military Mobilization."
76. Author interview with David Ginsberg on 11 October 2007.

Chapter 7. War and Feasibility

1. Most of this report was actually written by Nathan who was working for May at the time, although in a few months that working relationship would reverse.
2. Memorandum from Stacy May to Donald Nelson, "Feasibility of the Victory Program," National Archives, Planning Committee Document, Records Group 179, Box 1.
3. Ibid.
4. As this work has shown, although translating all of the complexities of the U.S. economy into dollar terms is not a perfect representation, all parties agreed (and continue to agree) that it was the best solution available. Also, by this time the president and many others in government had become familiar with this concept of translating the economy into national income accounts. This was to become a sticking point in later feasibility discussions, especially with General Somervell, who argued that such calculations could not be trusted and

did not reflect the true production outlook. This was probably just a negotiating ploy by Somervell: his personal files show him using the same financial translations in presentations to the joint staff prior to the height of the feasibility dispute in October 1942.

5. Memorandum from May to Nelson, "Feasibility of the Victory Program."
6. Ibid.
7. May and other civilian experts also failed to foresee that a new generation of materiel and munitions was about to move from the drawing board to the production line. These new weapons would require considerably more raw materials, money, and time to produce than the relatively simple items being churned out by U.S. factories in 1940–41. However, much of this extra cost would be erased as producers became more productive and reduced construction times often by orders of magnitude. Most of this increase in productivity was not captured in the early feasibility analysis, though it was being accounted for by mid-1942.
8. Memorandum from Stacy May to Donald Nelson, 4 December 1941, "Planning Committee Document," National Archives, Record Group 179, Box 1.
9. Ibid. This entire document is reproduced in Appendix 8, this volume.
10. Ibid.
11. According to the U.S Bureau of the Census (1975), "Private consumption was squeezed a bit in 1942, and then rose a bit in 1943 and 1944." However, most of the deflated amount of consumption was caused by a reduction in private investment, which was now to a great extent being done by the government. Consumers continued to spend freely throughout the war, using the black market to purchase items that were in limited supply due to rationing. Harrison, *The Economics of World War II*, 85–90.
12. Robert Higgs, "Wartime Prosperity? A Reassessment of the U.S. Economy in the 1940's" *Journal of Economic History* (1 March 1992): 41–60. Higgs takes aim at the "we never had it so good" hypothesis by using 1941 as his base year to judge wartime consumption levels against. His findings have ignited a debate among economic historians, but to the author appear to be another example of how modern statisticians can confuse economic models with reality. For an excellent analysis of the composition, quantity, and quality of consumer consumption, see Hugh Rockoff's essay, "The United States: From Ploughshares to swords," in Harrison, *The Economics of World War II*, 81–121.
13. The effects that labor, raw materials, and facilities had on feasibility were explained in a later study by Simon Kuznets, which is reproduced in a condensed version in Appendix 2, this volume. For further information, see Christman, "Ferdinand Eberstadt and Economic Mobilization"; Connery, *The Navy and Industrial Mobilization in World War II*; Jeffrey M. Dorwart, *Eberstadt and Forrestal: A National Security Partnership, 1909–1949* (College Station, TX: TAMU Press, 1991); Byron Fairchild and Jonathan Grossman, *The Army and Industrial Manpower,* (Washington, DC: Office of the Chief of Military History, Department of the Army, 1959); Industrial College of the Armed Forces, *Industrial*

Mobilization for War (1947); Koistinen, *Arsenal of World War II*; Novick, *Wartime Production Controls*; Smith, *The Army and Industrial Mobilization*; and "The United States at War."

14. Brigante, "The Feasibility Dispute,"116. This unpublished dissertation is the only detailed account of the particulars of the feasibility dispute. However, while Brigante's work details the actual dispute, he never researched or wrote about any of the massive strategic implications resulting from the dispute's resolution. Additionally, the author's research indicates that many of his comments on the motivations of the key players are not correct and that his analysis of how events unfolded prior to the dispute reaching a climax is very skimpy on details. Finally, Brigante did not document any of his assertions. To the best of his ability, the author tried to document as much of Brigante's story as possible from still existing records.
15. Brigante, "The Feasibility Dispute," 25.
16. Ibid., 27.
17. In early January OPM and SPAB would be combined into the WPB with Donald Nelson in overall charge.
18. Brigante, "The Feasibility Dispute," 29.
19. A copy of Beaverbrook's memorandum for Roosevelt dealing with this and other proposed increases can be found in Roosevelt's Safe Files in Box 2, Beaverbrook Folder, FDR Library, Hyde Park, NY.
20. Nelson, *Arsenal of Democracy*, 185.
21. Brigante, "The Feasibility Dispute," 31.
22. Woolley and Peters, *The American Presidency Project.*
23. Minutes of the Planning Committee, 27 January 1942, National Archives, RG 179.2.2.
24. Industrial College of the Armed Forces, *Industrial Mobilization for War* (1947), 275.

Chapter 8. The Great Feasibility Debate

1. Although what the concept of feasibility involves has been touched on in earlier chapters and will be again outlined in this chapter, some readers may profit from a deeper understanding of how the concept was viewed by the participants in this dispute. In that regard, a memorandum written by Simon Kuznets detailing the intricacies of the feasibility concept can be found in Appendix 1, this volume.
2. Brigante's study is full of personal and first-person details and is considered authoritative by economic historians who have reviewed it. However, it suffers from the major flaw that he did not document any of his claims and left no papers behind to help future historians check his facts.
3. Minutes of the Planning Committee, 26 February 1942, National Archives, RG 179, Box 4.
4. Ibid.

5. Ibid.
6. Minutes of the Planning Committee, 13 March 1942, National Archives, RG 179, Box 4.
7. Ibid.
8. Planning Committee Document 31, 14 March 1942, National Archives, RG 179, Box. 4. Because this is the baseline document that remained little changed in following feasibility studies, future historians will find it a valuable resource. The entire report is reproduced in Appendix 2, this volume. Note that although this book focuses on the relationship between GDP and feasibility, the report goes into great depth on other important areas dealing with overall feasibility: raw materials, industrial facilities (plant), and labor.
9. Brigante, "The Feasibility Dispute," 34.
10. Minutes of the Planning Committee, 16 March 1942, National Archives, RG 179, Box 4.
11. Ibid.
12. Ibid.
13. What is not mentioned in any of the works on this topic and is not adequately covered in either Kuznets' or May's studies (although Kuznets covers it in his later book, *National Product in Wartime*) is the effect of productivity increases. For instance, the cost per foot of aircraft had fallen by more than 80 percent by the end of 1944, so it was possible to limit spending to $72 billion annually and still count on a substantial increase in the amount of munitions delivered.
14. The letter can be found at Minutes of the Planning Committee, 16 March 1942, National Archives, RG 179, Box 4.
15. Minutes of the Planning Committee, 25 March 1942, National Archives, RG 179, Box 4.
16. Ibid.
17. Ibid.
18. Brigante, "The Feasibility Dispute," 48.
19. Minutes of the Planning Committee, 31 March 1942, National Archives, RG 179, Box 4.
20. This letter can be found in Roosevelt's Safe Files at the FDR Library, Hyde Park, NY. The letter has recently been placed on line and can be found at http://www.fdrlibrary.marist.edu/psf/box3/a43kk01.html (accessed 1 January 2009).
21. This note can be found in Roosevelt's Safe Files at the FDR Library, Hyde Park, NY. The letter has recently been placed on line and can be found at http://www.fdrlibrary.marist.edu/psf/box3/a43mm02.html (accessed 1 January 2009).
22. Minutes of the Planning Committee , 6 April 1942, RG 179, Box 4.
23. Minutes of the Planning Committee, 8 April 1942, National Archives, RG 179, Box 4.
24. Brigante, "The Feasibility Dispute," 53.
25. Ibid.
26. Kuznets' full explanation of this concept can be found in Appendix 1, this volume. An example-based explanation is provided by Nelson, *Arsenal of Democracy,* 380–82.

27. Somervell Desk Files, National Archives, Record Group 160, Box 6. Shipbuilding goals, for instance, were increased by more than a million tons.
28. Koistinen, *Arsenal of World War II,* 307.
29. The author was unable to find a copy of Kuznets' original report in any of the archive files. However, in the WPB records stored at the National Archives, there is a lengthy memorandum written by Robert Nathan that summarizes all of the key points of the Kuznets' study and that was used as the basis of discussion for the climactic feasibility meetings of 6 and 13 October. It is reproduced in Appendix 4, this volume. A copy can be found in the National Archives, RG 179, Box 1.
30. Ibid.
31. See Nathan's 6 October 1942 memorandum to the WPB (Appendix 4, this volume).
32. Brigante, "The Feasibility Dispute," 52; and Koistinen, *Arsenal of World War II,* 308. See Appendix 4, this volume.
33. Brigante, "The Feasibility Dispute," 60.
34. Ibid., 69.
35. Ibid., 70.
36. Ibid., 69.
37. Industrial College of the Armed Forces, *Industrial Mobilization for War* (1947), 287.
38. Brigante, "The Feasibility Dispute," 84.
39. As reproduced in Brigante, "The Feasibility Dispute." This letter is reproduced in its entirety in Appendix 5, this volume.
40. Ibid.
41. Somervell Desk Files, National Archives, Record Group 160, Box 6. This letter is reproduced in its entirety in Appendix 6, this volume.
42. Influential syndicated columnist Drew Pearson portrayed the dispute as a struggle to the finish in a series of columns from September through December 1942. These columns have been digitized and are available at http://www.aladin.wrlc.org/gsdl/collect/pearson/pearson.shtml (accessed 30 January 2008).
43. Koistinen, *Arsenal of World War II,* 311.
44. Brigante has written the most complete and accessible version of this meeting. Because he was able to interview persons who attended the meeting, his version must be taken as authoritative. The minutes of the meeting corroborate most of what Brigante says, although without the color. The minutes can be found in the National Archives, Minutes of War Production Board (6 October 1942; National Archives, RG 179.2.2, Box 3. The author was unable to find a copy of the Marshall letter either in the records of the WPB or in Somervell's files.

45. See Joel R. Davidson, *The Unsinkable Fleet: The Politics of U.S. Navy Expansion in World War II* (Annapolis, MD: U.S. Naval Institute Press, 1996), 36–40. Major naval procurement was mandated by law and Congress had already approved several million tons worth of production in July of 1942 (HR 7184). The WPB could not effect this procurement without the consent of Congress, although when the overall production cuts were made, the Navy took a small portion of the hit. However, the reductions in Navy procurement were far below those of the Army and did not affect the construction of major combat ships.
46. Brigante, "The Feasibility Dispute," 30.
47. Ibid.
48. Memorandum from Simon Kuznets to the Planning Committee, "Proposals for Adjustment of the Program," 8 October 1942, Minutes of the Planning Committee, 8 April 1942, National Archives, RG 179, Box 4.
49. Brigante, "The Feasibility Dispute," 97.
50. Minutes of the WPB, 6 October 1942. See Appendix 8, this volume.
51. Somervell Desk Files, National Archives, Record Group 160, Box 6.
52. Ibid. A copy of this letter is at Appendix 7, this volume.
53. Minutes of the WPB, 13 October 1942, National Archives, RG 179, Box 3.
54. Ibid.
55. Ibid.
56. Minutes of the Joint Chiefs of Staff, 20 October 1942, National Archives, Record Group 218.
57. Somervell Desk Files, National Archives, Record Group 160, Box 6.
58. A copy of this letter can be found in National Archives, records of the JCS, Record Group 218.2.1.
59. "U.S. War Production Objective, 1943," A Report by the Joint Staff Planners, with annexes, 26 November 1942, National Archives, records of the JCS, Record Group 218.2.1.
60. A good summary of the new munitions program can be found in Industrial College of the Armed Forces, *Industrial Mobilization for War* (1947), 290–93.
61. Brigante, "The Feasibility Dispute," 98.
62. Henderson, it should be noted, was fired or left his position as the head of the OPA when Roosevelt decided that the political cost of keeping him outweighed his obvious ability to keep inflation in check. Henderson had made too many enemies in business and in Congress.
63. Author interview with David Ginsberg on 11 October 2007. Nathan was later assigned to the Office of Strategic Services, but was medically released after a stay of several months at Walter Reed Army hospital for a back injury. Ginsberg left the Army in 1946 with the rank of major.

Chapter 9. Marshall's Commitment to a 1943 Invasion of Europe

1. Stewart, *American Military History*, 140. This quote is lifted directly from Maurice Matloff's *American Military History*, Vol. 2, *1902–1996* (Cambridge, MA: Da Capo Press, 1973), 419.
2. Maurice Matloff, *Strategic Planning for Coalition Warfare: 1943–1944* (Washington, DC: OCMH, Department of the Army, 1958), 21–22.
3. Minutes of the meeting held at Anfa Camp, 16 January 1943, are available in digital form from the Joint Chiefs of Staff History Office (Pentagon, Alexandria, VA). This resource has not been placed online, but is available on CD.
4. Some historians, notably Sir Michael Howard, noted that Marshall's commitment to a 1943 invasion was uncertain. However, while some—but by no means all—early World War II historians addressed this issue correctly, their position does not dominate the historical record.
5. For a brilliant explosion of the fallacy that there was a rift between British and American grand strategic conception on the wisdom of a cross-Channel invasion, see Richard M. Leighton, "Overlord Revisited: An Interpretation of American Strategy in the European War, 1942–1944," *American Historical Review* 68, no. 4 (July 1963): 919–37.
6. "Minutes and formal agreements," Arcadia Conference, Washington DC, 22 December 1941–14 January 1942. A copy of the minutes for all wartime conferences can be procured from the Joint Chiefs of Staff History Office (Pentagon, Alexandria, VA). Although these files have been digitized, they have not as of yet been posted to the Internet.
7. Winston S. Churchill, *Hinge of Fate: The Second World War*, Vol. IV (Boston: Houghton Mifflin, 1950), 287.
8. Sherwood, *Roosevelt and Hopkins*, 515. In a letter to Secretary of War Stimson, 15 April 1942, Marshall said, "Our proposal was formally accepted after an oral presentation by me and by Hopkins followed by general comments by members and Chief of Staff. PM in impressive pronouncement declared complete agreement." See Larry Bland, *The Papers of George Catlett Marshall*, vol. III (Baltimore: Johns Hopkins University Press, 1991), 162. Marshall reiterated this comment in a letter to the president on 18 April 1942 (Marshall Papers, 164).
9. Sherwood, *Roosevelt and Hopkins*, 535.
10. Guyer, "The Joint Chiefs and the War Against Germany," Section 4, 17.
11. A copy of this memo is available in FDR's Safe files and has been placed online at http://www.fdrlibrary.marist.edu/psf/box4/a44f02.html (accessed 1 January 2009).
12. Ibid. See online copy at http://www.fdrlibrary.marist.edu/psf/box4/a44f01.html (accessed 1 January 2009).
13. Hayes, "The Joint Chiefs and the War Against Japan." The British official history of World War II confirms this British position and how the British chiefs came to accept them. See J. M. A. Gwyer and J. R. M. Butler, *Grand Strategy, Volume III: June 1941–August 1942* (London: Her Majerty's Stationery Office, 1964), 617–24.

14. Sherwood, *Roosevelt and Hopkins*, 565.
15. Ibid., 567.
16. Guyer, "The Joint Chiefs and the War Against Germany," Section 5, 11. See Gwyer and Butler, *Grand Strategy*, 624–31 for a full account of these meetings.
17. Ibid., 8.
18. Harrison Gordon, *Cross Channel Attack* (Washington, DC: GPO, Department of the Army, 1951), 26.
19. Ibid., 14.
20. Twenty-fourth meeting of the Joint Chiefs of Staff, 10 July 1942, National Archives, Record Group 218. In *On Active Service in Peace and War*, Henry L. Stimson and McGeorge Bundy began a long-standing debate as to whether this was a serious proposal on Marshall and King's part. According to Bundy's interpretation of Secretary of War Stimson's biography, the proposal "was designed mainly as a plan to bring the British into agreement with Bolero." However, the actual quote from the Stimson *Diary* (p. 424) gives no indication that this was a ploy. As the *Diary* records, "I found Marshall very stirred up and emphatic over it [the British memo rejecting Bolero]. . . . As the British won't go through with what they agreed to, we will turn our backs on them and take up the war with Japan." A person planning a ploy is normally not as agitated as Marshall comes across. Moreover, if this plan was a ploy it would be critical to involve Stimson in it before it went to the president. However, there is no indication in the record of this proposal being a ploy. In fact, in the Minutes of the Joint Chiefs of Staff where this is discussed a ploy is never mentioned. The discussion revolves entirely around why this is a sound proposal and does not mention that it was not a real proposal but instead a method to pressure the British. This event is covered in the Marshall Papers in detail, without any indication it was a ploy (Bland, *The Papers of George Catlett Marshall*, Vol. III, 269–73). Moreover, when the president pushed back on this proposal, Marshall at first made an effort to defend his and King's position. This is an unusual approach to take for a ploy. One would assume that instead of defending his position Marshall would just inform Roosevelt that it was designed to force Britain's hand and was not a serious proposal. One would also assume that the joint chiefs would have brought the president into their thinking before forwarding such a radical proposal. Because Roosevelt's reply makes it obvious he was not so informed, both Marshall and King were taking a severe risk the president would lose faith in their ability and judgment. One should also note that at this level of leadership this kind of game is not played, at least not in this way. Anyway, it would have been just as effective a scare tactic, if that is what it was supposed to be, to bring in General Dill and tell him what Marshall and King were thinking, and let him back-channel it to the British chiefs. This could have been done without involving the president and risking his wrath. While the debate continues, all contemporary accounts indicate that both Marshall and King were serious about it. In fact, Marshall's deputy, General Handy, would return to this idea in November 1942. His unpublished memoirs

(Handy File, Military History Institute, Carlisle, PA) demonstrate that this was a serious proposal on the eve of the Casablanca Conference, as was the early proposal discussed here. Andrew Roberts in his new book, *Masters and Commanders* (London: Harper, 2008, 230–33), addresses this debate at some length and concludes that this was a serious threat and not a bluff.

21. Guyer, "The Joint Chiefs and the War Against Germany," Section 5, 15.
22. Ibid.
23. Hayes, "The Joint Chiefs and the War Against Japan."
24. Sherwood, *Roosevelt and Hopkins*, 576.
25. Ibid., 582.
26. Forrest C. Pogue, *George C. Marshall: Ordeal and Hope 1939–1942* (New York: Viking Press, 1966), 343.
27. Alex Danchev and Daniel Todman, *War Diaries: Field Marshall Lord Alan Brooke* (Berkeley: University of California Press, 2001), 280.
28. Memorandum from General Marshall to Field Marshall Sir John Dill, 14 August 1942; Bland, *The Papers of George Catlett Marshall,* Vol. III, 302.
29. British operations in Salonika, Greece, consumed enormous numbers of people and materiel for two years without significant result. The Germans, and later Allied critics, referred to it as the war's "largest self-sustaining prison camp."
30. Twenty-seventh meeting of the Joint Chiefs of Staff, 10 July 1942, National Archives, Record Group 218.
31. Sherwood, *Roosevelt and Hopkins*, 630.
32. Marshall, *The War Reports of General George C. Marshall*, 155–60.
33. Notes Taken at the Joint Chiefs of Staff Meeting, 25 November 1942, Minutes of the Joint Chiefs of Staff, National Archives, Record Group 218.
34. Maurice Matloff, *Strategic Planning for Coalition Warfare: 1941–1942.*
35. Guyer, "The Joint Chiefs and the War Against Germany," Section 5, 18.
36. Maurice Matloff and Edwin M. Snell, *Strategic Planning for Coalition Warfare: 1941–1942* (Washington, DC: Center of Military History, 1953), 363. See also Guyer, "The Joint Chiefs and the War Against Germany," and Hayes, "The Joint Chiefs and the War Against Japan."
37. Matloff and Snell, *Strategic Planning for Coalition Warfare: 1941–1942,* 365–66.
38. According to the "Determination of Army Supply Requirements" (National Defense University, Washington, DC). This document also demonstrates that the planners were now putting feasibility at the forefront of their considerations: "Before publication of this program, computed requirements were reviewed carefully with procurement and production representatives. . . . In some cases total requirements were modified in accordance with production capabilities. The program, as published, was considered to be capable with

the facilities available as of 1 January 1943 and generally within anticipated allocations of critical raw materials by the War Production Board.

39. The author could not find any record of exactly when Marshall was actually briefed on required force structure changes. However, included in "The Determination of Supply Requirements" there are copies of two memorandums. One, dated 14 December, was sent from Somervell to all of the Army's logistical chiefs, and was unlikely to have escaped Marshall's notice. In it he ordered the chiefs to make requirements reductions to bring them within feasibility limits in dollar terms. The other, dated 26 December, from the secretary of War and Marshall to the president, outlined the changes being made in the Victory Program, and presented these changes in dollar terms.
40. The Minutes of the Joint Chiefs of Staff only mention that this meeting occurred, but because of its secret nature do not give any details. Most of this account comes from Grace Hayes, "The Joint Chiefs and the War Against Japan" (unpublished manuscript). Guyer's unpublished history ("The Joint Chiefs and the War Against Germany") presents the same version of events. Since both of these authors were senior officers on the joint staff at the time of the meeting, their reports have substantial credibility.
41. King had made a similar estimate of the total Pacific war effort at a previous Joint Chiefs of Staff meeting. See "JCS Notes Taken at the Meeting," 25 November 1942, Minutes of the Joint Chiefs of Staff, National Archives, Record Group 218.
42. Both Guyer and Hayes agree on this point.
43. Hayes, "The Joint Chiefs and the War Against Japan."
44. Ibid.
45. As Admiral King is reported to have said, "Every time we brought up a topic those bastards had a paper on it." General Wedemeyer expatiated at great length on the superiority of the British staff system at Casablanca: "They swarmed down on us like locusts . . . with prepared plans . . . from a worm's eye's viewpoint it was apparent that we were confronted by generations and generations of experience in committee work, in diplomacy, and in rationalizing points of view. They had us on the defensive practically all the time" (*Wedemeyer Reports!*, 192).
46. Joint Chiefs of Staff Fiftieth Meeting, Minutes of the meeting held at Anfa Camp, 13 January 1943, available in digital form from the Joint Chiefs of Staff History Office.
47. Ibid.
48. JCS 50th Meeting Minutes.
49. Considering that the original Roundup plan called for forty-five divisions to land in 1943, one can see why Marshall's conception of the possible by this time had been radically scaled down.
50. Minutes of the Joint Chiefs of Staff meeting with President Roosevelt held at Anfa Camp, 14 January 1943. Available in digital form from the Joint Chiefs of Staff History Office.

51. Minutes of the meeting held at Anfa Camp, 16 January 1943. Available in digital form from the Joint Chiefs of Staff History Office.
52. Pogue, *George C. Marshall*, 12.

Chapter 10. Why Marshall Changed His Mind

1. Colonel Howard J. Vandersluis, "Relationship of the Joint Chiefs of Staff to Military Procurement," Industrial College of the United States Archives, Washington, DC (transcript of a 22 April 1946 speech at the college). See http://www.ndu.edu/library/ic1/L46–075.pdf (accessed 15 March 2009).
2. A good case can be made that Donald Nelson, as the production chief, was responsible for dealing directly with the Joint Chiefs of Staff and should have pushed the feasibility problems much harder in early 1942, and therefore must shoulder a share of the blame.
3. Memorandum for the Joint Chiefs, Untitled, 24 August 1942. A copy of this memorandum can be found in the Wedemeyer Papers Box 76, Hoover Institution, Stanford University, Stanford, CA. There is another copy attached to the "Army Mobilization Plan for 1943" in the National Archives, Record Group 165, 320.2.
4. Chief of Naval Operations to Chief of Staff, 27 August 1942, "Strength of Army for calendar year 1943," Record Group 165, OPD 320.2. Further information on this debate among the joint chiefs can be found in the Minutes of the Joint Staff, 1 September 1942, National Archives, RG 218.2.2.
5. Memorandum from president to Admiral King, 24 August 1942, Record Group 165, 370.01.
6. Memorandum from Somervell to Marshall, Joint U.S. Staff Planners' Directive J. P. S. 57/1/D, 17 September 1942, "Strength of Army for 1943," Somervell Desk File, National Archives, Record Group 160, Box 1.
7. Ibid.
8. Somervell Desk Files, National Archives, Record Group 160, Box 6.
9. Dr. Robert R. Palmer, "The Mobilization of the Ground Army, The Army Ground Forces Study No. 4," Historical Section—Army Ground Forces 1946, 11.
10. Ibid., 13.

Appendix 1. The Feasibility Concept

1. The original memorandum was written on April 13, 1942. The entire memorandum is located in the National Archives, "Records of the Planning Committee," RG 179, Box 4.

Appendix 2. The First Feasibility Study (14 March 1942)

1. National Archives, Records of the Planning Committee," RG 179, Box 4.

Appendix 3. Wedemeyer's Victory Program

1. A copy of this document can be found in the Wedemeyer Papers, Box 76, Hoover Institution, Stanford University, Stanford, CA. It has been reprinted: Kirkpatrick, *An Unknown Future and a Doubtful Present*. This appendix includes the entire study.

Appendix 4. Nathan's 6 October Memorandum for War Production Board Meeting

1. National Archives, Records of the Planning Committee," RG 179, Box 4.
2. On the basis of a level of munitions and construction output in December 1943 of WO to $85 billion (annual rate) the Bureau of Labor Statistics estimates war employment at 20 million persons. The present program, valued at $95 to $97 billion for 1943 (including the deficit for 1942) would call for a monthly output in December 1943 of $10.5 billion—i.e., an annual rate of $126 billion (this is on the basis of straight line projection from $5.5 billion output in December 1942). If we assume that employment increases proportionately to value of output the present objective would call for 10 million additional war employment in December 1943. Possibly an appreciably smaller number would be required; but even if it is scaled down to 7 million, the result would be a total deficit in December 1943 of 14 million (assuming armed forces at 10 million).
3. Chart was not with file in National Archives.
4. Chart was not with file in National Archives.

Appendix 5. General Somervell's Comments to War Production Board Proposals of 31 August 1942

1. As reproduced in Brigante, "The Feasibility Dispute."

Appendix 6. Simon Kuznets' Reply to Somervell's Comments on His Feasibility Proposal (Sent under Robert Nathan's Hand)

1. Planning Committee Records, National Archives, RG 179, Box 4.

Appendix 7. Letter from Robert P. Patterson (Under Secretary of War) to General Somervell, Post 6 October Feasibility Meeting

1. Planning Committee Records, National Archives, RG 179, Box 4.
2. Although the Navy would have to take some cuts, they were not nearly so great as Patterson may have hoped for.

Appendix 8. Minutes of War Production Board 6 October Meeting

1. Planning Committee Records, National Archives, RG 179, Box 4.
2. This section has been elided because the discussion does not pertain to the feasibility dispute.

Bibliography

Primary Sources

Speeches and Lectures

Post War Lectures given at the Industrial College of the Armed Forces

Armstrong, Donald (General): "Relations of JCS to Military Procurement"

Clayton, Lawrence: "Functions of the Federal Reserve System in War Financing"

Eccles, Henry E.: "Interdependence of Strategy and Logistics"

Fleming, Robert: "Federal Reserve System"

Foster, E. M.: "Financial Aid to War Suppliers"

Gay, Charles: "Financing Wars"

Goldenweiser, Emanuel A.: "Federal Reserve System"

Henderson, Leon: "Economic Controls and National Security"

Henderson, Leon: "Office of Price Administration During World War II"

Henderson, Leon: "Office of Price Administration in World War II"

Henderson, Leon: "Organizational Problems of the Price Administrator"

Henderson, Leon: "Price, Profit, and Wage Control"

Hunter, Louis: "Influence of Industrial Mobilization Planning in World War II"

Janeway, Eliot: "Appraisal of the War Production Board"

Knudsen, William: "Problems in War Production"

Lovenstein, Meno: "Financing War Expenditures"

May, Stacy: "Guns or Butter"

McCabe, Thomas: "The Role of the Federal Reserve in Wartime"

Mills, Earl (Admiral): "Navy Production Problems"
Murphy, Henry: "Financing National Security"
Nathan, Robert: "An Appraisal of the War Production Board"
Nimitz, Chester: "Industry and the Navy"
Rodgers, Raymond: "War Finance"
Scott, Frank: "Industrial Preparation for War"
Snyder, John: "The Role of the Federal Reserve in Financing War" (1950)
Snyder, John: "The Role of the Federal Reserve in Financing War" (1951)
Somervell, Brehon (General): "Problems of Production in WW II"
Staats, Elmer: "Relations Between Civilian Agencies and War Department"
Steiner, George: "Facts for War Production"
Vandersluis, Howard J.: "Relationship of the Joint Chiefs of Staff to Military Procurement"

Papers

Franklin D. Roosevelt Library, Hyde Park, NY
Harry L. Hopkins Papers
Henry L. Morgenthau Presidential Diaries
Joint Board Estimates of United States Overall Production Requirements
Plan Dog Case Files
Franklin D. Roosevelt Papers
Map File
Official File
President's Personal File (Safe File)
President's Secretary's File (Safe File)
George C. Marshall Library, Lexington, VA
George C. Marshall Papers
Hoover Institution on War, Revolution, and Peace, Stanford, CA
Albert C. Wedemeyer Papers (particularly boxes 76 and 77)
General Albert C. Wedemeyer Papers
Library of Congress, Washington DC
Henry H. Arnold Papers
Cordell Hull Papers
Ernest J. King Papers (copied at Naval Historical Center, Washington, DC)
Frank Knox Papers
William D. Leahy Papers
Robert P. Patterson Papers
National Archives and Records Service, College Park, MD
Record Group 38, Records of the Office of the Chief of Naval Operations

Record Group 59, Records of the Department of State

Record Group 80, Records of the Department of the Navy

Record Group 107, Records of the Office of the Secretary of War

Record Group 160, Records of the Headquarters Army Service Forces (including General Somervell's Desk Files)

Record Group 165, Records of the War Department General and Special Staffs

Record Group 179, Records of the War Production Board (including Minutes of Planning Committee meetings), particularly RG 179.2.1

Record Group 218, Records of the Joint and Combined Chiefs of Staff

Record Group 225, Records of the Joint Army-Navy Boards

Hayes, Grace, "The Joint Chiefs and the War Against Japan," an unpublished manuscript. This was meant to be a volume in an official history of the Joint Chiefs of Staff. A copy can be found in the National Archives, Record Group 218.2.2. An edited version was published by the U.S. Naval Institute Press in 1982.

Guyer, Lawrence, *The Joint Chiefs and the War Against Germany*, an unpublished manuscript. This was meant to be a volume in an official history of the Joint Chiefs of Staff. A copy can be found in the National Archives, Record Group 218.2.2.

National Defense University Library

"The Determination of Army Supply Requirements." This report (available in archival material stored at the National Defense University Library, Fort McNair, Washington, DC) was a restricted study prepared in 1946 by order of General Sommervell. This never-published document details the history of military production and supply from the perspective of the Army logistical agencies; it is supported by two full volumes of original supporting documents.

Naval Historical Center, Washington, DC

Ernest J. King Papers

Frank Knox Papers

William D. Leahy Papers

Samuel E. Morison Collection

Oral Histories

Andrew Goodpaster

John E. Hull

Forrest C. Pogue Interviews for the Supreme Command

Albert C. Wedemeyer

Robert J. Wood

U.S. Army Military History Institute, Carlisle, PA

Paul W. Caraway Papers

Lawrence J. Lincoln Papers
Guy Vernon Henry Papers
U.S. Joint Chiefs History Office
Minutes of Arcadia Conference
Minutes of Casablanca Conference
Minutes of Trident Conference
University of Wyoming, Laramie, WY
Stacy May Papers
Yale University Library, New Haven, CT
Henry L. Stimson Papers (Diary)

Books

Arnold, Henry H. *Global Mission*. Tab Books, 1949.

Blum, John Morton. *From the Morgenthau Diaries: Years of War, 1941–1945*. Houghton Mifflin, 1967.

Butcher, Harry C. *My Three Years With Eisenhower*. Simon and Schuster, 1946.

Campbell, Thomas M., and George C. Herring. *The Diaries of Edward R. Stettinius, Jr., 1943–1946*. Little Hampton Book Services, 1975.

Chandler, Alfred D. Jr. *The Papers of Dwight David Eisenhower: The War Years*. Johns Hopkins University Press, 1970.

Churchill, Winston S. *The Second World War*. Houghton Mifflin, 1948–53.

Harriman, W. Averell, and Elie Abel. *Special Envoy to Churchill and Stalin 1941–1946*. Random House, 1975.

Hull, Cordell. *The Memoirs of Cordell Hull*. Macmillan, 1948.

Ickes, Harold. *The Secret Diaries of Harold Ickes*. Simon and Schuster, 1954.

King, Ernst J., and Walter M. Whitehill. *Fleet Admiral King: A Naval Record*. W. W. Norton, 1952.

Kuznets, Simon. *National Income and Its Composition*. National Bureau of Economic Research, 1941.

Kuznets, Simon. *National Product in Wartime*. National Bureau of Economic Research, 1946.

Leahy, William D. *I Was There*. Whittlesey House, 1950.

Marshall, George C. *The War Reports of General George C. Marshall*. The United States News, 1947.

Nelson, Donald. *Arsenal of Democracy: The Story of American War Production*. Harcourt, Brace, 1946.

Stimson, Henry L., and McGeorge Bundy. *On Active Service in Peace and War*. Hippocrene Books, 1947.

Wedemeyer, Albert C. *Wedemeyer Reports!* Henry Holt, 1958.

Articles

Nathan, Robert. "GNP and Military Mobilization." *Journal of Evolutionary Economics* (April 1994).

"Streamlining the Army." *Time*, 9 March 1942.

Secondary Sources

Books

Anderson, Benjamin M. *Effects of the War on Money, Credit and Banking in France and the United States*. Oxford University Press, American Branch, 1919; and Carnegie Endowment for International Peace, 1919.

Army Industrial College. *World War Problems of Industrial Mobilization*. Government Printing Office, 1941.

Atkinson, Rick. *An Army at Dawn: The War in North Africa, 1942–1943*. Henry Holt, 2002.

Ballantine, Duncan S. *U.S. Naval Logistics in the Second World War.* Princeton University Press, 1947.

Beasley, Norman. *Knudsen: A Biography*. McGraw-Hill, 1947.

Bland, Larry. *The Papers of George Catlett Marshall.* Vol. 3. Johns Hopkins University Press, 1991.

Bogart, Ernest L. *War Costs and Their Financing.* D. Appleton, 1921.

Boyan, Edwin. *Handbook of War Production*. McGraw-Hill, 1942.

Brewer, John. *The Sinews of Power: War, Money and the English State, 1688–1783*. Harvard University Press, 1989.

Brigante, John. "The Feasibility Dispute: Determination of War Production Objectives for 1942–1943." Committee on Public Administration Cases, 1950.

Broadberry, Stephen, and Mark Harrison. *The Economics of World War I.* Cambridge University Press, 2005.

Brown, Ian Malcolm. *British Logistics on the Western Front: 1914–1919*. Praeger Publishers, 1998.

Buell, Thomas. *Master of Sea Power: A Biography of Fleet Admiral Ernest J. King.* Little, Brown, 1980.

Burk, Kathleen. *Britain, America and the Sinews of War, 1914–1918*. HarperCollins Publishers, 1985.

Burk, Kathleen. *Old World, New World.* Grove Press, 2007.

Butler, J. R. M. *History of the Second World War: Grand Strategy*. Naval and Military Press, 1957–72.

Catton, Bruce. *The War Lords of Washington*. Greenwood Press, 1948.

Chandler, David. *The Campaigns of Napoleon*. Scribners, 1973.

Christman, Calvin Lee. "Ferdinand Eberstadt and Economic Mobilization." Unpublished doctoral dissertation. History Department, Ohio State University, 1971.

Cline, Ray S. *Washington Command Post: The Operations Division.* Office of the Chief of Military History, 1951.

Clodfelter, Michael. *Warfare and Armed Conflicts: A Statistical Reference to Casualty and Other Figures.* McFarland, 1992.

Connery, Robert H. *The Navy and the Industrial Mobilization in World War II.* Princeton University Press, 1951.

Danchev, Alex. *Establishing the Anglo American Alliance: The Second World War Diaries of Brigadier Vivian Dykes.* Potomac Books, 1990.

Danchev Alex, and Daniel Todman. *War Diaries: Field Marshall Lord Alan Brooke.* University of California Press, 2001.

Davidson, Joel R. *The Unsinkable Fleet: The Politics of U.S. Navy Expansion in World War II.* Naval Institute Press, 1996.

Davies, Glyn. *A History of Money from Ancient Times to the Present Day.* University of Wales Press, 2002.

Doenecke, Justus D. *Storm on the Horizon: The Challenge of American Intervention, 1939–1941.* Rowman & Littlefield, 2003.

Dorwart, Jeffery M. *Eberstadt and Forrestal: A National Security Partnership, 1909–1949.* TAMU Press, 1991.

Dreisziger, N. F. *Mobilization for Total War.* Wilfrid Laurier University Press, 1981.

Eiler, Keith E. *Wedemeyer on War and Peace.* Hoover Institution Press, 1987.

Ellis, John. *World War II: A Statistical Survey: The Essential Facts and Figures for All the Combatants.* Facts on File, 1993.

Engels, Donald W. *Alexander the Great and the Logistics of the Macedonian Army.* University of California Press, 1980.

Fairchild, Byron, and Jonathan Grossman. *The Army and Industrial Manpower.* Office of the Chief of Military History, Department of the Army, 1959.

Fleming, Thomas. *The New Dealer's War: FDR and War Within World War II.* Basic Books, 2002.

Flynn, George Q. *The Mess in Washington: Manpower Mobilization in World War II.* Greenwood Press, 1979.

Frank, Tenny. *An Economic Survey of Ancient Rome.* Vol. I. Pageant Books, 1959.

Fraser, Cecil E., and Stanley F. Telle, eds. *Industry Goes to War.* Books for Libraries, 1941.

Friedman, Milton, and Ann Schwartz. *A Monetary History of the United States: 1867–1960.* Princeton University Press, 1971.

Galbraith, John Kenneth. *The National Accounts: Arrival and Impact, Reflections of America: Commemorating the Statistical Abstract Centennial.* Government Printing Office, 1980.

Gardner, Richard. *Sterling-Dollar Diplomacy.* Columbia University Press, 1969.

Gilbert, Charles. *American Financing of World War I.* Greenwood Press, 1970.

Gole, Henry G. *The Road to Rainbow: Army Planning for Global War, 1934–1940.* Naval Institute Press, 2003.

Goodwin, Doris Kearns. *No Ordinary Time: Franklin & Eleanor Roosevelt: The Home Front in World War II.* Simon & Schuster, 1994.

Gropman, Alan. *The Big L: American Logistics in World War II.* National Defense University, 1997.

Gwyer, J. M. A., and James R. M. Butler. *Grand Strategy.* Vol. III, *June 1941–August 1942.* Her Majesty's Stationery Office, 1964.

Hancock, W. K., and M. M. Gowing. *British War Economy.* Her Majesty's Stationery Office, 1949.

Harrison, Gordon A. *Cross-Channel Attack.* GPO, Department of the Army, 1951.

Harrison, Mark, ed. *The Economics of World War II: Six Great Powers in International Comparison.* Cambridge University Press, 1998.

Haythornthwaite, Philip J. *The World War One Source Book.* Diane Publishing, 1993.

Hooks, Gregory. *Forging the Military-Industrial Complex: World War II's Battle of the Potomac.* University of Illinois Press, 1991.

Horn, Martin. *Britain, France, and the Financing of the First World War.* School of Policy Studies, Queen's University, 1993.

Howard, Michael. *History of the Second World War: Grand Strategy.* Vol. IV. Her Majesty's Stationery Office, 1968.

Industrial College of the Armed Forces. *Emergency Management of the National Economy.* Author, 1954.

Industrial College of the Armed Forces. *Industrial Mobilization for War: History of the War Production Board and Predecessor Agencies: 1940–1945.* Author, 1947.

Industrial College of the Armed Forces. *Industrial Mobilization for War: History of the War Production Board and Predecessor Agencies, 1940–1945.* Vol. I. Government Printing Office, 1947.

Industrial College of the Armed Forces. *Mobilization Limitations in World War II.* Author, 1951.

Janeway, Eliot. *The Struggle for Survival: A Chronicle of Economic Mobilization in World War II.* Yale University Press, 1951.

Kennedy, David M. *Freedom from Fear: The American People in Depression and War, 1929–1945.* Oxford University Press, 2005.

Kirkpatrick, Charles E. *An Unknown Future and a Doubtful Present: Writing the Victory Plan of 1941.* Center of Military History, U.S. Army, 1992.

Koistinen, Paul A. C. *Arsenal of World War II: The Political Economy of American Warfare, 1940–1945.* University Press of Kansas, 2004.

Koistinen, Paul A. C. *The Hammer and the Sword: Labor, the Military, and Industrial Mobilization, 1920–1945.* Unpublished doctoral dissertation, University of California, 1964.

Kriedberg, Marvin A., and Merton G. Henry. *History of Military Mobilization in the United States Army, 1775–1945.* Department of the Army, 1955.

Larrabee, Eric. *Commander in Chief: Franklin Delano Roosevelt, His Lieutenants and Their War.* Harper & Row, 1987.

Laughlin, James L. *Credit of Nations: A Study of the European War.* Scribners, 1918.

Lauterbach, Albert T. *Economics in Uniform: Military Economy and Social Structure.* Princeton University Press, 1943.

Leighton, Richard M., and Robert W. Coakley. *Global Logistics and Strategy, 1940–1943.* Department of the Army, 1955.

Logistics in World War II: Final Report of the Army Service Forces: A Report to the Under Secretary of War and the Chief of Staff by the Director of the Service, Supply, and Procurement Division, War Department General Staff. Center of Military History, 1993.

Lowenthal, Mark M. *Leadership and Indecision: American War Planning and Policy Process, 1937–1942.* Praeger Paperback, 1988.

Lynn, John A. *Feeding Mars: Logistics in Western Warfare from the Middle Ages to the Present.* Westview Press, 1994.

MacCloskey, Monro. *Planning for Victory: World War II.* Richards Rosen Press, 1970.

Mathias, Peter, and Sidney Pollard. *The Cambridge History of Europe.* Vol. 8, *The Industrial Economies: The Development of Economic and Social Policies.* Cambridge University Press, 1989.

Matloff, Maurice, and Edwin M. Snell. *Strategic Planning for Coalition Warfare: 1941–1942.* Center of Military History, 1953.

Meltzer, Allan H. *A History of the Federal Reserve.* University of Chicago Press, 2003.

Menderhausen, Horst. *The Economics of War.* Prentice-Hall, 1941.

Miller, Edward. *War Plan Orange: The U.S. Strategy to Defeat Japan, 1897–1945.* Naval Institute Press, 2007.

Millett, John D. *Organization and Role of the Army Service Forces.* University of Michigan Library, 1954.

Milward, Alan S. *War, Economy and Society: 1939–1945.* University ~~of C~~alifornia Press, 1979.

Morton, Louis. *Command Decisions: Germany First: The Basic Concept of Allied Strategy in World War II.* Center of Military History, 2000.

Morton, Louis. *Strategy and Command: The First Two Years.* Center of Military History, 1961.

Murphy, Henry C. *The National Debt in War and Transition.* McGraw-Hill, 1950.

Murray, Williamson, MacGregor Knox, and Alvin Bernstein, eds. *The Making of Strategy: Rulers, States, and War.* Cambridge University Press, 1994.

Murray, Williamson, and Allan Millett. *A War to Be Won: Fighting the Second World War.* Cambridge University Press, 2000.

Nannery, James, and Terrence J. Gough. *U.S. Manpower Mobilization for World War II.* Army Center of Military History, 1982.

Nelson, Donald M. *Arsenal of Democracy, the Story of American War Production.* Harcourt, Brace, 1946.

Nelson, Otto. *National Security and the General Staff.* Infantry Journal Press, 1946.

Novick, David. *Wartime Production Control.* Da Capo Press, 1976.

Novick, David, and George Albert Steiner. *Wartime Industrial Statistics.* University of Illinois Press, 1949.

Novick, David, Melvin Anshen, and W. C. Truppner. *Wartime Production Controls.* Columbia University Press, 1949.

Ohl, John Kennedy. *Supplying the Troops: General Somervell and American Logistics in World War II.* Northern Illinois University Press, 1994.

Palmer, Robert R. "The Mobilization of the Ground Army, The Army Ground Forces Study No. 4." Historical Section, Government Printing Office, 1946.

Pogue, Forrest C. *George C. Marshall.* Viking Press, 1963–1987.

Pogue, Forrest C. *George C. Marshall: Ordeal and Hope 1939–1942.* Viking Press, 1966.

Pogue, Forrest C. *George C. Marshall: Organizer of Victory 1943–1945.* Viking Press, 1973.

Polenberg, Richard. *War and Society: The United States 1941–1945.* Greenwood Press, 1972.

Porch, Douglas. *The Path to Victory: The Mediterranean Theater in World War II.* Farrar, Straus and Giroux, 2004.

Raaflaub, Kurt A., and Nathan Rosenstein. *War and Society in the Ancient and Medieval Worlds: Asia, the Mediterranean, Europe, and Mesoamerica.* Cambridge University Press, 1999.

Roosevelt, Franklin D. *The Public Papers and Addresses of Franklin Roosevelt.* Macmillan, 1941.

Ross, Steven T. *American War Plans 1941–1945.* Routledge, 1997.

Ruppenthal, Roland G. *Logistical Support of the Armies.* Vol. I, *May–September 1944.* Department of the Army, 1953.

Ruppenthal, Roland G. *Logistical Support of the Armies.* Vol. II, *September 1944–May 1945.* Department of the Army, 1959.

Samuelson, Paul, and William D. Nordhaus. *Economics.* McGraw-Hill/Irwin, 2004.

Scitovsky, Tibor, Edward Shaw, and Lorie Tarshis. *Mobilizing Resources for War: The Economic Alternatives.* McGraw-Hill, 1951.

Sherwig, John M. *Guineas and Gunpowder: British Foreign Aid in the Wars with France, 1793–1815.* Harvard University Press, 1969.

Sherwood, Robert. *Roosevelt and Hopkins: An Intimate History.* Enigma Books, 2001.

Simpson, Mitchell. *Harold R. Stark: Architect of Victory, 1939–1945*. University of South Carolina Press, 1989.

Smith, Jean E. *Lucius D. Clay: An American Life*. Henry Holt, 1990.

Smith, R. Elberton. *The Army and Economic Mobilization*. Office of the Chief of Military History, 1959.

Somers, Herman M. *Presidential Agency: The Office of War Mobilization and Reconversion*. Oxford University Press, 1950.

Spiegel, Henry W. *The Economics of Total War*. Appleton Century, 1942.

Steiner, George A., ed. *Economic Problems of War*. John Wiley & Sons, 1942.

Stewart, Richard W. *American Military History*. Vol. 2, *The United States Army in a Global Era, 1917–2003*. Department of the Army, 2005.

Stoler, Mark A. *Allies and Adversaries: The Joint Chiefs of Staff, The Grand Alliance, and U.S. Strategy in World War II*. University of North Carolina Press, 2000.

Stoler, Mark A. *The Politics of the Second Front*. Greenwood Press, 1977.

Stubs, Kevin. *Race to the Front: The Material Foundations of Coalition Strategy in the Great War*. Greenwood Press, 2002.

Suetonius, Gaius. *The Lives of the Twelve Caesars*. Translated by J. C. Rolfe. Harvard University Press and William Henemann, 1920.

Thucydides. *The Landmark Thucydides: A Comprehensive Guide to the Peloponnesian War*. Free Press, 1996.

Tooze, Adam. *Wages of Destruction*. Viking Press, 2006.

Tucker, Spencer C. *The European Powers in the First World War: An Encyclopedia*. Garland Publishing, 1996.

U.S. Army Service Forces. *Annual Reports*. Government Printing Office, 1942–1945.

U.S. Bureau of the Budget. *United States at War: Development and Administration of the War Program by the Federal Government*. Government Printing Office, 1946.

U.S. War Production Board. *Wartime Production Achievements and the Reconversion Outlook, Report of the Chairman, War Production Board*. Government Printing Office, 1945.

U.S. War Production Board Chairman. *War Production in 1944*. Government Printing Office, 1945.

van Creveld, Martin. *Supplying War: Logistics from Wallenstein to Patton*. Cambridge University Press, 2004.

Vatter, Harold G. *U.S. Economy in World War II*. Columbia University Press, 1985.

Walton, Francis. *Miracle of World War II: How American Industry Made Victory Possible*. Macmillan, 1956.

Watson, Mark. *Chief of Staff: Prewar Plans and Preparations*. Army Center for Military History, Department of the Army, 1950.

Weigley, Russell F. *The American Way of War: A History of United States Military Strategy and Policy*. Indiana University Press, 1973.

White, Gerald. *Billions for Defense: Government Finance by the Defense Plant Corporation During World War II.* University of Alabama Press, 2005.

Whittlesey, Charles. "The Banking System and War Finance." National Bureau of Economic Research, Financial Research Program, "Our Economy at War." Occasional Paper 8. National Bureau of Economic Research (February 1943).

Articles

Carson, Carol. "The History of the United States National Income and Product Accounts: The Development of an Analytical Tool." *Review of Income and Wealth*, 21, no. 2 (1975).

Crouzet, François. "Wars, Blockades, and Economic Change in Europe, 1792–1815." *Journal of Economic History* 24, no. 4 (1964).

Ferguson, Niall. "Public Finance and National Security: The Domestic Origins of the First World War Revisited." *Past and Present* 142 (1994).

Friedman, Milton. "Price, Income and Monetary Changes in Three Wartime Periods." *American Economic Review* 42, no. 2 (May 1952).

Gatrell, Peter, and Mark Harrison. "The Russian and Soviet Economies in Two World Wars: A Comparative View." *The Economic History Review* 46, no. 3 (August 1993).

"GDP: One of the Great Inventions of the 20th Century." Bureau of Economic Analysis (January 2000). *Survey of Current Business,* Washington, DC. http://www.bea.gov/scb/pdf/BEAWIDE/2000/0100od.pdf.

Harrison, Mark. "Resource Mobilization for World War II: The U.S.A., U.K., U.S.S.R., and Germany, 1938–1945." *The Economic History Review* 41, no. 2 (May 1988).

Haydon, Frederick S. "War Department Reorganization, August 1941–March 1942 (Part I)." *Military Affairs* 16, no. 1 (Spring 1952).

Higgs, Robert. "Wartime Prosperity? A Reassessment of the U.S. Economy in the 1940s." *Journal of Economic History* 51, no.1 (March 1992).

Hitch, Thomas K. "Alternatives in War Finance." Department of Commerce, Washington, DC (October 1942). http://library.bea.gov/cdm4/document.php?CISOROOT=/SCB&CISOPTR=3443&REC=9&CISOSHOW=3435 (accessed 1 October 2007).

Kimball, Warren F. " 'Beggar My Neighbor:' America and British Interim Finance Crisis, 1940–1941." *Journal of Economic History* 29, no.4 (December 1969).

Leighton, Richard M. "Overlord Revisited: An Interpretation of American Strategy in the European War, 1942-1944." *American Historical Review* 68, no. 4 (July 1963).

Marcuss, Rosemary D., and Richard E. Kane. "U.S. National Income and Product Statistics: Born in the Great Depression and World War II." *Survey of Current Business*, Bureau of Economic Analysis, Washington, DC (February 2007).

Mathias, Peter, and Patrick O'Brien. "Taxation in Britain and France: 1715–1810: A Comparison of the Social and Economic Consequences of Taxes Collected for the Central Governments." *Journal of European Economic History* 5, no. 3 (1976).

Miller, Adolph C. "War Finance and Inflation." *Annals* (January 1918).

Neal, Larry. "A Tale of Two Revolutions: International Capital Flows 1789–1819." *Bulletin of Economic Research* 43, no. 1 (1991).

Nettels, Curtis P. "Cost of Production." *The Journal of Economic History* 3 (December 1943).

O'Brien, Patrick. "The Political Economy of British Taxation 1660–1815." *Economic History Review* 41, no. 1 (February 1998).

Ohanian, Lee E. "The Macro Economic Effects of War Finance in the United States: World War II and the Korean War." *American Economic Review* 87, no. 1 (March 1997).

Richard, T. A. "The Mining of the Romans in Spain." *Journal of Roman Studies* 18 (1928).

Robinson, Marshall A. "Federal Debt Management: Civil War, World War I, and World War II." *Economic History Review* 45, no. 2 (May 1955).

Rockoff, Hugh. "Price and Wage Control in Four Wartime Periods." *Journal of Economic History* 41, no. 2 (June 1991).

Simmons, Edward C. "Federal Reserve Policy and National Debt During the War Years." *Journal of Business of the University of Chicago* 20, no. 2 (April 1947).

Simonson, G. R. "Demand for Aircraft and the Aircraft Industry, 1907–1958." *Journal of Economic History* 20, no. 3 (September 1960).

Singer, H. W. "The Sources of War Finance in the German War Economy." *Review of Economic Studies* 10, no. 2 (Summer 1943).

Stein, Herbert. "Papers and Proceedings of the Ninety-Eighth Annual Meeting of the American Economic Association." *American Economic Review* 76, no. 2 (May 1986).

Warburton, Clark. "Monetary Policy in the United States in World War II." *American Journal of Economics and Sociology* 4, no. 3 (April 1945).

Welch, R. L. "The Necessity for an Economic Basis of International Peace." *Annals of the American Academy of Political and Social Science* 108 (1923).

White, Gerald T. "Financing Industrial Expansion for War: The Origin of the Defense Plant Corporation Leases." *Journal of Economic History* 9, no. 2 (November 1949).

Whittlesey, Charles. "The Banking System and War Finance." National Bureau of Economic Research Financial Research Program; *Our Economy at War*, Occasional Paper 8 (February 1943). (Reprints of this wartime research study can be ordered from the National Bureau of Economic Research, New York.)

Wicker, Elmus. "The World War II Policy of Fixing a Pattern of Interest Rates." *Journal of Finance* 24, no. 3 (June 1969).

Wright, J. F. "British Government Borrowing in Wartime, 1750–1815." *Economic History Review* 52, no. 2 (1999): 355–61.

Index

Page numbers followed by a *t* indicate tables. Page numbers followed by an *n* indicate notes.

L

M

About the Author

Jim Lacey was an active-duty military officer for twelve years and is currently a professor of strategy, war, and policy at the Marine War College and an adjunct professor in the Johns Hopkins National Security Program. He also works as a consultant on a number of projects for the U.S. military. Lacey has written for a number of publications, including the *New York Post* and the *New York Sun,* and appears regularly in *Military History* magazine and was an embedded journalist for *Time* magazine during the invasion of Iraq. Among his earlier books are *Takedown: The 3rd Infantry Division's Twenty-one Day Assault on Baghdad*, *Pershing*, and *The First Clash* (forthcoming).

The Naval Institute Press is the book-publishing arm of the U.S. Naval Institute, a private, nonprofit, membership society for sea service professionals and others who share an interest in naval and maritime affairs. Established in 1873 at the U.S. Naval Academy in Annapolis, Maryland, where its offices remain today, the Naval Institute has members worldwide.

Members of the Naval Institute support the education programs of the society and receive the influential monthly magazine *Proceedings* or the colorful bimonthly magazine *Naval History* and discounts on fine nautical prints and on ship and aircraft photos. They also have access to the transcripts of the Institute's Oral History Program and get discounted admission to any of the Institute-sponsored seminars offered around the country.

The Naval Institute's book-publishing program, begun in 1898 with basic guides to naval practices, has broadened its scope to include books of more general interest. Now the Naval Institute Press publishes about seventy titles each year, ranging from how-to books on boating and navigation to battle histories, biographies, ship and aircraft guides, and novels. Institute members receive significant discounts on the Press's more than eight hundred books in print.

Full-time students are eligible for special half-price membership rates. Life memberships are also available.

For a free catalog describing Naval Institute Press books currently available, and for further information about joining the U.S. Naval Institute, please write to:

Member Services
U.S. Naval Institute
291 Wood Road
Annapolis, MD 21402-5034
Telephone: (800) 233-8764
Fax: (410) 571-1703
Web address: www.usni.org